Closing the Capabilities Gap

Ortrud Leßmann
Hans-Uwe Otto
Holger Ziegler (eds.)

Closing the Capabilities Gap

Renegotiating social justice for the young

Barbara Budrich Publishers
Opladen & Farmington Hills, MI 2011

A CIP catalogue record for this book is available from
Die Deutsche Bibliothek (The German Library)

ISBN 978-3-86649-325-4

Die Deutsche Bibliothek – CIP-Einheitsaufnahme
Ein Titeldatensatz für die Publikation ist bei Der Deutschen Bibliothek erhältlich.

Verlag Barbara Budrich Barbara Budrich Publishers
Stauffenbergstr. 7. D-51379 Leverkusen Opladen, Germany

28347 Ridgebrook. Farmington Hills, MI 48334. USA
www.barbara-budrich.net

Jacket illustration by disegno, Wuppertal, Germany – www.disenjo.de
Printed in Europe on acid-free paper by
paper&tinta, Warsaw

Content

Ortrud Leßmann, Hans-Uwe Otto & Holger Ziegler

Introduction: Closing the Capability Gap and Renewing Social Criticism

The following volume collects perspectives from different disciplines such as educational science, economics, sociology, social policy and social work.[1] The task of the contributons is to critically assess what the Capability Approach may contribute to capture the issue of social inequality against the background of modern societies that are redefining their notion of "the public" and diminishing the collective responsibility for the vulnerable.

While the articles agree that the Capability Approach may provide an evaluative frame for assessing policies and politics in the fields of economy, education and social policy, they are controversial about whether and in how far the capability perspective makes a difference and provides value added in terms of promoting well-being on the level of individual persons – in particular for the worst off – but also in terms of enhancing justice on a social level.

As the title indicates the articles give particular attention to the topic of inequality towards the young who are in a particularly vulnerable period of life that has a decisive influence on their lives. Thus it seems to be reasonable for an introduction to assess what a capabilities perspective has to provide in order to analyse social inequality and to explore whether it is appropriate to conceptualize social disadvantages in terms of a capability gap.

A typology of approaches towards inequality

In order to classify the most relevant approaches to inequality Erik Olin Wright (2009) has recently suggested a helpful typology. Wright subdivides three clusters of inequality analyses: an individual-attributes perspective, an opportunity hoarding perspective and an exploitation and domination perspective. These perspectives – which may not exclude each other – might be regarded as basic elements of inequality research.

---

1 The volume collects contributions to an international and interdisciplinary conference which was collaboratively conducted by the Capability and Education Network of the Human Development and Capability Association, the 'Bielefeld Center for Education and Capability Research' and the Research School 'Education and Capabilities' of the state North Rhine Westphalia.

The individual-attributes perspective concentrates on the characteristics that allow clustering people in similar social status groups which may be called classes or social milieus. We find this perspective in different models of social stratification as for instance proposed by Lloyd W. Warner (1960), John H. Goldthorpe (1996), Dennis Gilbert (2002), Walter Müller (1977) or Karl Martin Bolte et al. (1968) but also within a social milieu approach suggested by Pierre Bourdieu (1984) and Stefan Hradil (1987).

Important examples of attributes which are significant in terms of inequality are for instance gender and race but also age and geographical location. However, next to the occupation in the labour market, one of the most commonly and systematically investigated attributes in line with this perspective to inequality is education or "human capital".[2] More sophisticated versions of the individual-attributes perspective include broader concepts such as cultural recourses, networks and sometimes even individual motivations and other (socially acquired) dispositions. Proponents of an individual-attributes approach argue that the sum of such attributes represents people's class or socio-economic status. The sum of such attributes aggregated on the level of the family of origin is considered as the "class background" of these persons.

Scholars who favour an individual-attributes perspective tend to devote special attention to this "class background" as it turned out to be an important factor for explaining to what degree persons are typically able to obtain what Pierre Bourdieu used to call economic, cultural and social capital in their own life course. From the individual-attributes perspective the correlation between the "class background" of people and the attributes they obtain in their own life course points to durable inequalities or the stability of class relations. There is no doubt that individual attributes and opportunities for persons to acquire these attributes are important. However, proponents who focus solely on individual attributes may fail to consider the nature of the positions and the corresponding attributes which are the metric of inequality in this tradition of assessing inequality:

> "Education shapes the kinds of jobs people get, but why are some jobs 'better' than others? Why do some jobs confer a great deal of power while others do not? And is there any relation between the power and wealth enjoyed by some and the lack of it experienced by others?" (Wright 2009: 104)

While the individual attributes approach might be appropriate to capture the distribution of economic, cultural and social capital it is less practical in grasping the social conditions and relationships within which goods, capitals and

2 Therefore the important results with respect to inequality which for instance the so called PISA-study (i.e. a large scale study within the Programme for International Student Assessment of the OECD) delivers might be considered as typical contributions to an individual-attributes approach to inequality.

socially acquired attributes are distributed. The two other perspectives have more to say about this issue.

What Wright calls the 'opportunity hoarding' perspective defines inequality with respect to person's "access to and exclusion from certain economic [and social] opportunities" and advantages (Wright 2009: 104). This perspective comes close to Weberian approaches to social closure as for instance suggested by Frank Parkin (1978), Raymond Murphy (1988) or Reinhard Kreckel (1992). Currently the 'opportunity hoarding' perspective is most sophistically elaborated by Charles Tilley (1998) who focuses on differential access that unequal categories have to value-producing resources.

Within the 'opportunity hoarding' perspective it is an important idea that the value of positions – or more exactly the advantages and privileges associated with them – depend on the scarcity of these positions. Therefore a basic mechanism is 'social closure' (Parkin 1978) which points to means and powers to exclude (potential) competitors from access to these positions. These closures might take place despite the individual attributes these competitors might have obtained. The difference between the individual-attribute perspective and the conceptualisation of inequality as product of opportunity hoarding processes is basically as follows:

From the opportunity-hoarding perspective the "advantages gained from being in a privileged class position are causally connected to the disadvantages of those excluded from such positions. In the individual-attributes approach, such advantages and disadvantages are simply the outcomes of individual conditions: the rich are rich because they have favourable attributes, the poor poor because they lack them; there is no systematic causal connection between these facts" (Wright 2009: 106f).

A third perspective to inequality is what Wright calls an "exploitation and domination" approach. This perspective which highlights power relations and socially created oppression is currently defended by Erik Olin Wright (1985) and John Roemer (1982). While exploitation points to the capacity to acquire benefits from the labour of other persons, or more precisely "from the labour of those who are dominated" (Wright 2009: 107), domination is a more comprehensive notion which might encompass exploitation as it points broadly to the capacity to control actions and conducts as well as the conditions of the actions and conducts of other persons.

Obviously these three fundamental approaches contain different informational bases of capturing social inequality. What is important is that an appropriate informational base of inequality should be able to grasp the fact that significance of inequality is not only about distributions of goods or capitals but also about hierarchical social relations i.e. relations in which some people have the capacity to "dominate, exploit, marginalize, demean, and inflict violence upon others", or more broadly "relations between superior and inferior persons" (Anderson 1999: 312). These distributions and relations are significant as they impact the quality people's beings and doings. The point of grasping inequality is therefore the identification of avoidable suffering and restrictions of human flourishing (i.e. the full realization and exercise of human potentials) (see Sayer 2009; Otto, Scherr & Ziegler 2010). These inequalities are 'social' insofar as they are features which are related to situations and dynamics of the social world and not only of the inner self. An adequate informational basis for capturing social inequality should be able to grasp material as well as relational features with respect to their significance for the live practices of the persons who are involved. We suggest that the Capability Approach might help to provide and to give reasons for establishing such an informational basis.

Classifying the Capability Approach as an approach to inequality

While the Capability Approach is an approach which does not provide a specific social or political economic theory it has started with the important question "Equality of What?" (Sen 1980) and "is concerned with showing the cogency of a particular *space* for the evaluation of individual opportunities and successes" (Sen 1993: 50). The focal variables are the "doings and beings" a person achieves in her life (functionings for short) and the capability for achieving these "doings and beings". The Capability Approach thus integrates aspects of the three perspectives to inequality mentioned by Wright.

With respect to attributes on the individual level it asks for those attributes that allow persons to lead a life they value and "have reason to value" (Sen 1999: 85). Thereby individual attributes may provide a fundament of what Onora O'Neill (2000: 203) calls "capacities and capabilities for action" (and interaction). These capacities are of course related to opportunities and hence contain at least conceptually an idea of social closure which is the critical point of the opportunity hoarding perspective to inequality.

Analytically the Capability Approach distinguishes between resources such as income and conversion factors (cf. Robeyns 2005). The latter can be differentiated further into personal and social conversion factors. For instance, Des Gasper (2002) makes a difference between S-capabilities, which indicate internal enabling skills as well as faculties, abilities, aspirations and attitudes and O-capabilities, which entail the control over resources, opportunities or options available to a person respectively the socially structured set of a person's attainable life-paths. These O-capabilities or social conversion factors can be further subdivided into 'socio-structural and cultural conversion factors' (such as social norms, gender roles, power relations, discriminatory practices etc.) and 'institutional conversion factors'[3] (such as entitlements, welfare and educational arrangements, collective provisions etc. but also the rationalities of collective decision-making processes). Also institutional classifications of persons into categories are a part of institutional conversion factors which may generate inequalities and constraints in the access to the means and freedoms of flourishing.[4]

An advantage of the Capability Approach can be seen in the inherently relational perspective of O- and S-capabilities. The Capability Approach combines the notions of 'individual' and 'social agency' and focuses on the interface of the question 'what an individual is able to do' and 'which opportunities are open for him or her' (Bonvin & Thelen 2003: 1). Despite the fact that the Capability Approach conceptualizes persons as active agents, it does not add to the solipsistic myth of an athletic in-control agent which obscures and denigrates the fact of vulnerabilities, (inter-)dependencies and needs of care from others.

A further crucial point of the capability approach is that it emphasises the significance of the informational basis of judgments. An informational basis of judgments of justice "specifies the variables that are directly involved in assessing the justice of alternative systems" (Sen 1992: 73). The capability perspective does not only suggest a specific form of such an informational basis of judgements of justice – namely a basis which allows an objective assessment of the state of a person (Salais 2008) but also implies to analyse what informational bases are used in a given social arrangement, whether it is objectively right, feasible and socially fair (cf. Salais 2008), what perspectives are privileged or neglected within this informational bases and what interests and whose needs are considered when authoritative informational bases of judgement in justice are selected and come into existence (cf. Bonvin 2009). Despite the criticism that the Capability Approach does not adequately address issues of power (cf. Navarro 2000) it simply seems to be obvious that power structures are a core concern of grasping inequality in terms of the informational space of capabilities.

It might well be that some scholars using the Capability Approach neglect the issue of power, hierarchies and domination. This however might rather be

3 As Sen (1999: 142) points out: "Individuals live and operate in a world of institutions. Our opportunities and prospects depend crucially on what institutions exist and how they function. Not only do institutions contribute to our freedoms, their roles can be sensibly evaluated in the light of their contributions to our freedom".

4 It is obvious that public organisations – which enable or constrain particular life courses and ways of conducting one's life – typically imply more or less restrictive views of what is a valuable being or doing. Therefore management reforms such as for instance towards more standardised managerial forms of service provision are not only a side issue but indeed a significant aspect of enhancing or diminishing the capabilities of the beneficiaries of social or educational services.

a shortfall in particular analyses than a conceptual failure of the Capability Approach. The control over one's political and material environment is explicitly mentioned and founded in Martha Nussbaum's list of central capabilities. In the absence of any special reason to argue otherwise Nussbaum is concerned with nothing else than the issue of power relations. Beyond the question about the contents of Martha Nussbaum's list, the central point of analysing power is based on the persuasive assumption that structures of power differentially shape person's room to manoeuvre. This is what the Capability Approach basically is about. It is therefore convincing to argue that the Capability Approach to inequality does not eclipse but on the contrary gives particular attention to the effects of structurally consolidated powers (Kreckel 2006: 15). Indeed capabilities can be perceived as synonymic to individual powers (Morriss 2002).

However the Capability Approach is not only concerned with the (positive) powers of individuals, but also with power structures and issues of domination. As Martha Nussbaum (1988: 145f.) figures out, the Capability Approach aims "at making people able to function in certain human ways" or "a fully human way" (Nussbaum 2000: 71). This comes close to a reversed version of Steven Lukes' definition of domination in his seminal work on power: "Domination occurs where the power of some affects the interests of others by restricting their capacities for truly human functioning" (Lukes 2005: 118). Against the background of such considerations the perspective of the Capability Approach to inequality thus comes close to an exploitation and domination approach insofar as an analysis of a person's capability set focuses on the real opportunities and the "opportunity freedom" of persons and this inherently involves the powers and capacities of not being dominated and exploited. At the same time personal and institutional powers and different forms of hierarchies and domination are also 'conversion factors'[5] which enhance or impede the 'conversion' of goods and services into states and practices people have reason to value or as G.A. Cohen (1993: 28) puts it into advantages i.e. a "heterogeneous collection of desirable states".

The Capability Approach thus formulates an idea about what is the point of inequalities and what kind of inequalities matter that goes beyond the question of domination and exploitation in that it asks for the degree to which individuals have the real and genuine capacity to take advantage of resources and life circumstances. This perspective also suggests to analyse the power dimensions of public institutions which deal with the issue of social inequality, social problems or, more broadly, of institutions which affect the life practices of persons. For example, if social welfare institutions utilize standardised, managerial measures and problem diagnoses, this implies a informational base of judgements which shapes the spaces of manoeuvre –

5 On the level of ,conversion factors' also a person's sense of powerlessness restricts his or her capabilities.

and therefore also the degree of the capability gap – of the beneficiaries of such services (cf. Bonvin & Rosenstein 2010: Otto et al. 2009). Therefore the analyses of such instutional strategies and rationalities – in particular those in the field of social policy and education (cf. Otto & Ziegler 2010) – are a central issue for theoretical and empirical investtigations on the fundament of the capability approach.

With such a perspective on inequality issues of freedom and autonomy take center stage. Using Isaiah Berlin's (1969) characteristic of freedom, the Capability Approach goes beyond a negative idea of liberty as non-interference and embraces a positive conception of liberty as the freedom to do and to be certain things. This focus points to the in-use-value of their opportunities and to the practical significance of opportunities. The idea of the Capability Approach is that inequalities arise not only from the varying extent to which they posses goods and assets but also from the relational positioning of persons towards these goods and assets. Ultimately inequalities matter in terms of their impact on the lives that people "seek to live and the things, relationships and practices which they value" (Sayer 2005: 117).

Thus, the analytical concern of the Capability Approach goes beyond other approaches to inequality in several ways: It takes individual attributes seriously, divides them into resources and conversion factors and asks what people with these resources and conversion factors can do or be in the context of a specific social, cultural and institutional environment. Thereby – like most of the established sociological and economical approaches to inequality – the capability approach assumes the idea that opportunities arise from interaction of social and personal influences. Within such an analysis however, the capability approach emphasizes the sets of abilities and entitlements of persons to live a life they value and have reason to value. Thus, it goes beyond a focus on the (undeniable) significance of (economic) positions and assets per se while it clearly highlights the importance of the (equal) access of individuals to the means she/he needs to develop to her/his potentials. The Capability Approach clearly shares major concerns of domination and exploitation approaches but goes beyond them in asking what life people value. Hence, the question of the practical value people can draw out of these positions and assets come to the forefront. In this respect the Capability Approach provides an evaluative framework for assessing inequality which is related to an emancipatory account which is anchored in conceptions of human flourishing and (avoidable) human suffering (respectively oppression).

Individual valuation, utilitarianism and welfare policy

There are basically two approaches that give particular attention to the individual valuation of life and its practical value: utilitarian welfarism and the Capability Approach. There are very good reasons to argue that a capabilities perspective is superior to utilitarian welfarism. These reasons are outlined in the following sections.

One cardinal objection to utilitarianism is that utilitarianism on the one hand side is sensitive to human suffering, but on the other hand side does not provide any reasonable and inherently consistent criterion which proscribes the suffering of a (even significant) minority of the population if this suffering contributes to the total benefit of the overall population respectively the aggregated total welfare of the whole society. Entitlements of single individuals and minorities might therefore be neglected from a utilitarian point of view. Thus utilitarianism is particularly unfeasible if it is used to grasp the situation of the most vulnerable.

Nevertheless proponents of utilitarian welfarism seemingly embrace the doctrine of 'agent sovereignty': "what is good for each person is entirely determined by that very person's evaluative perspective" (Arneson 1999: 116). Therefore welfarists argue that "in deciding what is good and what is bad for a given individual, the ultimate criterion can only be his own wants and his own preferences" (Harsanyi 1982: 39). Against this background subjective life satisfaction is considered by welfarists as the ultimate criterion to evaluate social conditions including inequalities.

A view in the literature reveals that the quest to assess individual's evaluation of their life satisfaction on the fundament of their cognitive assessment of their overall life quality has been adopted in sociological and psychological social indicators research. In economics happiness research is as well suggested to be "a new approach to measuring utility in the context of cost-benefit analysis" (Frey & Stutzer 2005: 208). For this purpose an increasing arsenal of psychometric measures of well-being has been developed and is credited "to contain substantial amounts of valid variance" (Diener 1984: 551).

With respect to distribution utilitarian welfarists typically seek to "maximize aggregate happiness as a social welfare function" (Frey & Stutzer 2007). Aggregate happiness does not take the inequality of the distribution of happiness across persons into account. Utilitarian welfarists rather prefer a state (of distribution), when it provides the most positive sum total of happiness. If u_p (a) respectively u_p (b) is the amount of happiness of person p experiencing state a respectively state b than state a is preferred to the state b whenever

$$\sum_{p=1}^{n} u_p(a) > \sum_{p=1}^{n} u_p(b)$$

Such a summation is particularly meaningful if we can reasonably assume happiness to be more than an elusive concept but rather a relatively global and stable attribute which is cardinally measurable and interpersonally comparable. Basically this seems to be the case (cf. Layard 2005; Ng 1996, 1997). Happiness might be – and is – measured in a comparatively simple way on the basis of psychometric survey and included in sociological, psychological and economic models.

However, at least in affluent countries inequalities in happiness only slightly correlate with material inequalities. In particular, happiness doesn't rise with rising incomes (Easterlin paradox). Furthermore most people – even those in social distress – actually seem to be happy or satisfied with their lives. Put differently: when the quality of life – and corresponding inequalities – in affluent countries are defined in terms of subjective well-being of their citizens, the world is seemingly fine even if there are undeniable and significant inequalities in terms of economic, social and cultural resources that these citizens possess. Even more disturbing is the fact that a range of studies suggest

> "that a variety of social programs that reduced social expectations among the disadvantaged might be hedonically beneficial as well. The key empirical findings here are that increasing the social isolation of subordinated groups often seems to make them happier by leading individuals to compare themselves to a narrower, less prosperous cohort in evaluating their circumstances. Thus, women reported themselves to be more satisfied with their incomes when they did not have much chance of getting traditionally male jobs at male pay. Black children in segregated schools have substantially higher self-esteem than blacks in integrated settings and than white children (without regard to school setting), while high-status blacks – who interact with more whites and expect to have lives more like theirs – were reported by some researchers to have low and falling rates of happiness" (Kelman 2005: 400).

As Mark Kelman (2005: 401) summarizes, it seems to be clear "that as long as individuals do as well as those around them who form a salient, recognized social group, they feel pretty satisfied". This implicates however that in terms of its impact on subjective well-being "stable and unquestioned hierarchy [...] seems to dominate fluidity (which leads largely to higher, disappointed expectations, or to self-blame for bad outcomes)" (Kelman 2005: 401). Also on the level of policies towards well-being the assumption of the protagonists of subjective well-being that "quality of life must be in the eye of the beholder" (Campbell 1972) has quite radical consequences: Taken serious, this perspective on well-being implies to be "indifferent between policies that increase people's opportunities and those that dampen their expectations if the two policies have identical impacts on subjective well-being" (Kelman 2005: 401).

Adaptive preferences and the Capability Approach

Even when dampening expectations is not embraced as a means of welfare policy people adjust their expectations in order to cope with unfavourable living conditions. This problem has been called the problem of "adaptive preferences" i.e. "preferences that have adjusted to their second-class status" (Nussbaum 2003: 33) respectively to circumstances which may be 'objectively' unfavourable. Adaptive preferences point to the fact, that while "people's own assessment of their degree of satisfaction [...] is partly determined by their level of aspiration" (Erikson 1993: 77), it is known that by-and-by people in distressed situations become accustomed and tend to conform to unfavourable circumstances. As David Swartz (1997: 103) puts it, the process of adaptive internalisation „tends to shape individual action so that existing opportunity structures are perpetuated. Chances of success or failure are internalized and then transformed into individual aspirations or expectations; these are then in turn externalized in action that tends to reproduce the objective structure of life chances". Referring to processes of adapting preferences, some commentators even suggest that "measuring how satisfied people are is to a large extent equivalent to measuring how well they have adapted to their present" (Erikson 1993: 77).

Since a "utilitarian calculus gives sanctity to that distortion"[6] (Sen 1984: 309) happiness and life satisfaction as proxies for utility are rather "inadequate as a basis of social choice" (Nussbaum 2000: 139) and subsequently are misleading as a fundament for social policy. This is particular the case against the background of the fact that policies and ideologies that obscure injustice, oppression and inequality may well lead to happiness while consciousness-raising may induce dissatisfaction.

"[T]he trouble comes when social policy is driven by people's actual preferences. If what people in oppressed circumstances want is conditioned by their presently-feasible options,

6 As Sen figures out more recently: "The utilitarian calculus based on, say, happiness can be deeply unfair to those who are persistently deprived, such as the traditional underdogs in stratified societies, oppressed minorities in intolerant communities, precarious sharecroppers living in a world of uncertainty, sweated workers in exploitative industrial arrangements, subdued housewives in deeply sexist cultures. The hopelessly deprived people may lack the courage to desire any radical change and often tend to adjust their desires and expectations to what little they see as feasible. They train themselves to take pleasure in small mercies. The practical merit of such adjustments for people in chronically adverse positions is easy to understand: this is one way of being able to live peacefully with persistent deprivation. But the adjustments also have the incidental effect of distorting the scale of utilities in the form of happiness or desire-fulfilment. In terms of pleasure or desire-fulfilment, the disadvantages of the hopeless underdog may thus appear to be much smaller than what would emerge on the basis of a more objective analysis of the extent of their deprivation and unfreedom" (Sen 2009: 282f.).

no social action would seem to be called for to improve the lot of such oppressed people who do not express dissatisfaction with their circumstances" (Bruckner 2009: 311)

The problems of subjective approaches of assessing well-being are obvious. Nevertheless it is still convincing that inequalities matter most in terms of their impact on the lives, that people -"seek to live and the things, relationships and practices which they value" (Sayer 2005: 117). The problem of adaptive preferences has motivated the move of the Capability Approach in a more objectivist direction (Sen 1987) in terms of an assessment of real structural opportunities and the effective scale and scope of possibilities of beings and doings rather than the mearly subjective satisfaction with present states. Yet, an assessment of 'objective' resources and positions is not a sufficient information base for well-being. The insight of Andrew Sayer stresses the significance of use value and internal goods and does not necessarily make a point for subjective approaches to well-being. The idea is to not only focus on cash or in-kind resources, but rather take a whole configuration comprising resources as well as individual and social factors into account which allow individuals to convert resources into valuable states and activities (cf. Bonvin 2009). A person's capability set consists of all valuable states and activities feasible for her. It can thus be said to summarize the whole configuration of resources and conversion factors. Following this perspective Sayer argues that the inequalities that matter most "effect what Amartya Sen calls [... people's] 'capabilities' to engage in ways of life they have reason to value."

Objective well-being and autonomy

The Capability Approach attempts to reconcile the competing demands associated with the values of equality, recognition, liberty and human flourishing. The central issue of the Capability Approach is the issue of a good life, respectively a conduct of life which allows to individuals to realise their potentials. Thereby the Capability Approach is concerned with the cultivation, and just distribution of the (real) freedom and the well-being of persons. As Martha Nussbaum summarises the Capability Approach:

"We ask not only about the person's satisfaction with what she does, but about what she does, and what she is in a position to do (what her opportunities and liberties are). And we ask not just about the resources that are sitting around, but about how those do or do not go to work, enabling [this person] to function in a fully human way" (Nussbaum 2000: 71).

According to Nussbaum, the essential public function is to "make available to each and every citizen the material, institutional, and educational circumstances in which good human functioning may be chosen; to move each and every one of them across a threshold of capability into circumstances in which they may choose to live and function well" (Nussbaum 1999: 24). However, the Capability Approach neither aims at imposing an understanding of what is good on the agents, nor to constrain their freedom of doing and being with respect to that aim, nor does it support (the government) "to force people into excellence" (Hurka 1993: 147). On the contrary: The Capability Approach represents an approach that is concerned with the scope of self-determination and autonomy to render a good life possible. The Capability Approach takes seriously the focus on the scope of opportunities and the freedom of people to live lives they value in a systematic fashion by differentiating between functionings and chances of realisation, respectively capabilities. Functionings refer to the question if people actually are or do something specific. In contrast to this, the perspective of capabilities is directed at the *objective set* of opportunities to realise *different combinations* of certain qualities and functionings. Considering the chances of realisation, it is the *real, practical freedom* of people to *decide* for or against the realisation of certain functions and lifestyles, i.e. to be able to develop and to realise one's own conception of a good life that matters (cf. Sen 1992, 1999). This objective real freedom and the suitable institutional conditions enabling and facilitating this freedom is considered to be the good to be advanced. This means the Capability Approach is less concerned with establishing a coercion and discipline towards the "good" (Nussbaum 1998) i.e. the stipulation of a particular way of living, but rather with a definition of basic opportunities and capacities as well as their implementation that people are entitled to and which can be understood as the basis of the pursuit and realisation of *various* potentials, plans or designs of a good life (cf. Nussbaum 2000, 2006).

With respect to research the Capability Approach thus implies the task to formulate a realist conception of the possible, not just the actual. Against the background that such a formulation has to emanate from a diligent analysis of actual social realities, Amartya Sen (2009) has recently pointed out that the Capability Approach is a "comparative" rather than a "transcendental" approach for conceptualising social justice. Sen calls theories that sketch the state of 'perfect' justice "transcendental". Such theories might be misleading for advocating justice in the context of non-ideal circumstances in contemporary societies since an idea of the perfect just state is neither necessary nor sufficient to give directions for choosing within a reality in which ideal alternatives are neither likely to be viable nor to be feasible.

Despite the fact that we might not come to a reasoned agreement about the nature of a perfectly just, ideal state (cf. Sen 2009: 10ff.) the problem is that transcendental theories to justice aim only at identifying "social characteristics that cannot be transcended in terms of justice, and its focus is thus not on comparing feasible societies, all of which may fall short of the ideals of perfection. [... It] concentrates primarily on getting the institutions right, and it is not directly focused on the actual societies that would ultimately emerge" (Sen 2009: 6). Instead of constructing what a unique set of perfectly just institutions or societies might counterfactually be, Sen argues in favour for a comparative framework for evaluating justice and informing practical decision making which focuses on what feasible alternatives, actions or states are practically (relatively) more just than others (i.e. more appropriate in providing means and freedoms to flourishing) and what measures might lead to partial progress i.e. what measures might be promising in order to make (imperfect) states of affairs more just than they currently are. This comes close to the suggestion that instead of conceiving justice in terms of an "affirmative state – of formal equality, equal capacity, or shared freedoms" – it might be more convincing to conceptualize justice in term of "a never-ending effort to make social relations less arbitrary, institutions less unjust, distributions of resources and options less imbalanced, recognition less scarce" (Wacquant 2003: 12). This may come close to what John Dewey (1927) used to call 'democratic experimentalism' which involves a constant (re-)evaluation and improvement of situations and arrangements respectively a direction of movement rather than technologically deducing form an unmodifiable institutional property of a transcendental, determined ideal which might be decoupled from real life situations.

Sen's way of a avoiding a substantive, morally authoritarian, perfectionalist conception of the good as an ultimate destination is to thoughtfully figuring out what could make the world less unjust, for this task approaches which construct unitary states of perfect justice – or what Thoedor W. Adorno (1995, 2000) would have called "positive utopias" – or other kind of knowledge about the non-arbitrary nature of 'pure' justice in abstract terms, is neither necessary nor particularly helpful. However the metric Sen proposes for a comparative approach to justice *is* capabilities which encompasses the real freedom to develop and realise one's own conception of a good life.

Sen's suggestion in favour of "comparative" approaches to conceptualise social justice reflects the demand that an ambitious theoretical approach to capturing social inequality has not only to be philosophically sound but also to prove itself in a complex empirical reality. In particular the conceptualisation of the Capability Approach as a comparative approach renders it possible – but also points to the requirement – to apply the Capability Approach in empirical investigations.

The contributions in this volume are therefore not in the first place abstract discussions about the philosophical foundations of the Capability Approach but rather (empirical) applications of the Capability Approach against the background of social chance, political dynamics and welfare reforms in modern societies. In particular the issue of inequality in childhood and youth is analysed within the evaluative framework of the Capability

Approach. Put together the contributions assess whether the application of the Capability Approach makes a difference, whether it may have unintended side effects and eventually whether and in how far it is appropriate to reformulate social inequality in childhood and adolescence in the language of capabilities and thus subsequently to reformulate the public policies in terms of the task of closing the capability gap.

The young, freedom, agency and well-being

To apply the Capability Approach to childhood and adolescence seems to be both a particular necessity and a particular challenge. Enhancing the real freedom to develop and realise one's own conception of a good life is especially important in the case of young people. They are in a crucial stage of life. While still under some parental and societal care they are expected to make up their mind about what kind of life they want to lead. Yet, their freedom to do so is restricted in many ways. Often they are mainly seen as a focus group of educational strategies in the form of investments in human capital. The young are one of the groups with the highest risk of poverty. Policy tends to view them as patients for whom the parents and the government has to care. The Capability Approach could imply a substantial shift of perspectives. Instead of viewing them mainly as patients the capability perspective opens up the route to see them as agents without burdening them with the exclusive responsibility for their successes and failures in leading a good life. By focussing on the real opportunities they face, the Capability Approach can take account of the restrictions entailed on them by the institutional and social setting as well as of what it mean to lead a life one values and has reason to value.

However, the Capability Approach does not really discuss young people as agents. Its main advocates rather make some short remarks on children. Nussbaum (2000: 89f.) holds that in the case of children it is "perfectly legitimate" to require certain types of functionings instead of looking at their capabilities because "Exercising a function in childhood is frequently necessary to produce a mature adult capability". In a similar way Sen (2006: 10) argues that the promotion of children's "freedom may well have to be, often enough, in the hands of others". He views the task of public policy mainly in providing and maintaining opportunities to young persons "in line with what they can be reasonably expected to want". There is agreement that education is important but it is not qualified as to whether this comprises more than primary education. Apart from the general idea that children and adolescents have to be prepared for taking part in society and for participation in public reasoning in particular, the Capability Approach does not elaborate how that can and should be ensured. Thus, there is a theoretical capability gap concerning justice for the young to be filled.

Empirical Research with respect to the capability gap is needed

In general research on the basis of the Capability Approach is on the one hand about whether people have access to what they reasonably aspire to be and to. On the other hand, and most importantly, capabilities oriented research on well-being is also about whether people have the real and genuine freedom to choose among such options but also to participate in the process of creating options. In the centre of concern is therefore "the extent of freedom (negative and positive) people have to achieve doings and beings that they (have reason to) value" (Wolff & de-Shalit 2007: 37). In terms of inequality therefore, the fundamental metric is "the capability each has to enjoy valuable activities and states of being" (Alkire 2002: 4).

This should apply not only to mature adults, but also to the young who live through crucial stages of human life. The young are especially vulnerable to deprivation in terms of the functionings they actually achieve as well as in terms of their freedom to voice their concerns and to develop their own views of what constitutes a good life.

From the view point of the Capability Approach the important factors are the range and quality of the spectrum as well as the number of those opportunities and capacities of people to be able to realise doings and beings important to their own concept of a good life that can effectively be realised and differentiated. This is to be measured and reconstructed *empirically*.

In order to do so it is seemingly necessary to overcome a gap between different disciplines concerned with the Capability Approach. The Capability Approach highlights the need to work cross disciplinary.

This volume is part of this task. The contributions of the volume critically assess what the Capability Approach has to provide in order to appropriately grasp social inequality and to broaden the information base in capturing and promoting social justice.

The contributions of this volume are subdivided into two broad sections. The articles in the first section "Renegotiating Social Justice" argue from a more general and connectional perspective assessing the potential and feasibility of the Capability Approach to inform both public policy and social and educational research. The second section "Capability Gaps of the Young" scrutinises the implications of a capability perspective for investigating socially unequal childhood and adolescence. Both sections together map innovative perspectives for analysing what is needed in order to diminish the capability gap in the life of young persons and to promote social justice in current societies.

References

Adorno, T.W. (1995): Negative Dialectics. New York.

Adorno, T.W. (2000): Culture industry reconsidered. In: O'Connor, B. (Ed.): The Adorno Reader. Oxford.

Alkire, S. (2002): Valuing Freedoms: Amartya Sen's Capabilities Approach and Poverty Reduction. Oxford.

Anderson, E. (1999): What is the Point of Equality? In: Ethics 109, 287-337.

Arneson, R. (1999): Human Flourishing Versus Desire Satisfaction. In: Social Philosophy and Policy, 16, 113-142.

Berlin, I. (1969): Four Essays on Liberty. Oxford.

Bolte, K.M., Kappe, D. & Neidhardt, F. (1968): Soziale Schichtung. Opladen.

Bonvin, J.-M. (2009): Der Capability Ansatz und sein Beitrag für die Analyse gegenwärtiger Sozialpolitik. In: Soziale Passagen, 1, 1, 8-22.

Bonvin, J.-M. & Thelen, L. (2003): Deliberative Democracy and Cpabilities: The Impact and Significance of Capability for Voice. Paper presented at the 3rd Capability Conference 2003 in Pavia.

Bonvin, J.-M. & Rosenstein, E. (2010): Jenseits evidenzbasierter Steuerungsmodelle: Kognitive Rahmen und ihre normativen Implikationen in ‚Steuerungsmodellen zur sozialen Integration'. In: Otto, H.-U., Polutta, A. & Ziegler, H. (Eds): What Works – Welches Wissen braucht die Soziale Arbeit? Opladen, Farmington Hills.

Bourdieu, P. (1984): Distinctions. A Social Critique of the Judgment of Taste. Cambridge.

Bruckner, D (2009): In Defense of Adaptive Preferences. In: Philosophical Studies, 142, 3: 307-324.

Campbell, A. (1972): Aspiration, Satisfaction and Fulfillmen. In: Cambell, A. & Converse, Ph. (Eds.): The Human Meaning of Social Change. New York.

Cohen, G.A. (1993): Equality of What? In: Nussbaum, M. & Sen, A. (Eds.): The Quality of Life. Oxford.

Dewey, J. (1927): The Public and its Problems. New York.

Diener, E. (1984): Subjective Well-Being. In: Psychological Bulletin 95, 3, 542-575.

Erikson, R. (1993): Descriptions of Inequality: The Swedish Appraoch to Welfare Research. In: Sen, A. & Nussbaum, M. (Eds.): The Quality of Life, 67-83.

Frey, B. & Stutzer, A. (2005): Happiness-Research: State and Prospects, Review of Social Economy, 62, 2, 207-228.

Frey, B. & Stutzer, A. (2007): Should National Happiness Be Maximized? University of Zurich, Institute for Empirical Research in Economics. Working Paper 306.

Gasper, D. (2002): Is Sen's Capability Approach an Adequate Basis for Considering Human Development? In: Review of Political Economy 14, 4, 435-461.

Gilbert, D. (2002): The American Class Structure: In An Age of Growing Inequality. Belmont.
Goldthorpe, J. (1996): Class analysis and the reorientation of class theory: the case of class persisting differentials in educational attainment. In: The British Journal of Sociology, 47, 481-505.
Harsanyi, J. (1982): Morality and the Theory of Rational Behaviour. In: Sen, A. & Williams, B. (Eds.): Utilitarianism and Beyond, Cambridge.
Hradil, S. (1987): Sozialstrukturanalyse in einer fortgeschrittenen Gesellschaft – Von Klassen und Schichten zu Lagen und Milieus. Opladen.
Hurka, Th. (1993): Perfectionism. Oxford.
Kelman, M. (2005): Hedonic psychology and the ambiguities of "welfare." In: Philosophy and Public Affairs 33, 4, 391-412.
Kreckel, R. (1992): Politische Soziologie der sozialen Ungleichheit. Frankfurt a.M., New York.
Kreckel, R. (2006): Soziologie der sozialen Ungleichheit im globalen Kontext. (Der Hallesche Graureiher 2006-4). Halle, Institut für Soziologie.
Layard, R. (2005): Happiness: Lessons From a New Science, New York & London.
Lukes, S. (2005): Power: A Radical View. 2nd edition. Basingstoke.
Morriss, P. (2002): Power: A Philosophical Analysis. 2nd edition. Manchester.
Müller, W. (1977): Klassenlagen und soziale Lagen in der Bundesrepublik. In: Handl, J. et al. (Eds): Klassenlagen und Sozialstruktur. Frankfurt a.M. & New York.
Murphy, R. (1988): Social Closure. The Theory of Monopolization and Exclusion. Oxford.
Navarro, V. (2000): Development and Quality of Life: A Critique of Amartya Sen's Development as Freedom. International Journal of Health Services 30, 661-674.
Ng, Y.-K. (1996): Happiness Surveys: Some Comparability Issues and an Exploratory Survey Based on Just Perceivable Increments. In: Social Indicators Research, 38, 1-27.
Ng, Y.-K. (1997): A Case for Happiness, Cardinalism, and Interpersonal Comparability. In: The Economic Journal, 107, 1848-1858.
Nussbaum, M. (1988): Nature, Function, and Capability: Aristotle on Political Distribution. In: Oxford Studies in Ancient Philosophy (supplementary volume), 145-184.
Nussbaum, M. (1998): The Good as Discipline, the Good as Freedom. In: Crocker, D. & Linden, T. (Eds.): Ethics of Consumption: The Good Life, Justice, and Global Stewardship. Lanham.
Nussbaum, M.(1999): Gerechtigkeit und das gute Leben. Frankfurt a. M.
Nussbaum, M. (2000): Women and Human Development. Cambridge.
Nussbaum, M. (2003): Capabilities as Fundamental Entitlements: Sen and Social Justice. In: Feminist Economics, 9, 33-59.
Nussbaum, M. (2006): Frontiers of Justice: Disability, Nationality, Species, Membership. Cambridge.
O'Neill, O. (2000): Towards justice and virtue, a constructive account of practical reasoning. Cambridge.
Otto, H.-U., Polutta, A. & Holger, Z. (Eds.) (2009): Evidence-based Practice – Modernising the Knowledge Base of Social Work. Opladen, Farmington Hills.
Otto, H.-U., Scherr, A. & Ziegler, H. (2010): Wieviel und welche Normativität benötigt die Soziale Arbeit. In: neue praxis 2, 137-163.

Otto, H.-U. & Ziegler, H. (Eds.) (2010): Education, Welfare and the Capabilities Approach – A European Perspective. Opladen, Farmington Hills.
Parkin, F. (1979): Marxism and Class Theory: A Bourgeois Critique, Cambridge.
Robeyns, I. (2005): The Capability Approach: A Theoretical Survey. Journal of Human Development 6, 1, 93-114.
Roemer, J. (1982): A General Theory of Exploitation and Class. Cambridge.
Salais, R. (2008): Capacités, base informationelle et démocratie délibérative. Le (contre)-exemple de l'action publique européenne. In : De Munck, J. & Zimmermann, B. (Eds.) : La Liberté au prisme des capacités. Amartya Sen au-delà du libéralisme, Paris, Editions de l'EHESS.
Sayer, A. (2005): The Moral Significance of Class. Cambridge.
Sayer, A. (2009): Who's Afraid of Critical Social Science? In: Current Sociology, 57, 767-786.
Sen, A. (1980): Equality of what? In: Sen, A. (Ed.): Choice, Welfare and Measurement. Oxford.
Sen, A. (1984): Resources, Values and Development. Oxford.
Sen, A. (1992): Inequality Reexamined. Oxford.
Sen, A. (1993): Capability and Well-Being. In: Sen, A. & Nussbaum, M. (Eds.): The Quality of Life. Oxford.
Sen, A. (1999): Development as Freedom. New York.
Sen, A. (2006): Children and Human Rights. New Delhi: Institute for Human Development.
Sen, A. (2009): The Idea of Justice. Cambridge.
Swartz, D. (1997): Culture and Power: The Sociology of Pierre Bourdieu. Chicago.
Tilly, Ch. (1998): Durable Inequality. Berkeley, CA.
Wacquant, L. (2003): Pointers on Pierre Bourdieu and Democratic Politics. In: Constellations, 11, 1, 3-15.
Warner, L. (1960): Social Class in America: A Manual of Procedure for the Measurement of Social Status. New York.
Wolff, J. & De Shalit, A. (2007): Disadvantage. Oxford.
Wright, E. (1985): Classes. London.
Wright, E. (2009): Understanding class: Towards an integrated analytical approach. In: New Left Review, 60, 101-116.

Part I – Renegotiating Social Justice

Robert Salais

From Social Citizenship to Social Capability in an Enlarged Economic Europe

The concept of social citizenship[1] as it has developed since T.H. Marshall[2] has given rise to a body of criticism. This criticism focuses notably on the body of thought that underpins the concept, its teleological view of the history of rights, and its idealised presentation of the welfare state. Section 1 focuses on two fundamental flaws that make it difficult to envision the future of social Europe without a wide redefinition of this concept. These flaws are: 1. the absence of any reference to work as social and productive activity; 2. its neglect, paradoxically, of concerns related to social inclusion. Enlargement has become, surreptitiously, a social laboratory in which competing conceptions of European policy reform are tested. Five years later, enlargement has, above all, contributed to put in danger the meagre progress towards European citizenship observed before. Until now and maybe still for some years in effect, people from the new Member States are not entitled, due to varied but quite general, national restrictions, with the freedom to move and to reside in other Member States. This has direct and indirect effects on European citizenship, especially on national social legislation. One of the major issues was – and still remains – the fear of social dumping practices, stemming from the acceding countries. However the effective risk of social dumping cannot be properly assessed without stressing the major problem, which is the lack of autonomous economic development for these countries. Such a lack of autonomy has been recently revealed to its full extent and implications by the economic crisis (Section 2). Section 3 confronts a citizenship based on minimum welfare transfers and standards, with a formulation in terms of social capability, which in our view is better suited to the challenges of economic development. We conclude with some remarks with regards to the underlying political approach.

1 This paper is a revised and updated version of a contribution published in Lars Magnusson and Bo Stråth, (eds.) (2004): A European Social Citizenship? Preconditions for Future Policies in Historical Light, Bruxelles, 179-200.

2 Marshall, 1950, in particular. For the critics made, see the introduction of Magnusson and Strath, 2004, *op. cit.*

1. Fundamental flaws of the concept of social citizenship

Since the end of 1990s, the European political debate has converged towards the idea (false or true, no matter) that social protection systems are too costly and that enlargement could give businesses a chance, for a time, to reduce labour costs without (overly) affecting product quality or economic efficiency. Such expectations place work at the heart of the social reform in Europe, for the European Union as well as for its Member States. The second concern of the European Union is about social inclusion for all, the idea being that social expenditure should be considered as a "productive factor". Both ideas draw attention on the ways by which social expenditure can become an investment into human capital (in other words, into intensity and quality of work). Can social citizenship be the right institutional vector to convert social expenditure into efficient human capital and effective access to employment? Or is, too often, social citizenship mainly a political façade that dissimulates something different, namely the need to keep the poor under social control (paragraphs 1.1 and 1.2)? One needs to eliminate a misleading ambiguity between two models of social citizenship, the Anglo-Saxon (which is dominant) and the Scandinavian ones. Almost everything opposes these two models. Clearing up the difference helps to understand that what Europe needs is not a general normative model, but a pragmatic approach to social progress (paragraph 1.3).

1.1 Social citizenship and work

Social citizenship originates from the Anglo-Saxon conception of social rights. Social rights according to T.H. Marshall do not take their justification from participation in the creation of wealth (in other words, from work), as a counterpart for the social effort granted by the community. In Marshall's conception, social rights give a right to share the existing wealth, but not to participate in its creation. This is the first flaw that undermines the concept of social citizenship.

In a market democratic economy composed with active "market" citizens, contributing to the financing of social protection by one's own personal activity (whatever the institutional system) establishes a claim for protection that the society owes and must honour to those who are or have been active, and to their family. As a social activity – and on the condition that all useful activities are included, not only paid activity in the strict sense – work thus becomes the source of the political legitimacy for the right of access to this protection. Furthermore, participating in a wealth-producing activity gives participants the right to take part in collective decisions regarding the financial bases of social protection and the ways in which these funds are used.

The strength of civil and political rights comes from the "social *contract*", i.e. from the system of mutual duties and rights that they guarantee in a political society. An active participating social citizenship places itself in a comprehensive conception of fundamental rights in which civil, political, economical and social rights form a united set in which the realization of one of these rights is a support for the realization of the others.

But at the turn of the 19th to the 20th century, British social reformers (of who Marshall pursued the philosophy) have other political concerns. They were thinking of passive social citizenship rather of an active one. They deemed that founding rights upon work activity would favour the corporatist power of trade unions and their control of the market and working conditions (tariff negotiation, financial support for strikes, control of apprenticeship training and mobility).[3] They were eager to cut off any possibility of material support, hence to offer rights that were not founded on work. Their target was, in particular, the workers excluded from professional and trade systems, with a political intent to divide. For the main preoccupation of these reformers was to create a labour market freed from what they consider to be rigidities that hinder its optimal operation. Hence, from the outset, the justification of social rights in Anglo-Saxon countries is remaining vague and insecurely anchored, because it cannot truly assume its ultimate goals. According to T.H. Marshall's well-known phrase (Marshall 1950), social rights emerge, after civil rights and political rights, as "as the full range of rights, from the right to share the social heritage, to the right to live as a civilised being, in keeping with prevailing societal standards". The apparent liberty granted to individuals remains but a formal right, for individuals have no effective material basis – participation in the collective effort – to support their claims.

1.2 Social citizenship and inclusion

The second concern about social inclusion for all (EC 2003) arose in Europe. It was about finding economic justification and reassessment of social expenditures, in order to safeguard as most as possible the European social model. The underlying basic issue is how to create positive links between the economic effectiveness of social protection and expectations of social justice.

The second flaw that undermines the social citizenship Marshall's approach is that it could not work in favour of effective social inclusion. The European Union's emphasis on social inclusion stems from another tradition, that of the philosophies of social justice for which integration of all individuals into society is a fundamental objective.

---

3 Mansfield, Salai, Whiteside, 1994.

In philosophies of social justice (among the most eminent ones are those of John Rawls and Amartya Sen), the objective of participation for all remains central. Disagreement between people may persist within a society – as everybody knows that there are many possible options – as to the specific methods of evaluation of the value of individual contributions and of the level of social support in terms of efficiency and justice, but regardless of this disagreement, one must find the way for participation for all. This aim is nothing other than a concern for social ties: the aim is to ensure what could be called the first stage of solidarity. In such a solidarity framework, everything that it is possible to do at the different levels of social organisation must be undertaken to give each individual the chance to participate. Each individual must be put in a position to demonstrate his or her capability to make a valuable contribution, via an activity (work, in this sense). This objective holds whatever the scale by which value is estimated (be this value economic, cultural, political or social) and whatever the form of collective support granted to the individual. To be achieved, this requires that public policies create for each person a set of material, social and economic conditions that help her to develop her capabilities.

Some will retort that Anglo-Saxon countries, the original sphere of the concept of social citizenship, have pushed work to the fore as a factor of inclusion in their recent social reforms, such as workfare in the United States or its British counterpart, the New Deal. This is a mistaken and misleading view. For these reforms confuse personal duty (which presupposes the exercise of free will) with external obligation that negates the primacy of individual liberty. And they conceive public policies as devices to oblige people to take in charge external obligation in their behaviour. The social citizenship such reforms afford is a second-class citizenship, a reminder of the time when, even at the turn of the 19th century, the poor had to relinquish their civil rights when they entered the workhouse (so aptly named). In effect, the innovation of recent reforms has been to re-establish not work as a core value, but the *obligation to work* as a political instrument. In its gentler version, the pressure to work is exercised by a system of incentives and penalties. For young people in particular, the acceptance of a task, no matter which, becomes under this system a criteria of merit that resuscitates the old moral criteria formerly reserved for the poor. Reminiscence of such conceptions is visible even in the so-called "Third way": "Unemployment benefits, for example, should carry the obligation to look actively for work, and it is up to governments to ensure that welfare systems do not discourage active search. As an ethical principle, 'no rights without responsibilities' must apply not only to welfare recipients, but to everyone" (Giddens 1998: 66). It can be remarked that historically speaking the United Kingdom is the only country in the European Union that does not possess a charter of fundamental rights[4], and that the legal notion of citizenship was instituted there only in 1948. Furthermore, the flat-rate support payments recommended under Beveridge's full-employment model have been in practice largely implemented in the form of means-tested payments. The obligation to work denies the question which is the point of departure of all theories of justice: how can the fundamental rights of individual and collective liberties be reconciled with the creation of a society in which people can live together? As pointed out by Amartya Sen, the requirement of participation must be founded on effective freedom, in other terms on capabilities. Only this development can create a dynamic interaction between rights and duties. This issue will be addressed in Section 3.

Thus there is deception. As for the mistake, it lies in the fact that in these countries the scope and quality of social citizenship are subordinated to the amount of funding that the State budget is willing to allocate annually. Social citizenship is dependent on taxes, always unpopular and too high. It is subject to the vagaries of the political market, potential targets for budget restrictions when public deficits must be reduced, as is the case today under the pressure of growing public deficits and on the name of the Stability and Growth Pact. Quite often social citizenship is fragmented into a series of temporary, specific and local welfare programmes, as in the United States. Far from emerging as a development of political citizenship, social citizenship risks to be subject to the whims and wishes of those who vote. A visible consequence is the disappearance of a growing number of individuals, particularly young people, from any social register (voter rolls or social agencies – or censuses as in Great-Britain). Under this conception, social citizenship is at risk of excluding, rather than including, because the conditions imposed are so repulsing to the people who should be the first to benefit.

1.3 The two conceptions of social citizenship

In his work on the three worlds of welfare capitalism[5] Esping-Andersen (1990) went to considerable lengths to avoid the logical dead-ends in the concept of social citizenship. He sought to bestow scientific and political legitimacy on a number of models for social protection, among which the liberal model (called "residualist") figures as a foil. The aim was to erect the Scandinavian model as the true model of social citizenship. So it might seem possible to re-examine the Scandinavian model of social citizenship, and use it as the matrix for discussion and social reform in Europe. For, apart from politi-

4 And, recently, the UK agrees on the Lisbon Treaty under the condition of opting out of the European Charter of Fundamental Rights; it will not, thus, apply to the UK (nor to Poland and the Czech Republic).

5 Another concept introduced by T.H. Marshall.

cal problems[6], it must be recognised that despite the shift towards activation in northern countries (Abrahamson 2000) the latter are still fundamentally different from Anglo-Saxon countries and in fact closer to the countries of continental Europe. As a general rule, a large majority of social protection systems in Europe (as well as within the OECD) continue to operate under rules of funding and provision that are based either on work (for the major part) or on the universalistic model. When combining the OECD database SOCX and the International Labour Organisation's ISSADOC database, it becomes apparent that in the mid-1990s, out of 163 systems characterised for OECD countries, only 22 relied on means-testing (for the most part in Anglo-Saxon countries). One hundred and eight systems distributed their aid according to rules based on work, and 33 according to universalistic rules. The northern and continental EU countries devote a larger share of their GDP to social expenditures than do Anglo-Saxon countries (even after correction for the effects of taxation).[7] Until now there has been no dramatic move away.

Graphs 1 A to D[8] (Annex) show that even in the countries most typical of EA's models (Sweden and the United Kingdom, for example), expenditure for a given risk generally comes from several types of regimes (means-tested; work-based; universalistic). They also show that the analysis should not be restricted to monetary payments, but must include in-kind expenditures that are publicly funded (among which are found notably hospitals, retirement homes, day-care centres, and their staff). Sweden, a universalistic country according to EA's typology, also has retirement and unemployment regimes based on work. The country gives more weight to expenditure for infrastructure. The United Kingdom, a "residualist" country, nonetheless has universalistic-type pension and healthcare systems, even if they are sometimes not very generous. No country deals with a unique model to implement its social protection system.

More specifically, graphs 1 A to D show the average value the community places on a retiree, an unemployed person and a family respectively, in each country of the European Union (the United States is included for purposes of comparison). It can reasonably be assumed that these orders of magnitude, pertaining to the mid-1990s, are still valid today. In each case the data refers to annual social expenditures per beneficiary. These expenditures have been divided by the average remuneration in the country, so as to correct the national efforts for differences in per capita productivity, and improve the comparison. Indeed logically it is easier for a rich and highly productive

6 In his recent work Esping-Andersen himself no longer seems to be convinced that such an attempt would be useful. Instead he focuses on seeking compromises between the northern and the Anglo-Saxon models, if indeed such compromises are possible.

7 Salais, 2003. In each country the systems are broken down into four types of social coverage: old age, labour accidents, family support, unemployment compensation.

8 Graph 1D (unemployment) has been already published in Salais 2003.

country to fund social expenditures than for a poor and less productive country. After correction, the figures show that, for the community as a whole, an unemployed person is worth on average 0.8 of a worker in Sweden, compared to only roughly 0.2 in the United Kingdom; a retiree is worth 0.6 of a worker in Sweden, as against 0.4 in the United Kingdom. This gives, indirectly an estimate of the social and economic value of a person in each country. As a human being every person deserves to benefit from the solidarity of the community (in a context of expectations of reciprocal efforts). As a repository of capabilities, every person represents an economic value, which justifies the investment in social expenditures made for the person. In short, all else being equal, we can conclude that the countries with low social expenditure per capita accord little value to the individual.

Esping-Andersen (EA) unfortunately neglected the political qualities of the third model, based on work, that he offhandedly called "conservative-corporatist". This last model is only characterised by default in his works. EA missed the turn here. For, as we emphasise before, this model remains the dominant one in Europe. Instead of seeking compromises between the northern and the Anglo-Saxon models, it would be closer to reality and to actual possibilities to look for viable compromises between the northern and continental models, on a European scale.

Hence several aspects appear to dramatically undermine the relevance of the concept of social citizenship in the European debate. For social citizenship has been implemented in two diametrically opposed ways, a minimalist one coming from Anglo-Saxon countries (which, in Europe, means the UK), a more promising one that has been implemented under two different variants in the Nordic and continental parts of Europe. Unfortunately, the European discourse on social citizenship borrows most of its features from the Anglo-Saxon conception. As we have seen, by rejecting any foundation on work, though it is dominant in the EU, such a conception puts an excessive limitation on the scope of *justifiable* social protection. Lastly, and not least, the desire to establish a general normative model at the outset (the so-called rational "constructivist" approach) before engaging a reform action, is doomed to defeat, in light of historical trends and the practices observed. For the history of social rights is dominated by political pragmatism, not by dogmatism.

If one wanted to develop a right conception of social citizenship for Europe, it would be necessary, in any event, to determine a guiding principle to be used in all times and places to materialise this concept. Such a principle should allow diverse situations of action to be evaluated, despite their variety, through a common approach. As shown in the next sections, this requires reinterpreting social citizenship as effective provision of social capability.

2. Enlargement of Europe, social dumping and inequality of capabilities

There exists, undeniably, some risk of social dumping due to enlargement, although it is localised, and although the fears of having Western European countries invaded by hordes of Eastern population have not been materialised. Preventing social dumping will require economic development based on equality of capabilities. Paragraph 2.1 recalls the main traits in new member States with regards to productivity and social expenditure. As an alternative to an economic evaluation founded on price competition and the perfect market, we posit a social evaluation founded on capabilities and effective freedom of choice. Paragraph 2.2 compares the risk of social dumping for the European Union with the risk of the absence of any logic of economic and social development in the new Member States.

2.1 Productivity gaps and inefficiency of social expenditures in new Member States

Two macro-economic observations that contrast the new Member States on the one hand and "old" EU Member States on the other hand will serve as our point of departure. Among the latter we distinguish the sub-group of countries with (relatively) low per capita income (measured by per capita GDP): these are the southern countries included in the previous round of enlargement–Spain, Greece, Portugal. It is important to keep in mind that per capita income is also an overall indicator of the productivity of the economy in question.

These two observations are the following:

1. Shares of GDP that before their accession the "new" countries devote to social expenditures (education, health, social security, welfare) are equivalent to that of "old" EU countries (Table 1).
2. The per capita productivity (per capita GDP) of the "new" countries, by contrast, is on average three times lower than that of "old" EU countries (Figures 1 and 2).

Table 1:

Source: EPI, Fiscal Policy in Transition, CEPR, 1997

Public Expenditure (% of GDP)							
Country	**Total**	**Current**	**Consumption**	**Subsides**	**Social Security and Welfare**	**Interest**	**Capital**
Belgium	54,7	52,6	14,2	2,9	24,8	10,7	2,0
Danmark	57,6	55,3	24,7	3,0	20,5	7,2	2,3
France	50,2	46,6	18,3	1,6	23,5	3,1	3,6
Germany	45,8	42,3	18,5	1,9	19,3	2,6	3,5
Ireland	44,5	43,5	14,6	4,4	16,4	8,0	1,3
Italy	53,2	48,3	17,4	2,2	18,9	9,7	4,9
Netherlands	56,3	52,3	14,9	1,6	29,1	6,7	4,0
UK	42,9	38,1	20,0	1,1	13,7	3,4	4,7
Portugal	42,7	40,2	19,7	1,5	10,5	8,6	2,4
Spain	41,5	35,5	14,2	1,6	16,1	3,6	6,0
Greece	53,9	51,0	21,9	1,8	16,1	11,2	2,9
Poland	49,8	47,3	14,9	1,8	21,0	5,3	2,5
Hungary	55,3	49,9	18,7	3,5	18,8	8,9	5,3
Czech Republic	49,8	42,2	18,2	3,4	19,4	1,3	7,7
Slowakia	47,3	42,3	14,8	4,8	20,5	2,2	5,0
Slowenia	46,2	43,2	7,9	3,7	28,6	1,5	3,0
	Total	**Current**	**Consumption**	**Subsides**	**Social Security and Welfare**	**Interest**	**Capital**
Average EU	49,4	46,0	18,0	2,1	19,0	6,8	3,4
Average Low-Income EU	46,0	42,2	18,6	1,6	14,2	7,8	3,8
Average CEFs	49,7	45,0	14,9	3,4	21,7	3,8	4,7

Table 1 reproduces the Table 3.6 from EC, 1999, part B: 108.

Figure 1:

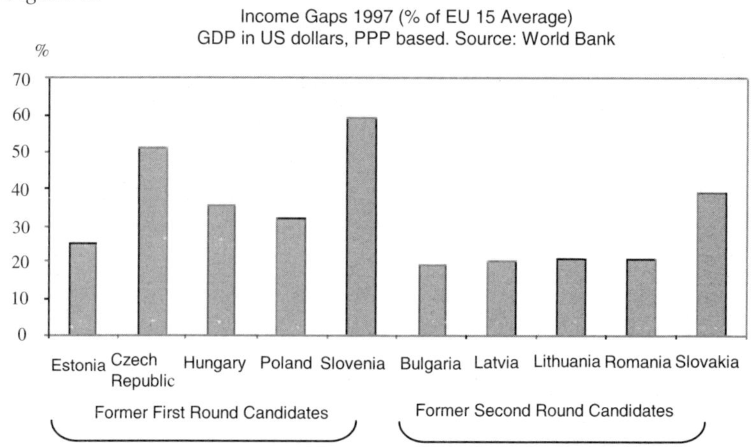

Figure 2:

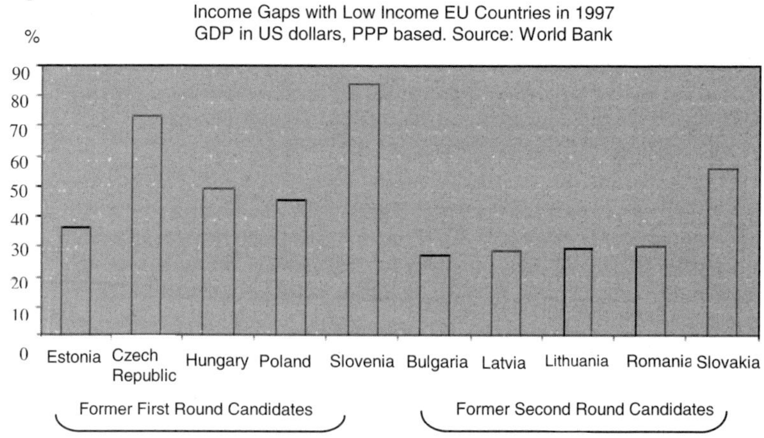

Figures 1 and 2 reproduce the figures 3.1 and 3.2 from EC, 1999, part B: 96.

The percentages vary, of course, from one country to another. At the end of the 1990s the income and productivity gap ranges from 1 to 10 for countries in the second wave of applicant countries (Romania, Bulgaria); it is between 1 and 2 for Slovenia. And yet, the new Member States devoted a higher percentage of their GDP to social expenditures than the one that can be observed, not only in Spain, Greece and Portugal, but in the United Kingdom as well.

If one takes seriously the objective of making social expenditure fundamentally a productive factor, the main problem that arises for the new Members is less the intensity than the low productivity of their social expenditure, given the limited effectiveness and mediocre quality of their human capital. This problem did not arise to this degree at the time of the previous enlargement. Ten years after the fall of the Berlin wall the gap had not narrowed. Twenty years later, in 2009, the gap has a little bit narrowed, but even the best-rated country, Slovenia, has its GDP per person equivalent to 60% of western European average. The least advantaged countries, Romania and Bulgaria, still stand under 20% of the western European average.[9] Econometric analyses made in 1999 estimated that it would take an average of 30 years for the GDP of acceding countries to converge towards the EU average (EC, 1999, Part B: 101). In 2009, that ultimate goal remains as remote as it was in 1999. And a true assessment should take on board the effects of the current economic crisis (especially public deficit and the lack of financial resources to invest).

In Sen's sense (see below, Section 3) the new Member States are faced with a dramatic problem in converting social expenditure into capabilities. More than the risk of social dumping, what is stressing is the lack of autonomous development, and of an economic development that would result in improved capability.

2.2 Social dumping or autonomous economic development

An assessment of the risk of social dumping must look at both sides of the issue. The cost of labour was impressively low at the beginning: in the proportion from one to five or six, depending on the country. But productivity was on average low and the quality of work relatively mediocre to begin with. And labour costs are the most often a modest part of total costs. Competition also has two sides: competition on prices, and competition on quality and innovation. All of these parameters must be assessed actively and simultaneously. This exercise, which we only briefly sketch out here, is needed to provide factual economic arguments (less easily falsified) in response to stances that aim to have a political influence, via enlargement, on the structural reforms of the labour market and social protection in the EU.

In price competition and displacement of jobs, what counts is the unit cost, i.e. the cost of remuneration per unit produced. Labour may be cheap, but the potential "promises" can be fallacious. If that labour produces less per unit of time, the hoped-for gains are lost. On the other hand, other hidden costs must be added to the direct unit cost – these are costs tied to the absence of infrastructure for production (transport, communication, energy), organisa-

9 Source: The Economist, 7-13 November, 2009: 26. See also EC 2006.

tional tasks (local public administration, banks, degree of compliance with contracts, for example) and social needs (housing, worker transportation, healthcare, schools, day care centres, etc.). These indirect costs have a negative impact on company performance, internally and on the market. As the economic studies undertaken to prepare for enlargement have concluded, the risk of widespread social dumping can be discounted, especially as the economies of the acceding countries are small in terms of GDP, compared to those of the EU countries. The economic shock that they could generate would be small. However, there are risks of localised dumping and a subtler influence on legal and social regulations on work in Europe.

The localised risks of social dumping pertain to standard products and services that are easy to produce, and for which local labour can conceivably learn to adopt "western" standards of performance and quality of work (and organisation). The labour that is threatened in the "old" EU Member States is unskilled and low-skilled labour. The regions that are threatened are those where this type of production is located, typically the regions on the western and southern edges of the EU that in the 1970s and earlier received funds to invest in this type of production. Experience with implantation in acceding countries shows a significant gap between "Western" and "Eastern" standards. The learning curve is long and costly, even for common consumer products. It apparently pushes some companies to buy businesses in Eastern Europe, keep the employees as long as needed to fulfil the social clauses, and then close the businesses and supply the market directly from their factories in Western Europe. Generally speaking, the structure of trade between the EU and the acceding countries shows that the EU exports sophisticated products with high unit value, and imports low-value standard products from the acceding countries.[10] These imported products are often integrated as components in more elaborate EU products that are then exported to the acceding countries, and elsewhere (products such as standard cast-metal parts or wiring components for car assembly plants). Enlargement is a good business for European firms. France, for instance, had in 2002 a favourable trade balance with the PECO of around 2.4 billions Euros.[11] This intertwining of economies does not facilitate autonomous economic development. Since the transition to a market economy, direct investment has targeted first of all major urban centres (such as Budapest, Prague, Warsaw, Bratislava, etc.) and the regions, often already more developed than others, that are close to western borders (notably with Germany and Austria).

---

10 68% of exports of acceding countries were already directed towards the EU (in 2002). Even for agro-food products, European financial aids will not be able to compensate the difficulties to learn health standards required by the EU. For a long time, Polish peasants will only be able to export raw materials like milk or grains without any value-added transformation (CEPII Report 2002).

11 Source: DREE, French Ministry of Finances, 2003.

More pernicious and with long term effects could be the status of European second-class citizenship attributed to the persons and workers of the new Member States. Though freedom of movement and to reside is part of the European four fundamental economic freedoms (persons, services, goods, capital) and should have been untouchable (as it was for the enlargement toward Sweden, Denmark and Finland), the Accession Treaties have allowed old Member States to put durable restriction on that freedom for citizens coming from the new member States[12] (Carrera 2005; Kochenov 2003; Maas 2005). Effects are pernicious for these people of course first, but also for the citizens of the old Member States, particular for their national labour law and social protection. The final effects are subtler than pure limitations of freedom and much dangerous in the long run for these protections in all European countries, old or new.

Eastern workers can move freely toward the Western countries, under three statuses: being regularly recruited by a Western firm with a regular contract (for instance in Germany through a German-law contract of work); working as an independent, legally registered in the country where he moves; or recruited as posted worker and called to work by the firm that recruited him in a Western country for definite and limited periods (for instance, Latvian workers hired for posted work in Finland by a Latvian subsidiary of a Finnish firm – the case law *Viking* of the European Court of Justice[13]). The second and third cases are under the application of the freedom of services, on which no restriction has been put in Accession Treaties. In the first case (regular worker) the person benefits of the whole law and social protection of the country where he works. In the second case he has no benefit to social protection, being submitted to the economic law of the country but, in theory at least, he can charge her services at tariffs equal or close to the country's standards (market freedom). In the third case, as posted worker, he continues to be submitted to the law of her own country (Latvia in the *Viking* case); which means much lower wages and much less law and social protection for him, increased benefits and more flexibility for the hiring Western firm, and a legal way for the firm to escape Western labour markets so-called "rigidities".

It is easy to understand, for everybody and, all the more, for an employer, the gains attached to the recruitment of Eastern workers as posted workers or through a (most often false) status of independent. Legal recruitment through labour contract appears for such employers in all respects too costly. One knows, too, though they are difficult to number, that many Eastern people work as clandestine workers in Western countries at work and wage conditions inferior to the national legal standards. We have no enough room to develop more. It is enough to say that the efforts to develop in Europe social

12 Exceptions were Ireland, Sweden and the UK, though the economic crisis has led these countries to be less tolerant.

13 See, among others, Joerges and Rödl, 2008.

citizenship at a par of market citizenship are seriously undermined by such an evolution.[14] It favours, for the European Court of Justice, the coming back to a narrower and purely market-oriented jurisprudence that, more than ever, give priority and dominance of economic freedoms over social rights. Furthermore, an in-depth reading of the European Charter of Fundamental Rights (to come with the signature of the Lisbon Treaty) reveals a regrettable lack of judicial enforceable resources (Kenner 2003, chap. 12).

It is hard to assess the long-term dynamics of cost competition, within Europe, in the low and middle range segments of the product markets. It depends on contradicting elements. It is in the common interest of Eastern and Western Europe peoples to see this segment become weaker. The only way to fight against social dumping is not to protect Western markets from Eastern immigration and products. It will be achieved through a process to improve product quality and bolster innovation in the acceding countries. Such a process would prime a virtuous circle. The forces of competition structuring the economies of the acceding countries would increasingly integrate competition by quality and innovation. In this dynamic process the market would grow in scope and depth. New opportunities for profitable investment would emerge, leading to job creation and wage growth, and not just delocalisation. A growing mass of income would be distributed, creating domestic demand with rising expectations of quality. The evident features of a market with strong potential would attract new investors, with qualitatively more elaborate plans. And so it would continue. As remuneration and productivity gaps narrow, the material conditions for competition would be unified across all of Europe via a process of rising product and labour quality.

But under what conditions is such a virtuous circle possible? It could be difficult to achieve, due to two factors: the low quality of human capital to begin with, and the strategy of foreign investors (mostly European). A great deal will depend on the policies enacted by the EU.

2.3 Work and human capital in the acceding countries

A virtuous circle should assume high quality and motivated human capital, espousing a development perspective. Work is a key issue for such a virtuous circle. After a superficial and rather optimistic initial survey, based on apparently sizeable investment in education, particularly in vocational training and apprenticeship, evaluations tended to be more pessimistic. The labour workforce (men in particular) released by the massive shutdowns of the former socialist industrial sector, has revealed to be largely unemployable under the standards imported by foreign investors. Skills are outdated. Few workers

---

14 At a point that the question posed by Reich, 2001, union citizenship: metaphor or source of rights? has not yet received a convincing answer.

have completed secondary school, much less institutions of higher education. They are, for obvious reasons, entirely unaccustomed to the rules of the labour market and to employers' expectations in this market. Professional and geographical mobility, aptitude for learning or pride in a job well done, all are attitudes that were not valued under the previous economic regime. There are more developed areas, of course, and the new generations arriving on the labour market will have more and more of the qualities that the market is looking for, but full demographic renewal takes time, at least 30 years and presumably more. This is one of the factors explaining the low efficiency of social expenditures; added to this is the fact that these expenditures have had to finance the rise in unemployment, and the reduced number of jobs on offer: forced or early retirement for old workers, lay-offs, official or disguised unemployment. These are passive expenditures, and furthermore do not ensure a sufficient minimum income. To put these economies on the road to quality, what is needed is on the contrary a massive investment in human capital, at the price of a major unrelenting and properly distributed effort, both quantitative and qualitative.

The second difficulty – that could run counter to a strategy of investment in human capital – arises from another fundamental difference with the previous enlargement towards southern Europe. There is practically no existing local capitalism, at least not sufficiently well established or developed: no entrepreneurial class or investors, no workers trained up to standards of output and quality, no system of conventions and mutual expectations that are necessary for the efficient and equitable functioning of a market economy. The initial material, financial and human capital (mostly State-owned) was massively devalued during the transition period. The social consequences, as we have recalled, are unemployment, shrinkage of the active population, poverty, loss of working skills – all of which increase with distance from the western border and from major urban centres. The economic consequences are equally significant. Economic renewal and revival will depend, for a long time to come, on the intensity and nature of foreign direct investment (FDI). The main risk is that these investors might behave like *predators*, intelligent of course and even civilised, but predators nonetheless.[15] This has been verified by the fast retreat of most of foreign capital with the 2007-2008 economic crisis. Admittedly it would be an insult to consider all investors who take risks in buying (albeit at a very low price) obsolete enterprises as potential predators. The existence of potential markets is also a factor in implantation. But these markets are not enormous in size (the ten acceding countries represent 20% of the population of the enlarged Europe, but 5% only of its GDP). The absence of pre-existing and mature local capitalism complicates the process of obtaining balanced productive and financial compromises in order to

15 On the economics of predatory behaviour, see Milgrom and Roberts, 1982.

move upwards in the quality range. Furthermore, predatory appetites could turn out to be fairly limited, in the long run, in the face of local problems that may become long-lasting, and in light of better opportunities elsewhere (especially in Asia). The new Members were looking with fascination to the example of the "Irish tiger" (now in great difficulty). Like Ireland, they have reduced their taxes on profit at a dumping level, but the effect risks to be marginal. It may be too late for an "Irish tiger" strategy in the acceding countries, based on subcontracting for work in new technologies.

In those countries political authorities, for most of them, are weak or complacent in the face of powerful economic interests that come to invest. The European Commission is above all concerned with transferring the "Community *acquis*" within institutions (and among these, competition policy comes well before employment and social dialogue). It neglected the need to improve the "democratic quality" in political collective choices in those countries. The threat to condition the arrival of European funding to the rhythm of national *acquis* transpositions (and more generally to the Copenhagen criteria that should have guided the accession process) has not been really mobilised (Kochenov 2006). For the Commission, the enlargement process was, above all, strategic and political; it was not to create the conditions for these countries to become member of the EU at a par with those already in place. The Commission refuses to negotiate any special conditions that could facilitate a transition process in order to lay the foundations for endogenous development. The transplantation of "*acquis*" risks has been, presumably, more formal than effectively implemented, following in that durably implanted traditions in ex-socialist countries. At least that will be a long way, even if much has been already made.

What might be the strategy of intelligent predators, without any serious opposing forces? It could be, on the one hand, to obtain improvement in human capital and infrastructure in the immediate neighbourhood of their implantations, and on the other hand to maintain a sufficient differential in remuneration in the medium term, compared to average remuneration in the EU. For instance to profit from low wages, Philips has delocalised qualified jobs in services from Ireland to Lodz in Poland. The condition was that the Polish state takes in charge social contributions and the funding of professional training.[16] Such a strategy creates pockets of development, surrounded by zones of high unemployment. Investment is scattered, without overall coherence. There would be neither subsequent virtuous cycle of growth, nor significant progress in terms of jobs. European social funds (ESF, structural funds) are capped for the coming years. Deployment of these funds in Eastern Europe is fraught with political tension; the rules pertaining to these funds have yet to be learned and require reforms. As with economic and monetary

16 Source: Le Monde, 27 January 2004.

union in the 1990s, strict budget discipline will be the standard for governments that hope to converge towards the Euro currency as quickly as possible. Until now only Slovakia and Slovenia were able to join the Eurozone. With the economic and financial crisis, other new Members States are struggling hard below the line to join the Maastricht criteria. Dates for joining the Euro are postponed with regards to initial expectations and have become uncertain.

3. From social citizenship to social capability

We have seen in Section 2 that the risk of social dumping (evaluated according to a principle of price competition) must be balanced against the difficulties of endogenous development (competition in terms of quality). Section 3 will compare and contrast two pathways. The first path recommends instituting Europe-wide minimum welfare provision and rights, which would utilise a conventional justification based on social citizenship. The second path steers European policy towards a quest for balanced endogenous economic development, taking advances in effective capabilities and freedoms as both means and ends. In this perspective social citizenship is reformulated as social capability.

3.1 Citizenship and minimum welfare provision

Does the social citizenship approach have any chance of rising to the challenges of enlargement, in the structural conditions described above? The advocates of a liberal Europe, mostly restricted to a single and deregulated market, have already proposed their solution regarding citizenship. In enlargement they see a political opportunity to move ahead with this solution. It is best to let the 1999 Report on Enlargement speak for itself.

"In the case of transfers meant to guarantee a minimum welfare level to citizens, any tendency of poor people to move towards more generous jurisdictions and of rich tax-payers to move out of them makes it more difficult for local constituencies to implement their own preferred exclusion-preventing systems. Hence poor policy coordination can potentially generate a "race to the bottom" and/or excite political sentiment against free personal mobility. To ensure the long-run sustainability of social protection and free personal mobility within the EU, the social rights of European citizens could be defined in the form of minimum welfare standards at the EU level (Atkinson 1998[17]; Bean et al. 1998; Bertola et al. 1999). The wide income differentials among current and prospective EU members do imply that minimum-welfare transfers and services may also need to be co-financed at the

17 Reference not found into the Report.

EU level. The size of the relevant budget line, however, could be smaller than that of the current Structural, Cohesion, or Common Agricultural Policy funds (which currently amount to some 60 billion Euros and would more than suffice to lift all Europeans out of extreme poverty). Moreover, a poverty-prevention programme could in principle be run along the same lines as those existing funds and hence require no institutional reforms... Since entitlement to poverty-prevention transfers is based on citizenship (rather than on past contributions), proper implementation of any centrally co-funded minimal welfare program is intimately related to the intensity and character of migration flows from the EU, or from newly acceding countries during the transition period... A pan-European safety net would also contribute to ease social tensions in that it could be established as a European citizenship right. In the spirit of social cohesion, all EU legal residents could be fully integrated into such a system of minimal welfare provision. This would also provide a strong rational for EU-wide immigration policies" (Report on enlargement 1999, Part B: 32).

One does not know what future has been reserved to these ideas after 2004. No doubt, nevertheless, that they continue in the long run to inspire the dominant European thinking, especially for the reforms of European social policies and structural funds.

There is no contesting the need for a safety net, which under certain conditions, locally and *as a last resort* would prevent people from falling into extreme poverty. Exclusion takes many forms, but the first of them is the absence of any income. The above proposals are not restricted to basic allocation. However, the overall line is coined in terms of poverty-prevention and welfare programs, that old Anglo-Saxon tradition of "passive" citizenship we have seen Section 1. It is structured along the provision of basic income, without due concern about social and labour market inclusion. It is taken for granted that economic development has no link with social development.

Maybe it would be better to say that we are facing a multiple-targeting warhead missile to control European policy thinking. The immediate target is the risk of massive immigration flows towards the EU. To prevent these flows it is important to *fix* the population (and precisely the out-of-work poor) where they are, in the East and the South.[18] The second target is constituted with the social obstacles that block industrial conversion in these regions or in Europe, or render them more costly (in terms of promises and financing). The market is assumed to be efficient; those who are ejected from its sphere must be treated by social policies. Doling out a minimum allocation (modulated according to local cost of living) makes it possible to keep the minimum wage as low as possible, and maintain the advantage in terms of remuneration costs for underprivileged regions. For those who have jobs, remuneration would be uncoupled from income.

The third and in the long run most important target seems to be EU structural policies (among them, the most strategic being the reform of the Agri-

18 Selective immigration of qualified workers, by contrast, is welcome in countries like France or the UK.

cultural Common Policy). Basic allocation and minimum standards, whatever their precise technical or administrative formulation, would cost nothing to businesses, or to EU governments. It would be Europe's responsibility, and would yield savings in the European budget. This could fit well with the desire to block the European budget at 1% of the Europe GDP, as expressed by the major Western economies. Furthermore, no matter how favourable these structural policies are to market solutions and how limited funding is, they still represent a danger, because they offer opportunities for *economic* protest to actors and political authorities that seek for other solutions. Nonetheless, it is pertinent to underscore the formal homology, in terms of model for action, between the proposal and the Speenhamland model, source of the British law on poor people, made famous by Polanyi, 1944. These two models stem from an objective of holding the local population in place. Historiography since Polanyi has clearly demonstrated the economic role of the Speenhamland model. For the land-owning lords the aim was to keep poor seasonal workers in the parish during the agricultural off-season, in order to have abundant labour for the heavy work in spring and summer.

3.2 Generating social capability

Let us return to the facts outlined in Section 2. In spite of considerable efforts deployed by the new Member States, the restructuring of their economies is far from complete and it is probable that the current economic crisis would be the opportunity to do more than previously expected. Henceforth restructuring takes places via integration of the "Community *acquis*", and is subordinated to the strategies of foreign investors, European and non-European, who have bought up the bulk of production capacities and of the banking system. Take the regions that have been left out of the process or that have suffered the shutdown of obsolete enterprises. Unemployment is high, there are no jobs, the income shortfall is blatant, collective services (healthcare, housing, environment, public transportation), though European funding has come to renovate or create them, remain in a state of advanced decrepitude, investment and maintenance have been neglected for decades, the spirit of initiative has disappeared and dependency reigns. The observation that should be made is not that of a situation of poverty, but more in-depth of an absence, in some instances a nearly total absence, of *effective freedoms*. Prescribing minimum welfare transfers and standards presupposes that the beneficiaries have some room for choice in which they can make rational decisions. Today in these places there is no such room for effective choice in which life projects can be planned and realised, much less a possibility for rational conduct (outside of the bold ones who are ready to move to the West, beyond legal obstacles).

In these circumstances causes are overlapping, and generate vicious circles. There are no jobs, because transport infrastructure is mediocre, among other reasons. There is no profitable investment in transport means because effective demand is weak, given the general poverty. Work qualifications are unsuitable, which keeps foreign capital from investing; but without creation of jobs there can be no apprenticeship to update work standards. Even if money were available, the actors lack the skills to elaborate viable modernisation projects that are adapted to needs. The direct connection between resources and outcomes cannot be established. Beyond the lack of funding, the key problem is actors' *power to convert* financing into valuable outcomes, i.e. into effective access to life and work opportunities, at individual and collective levels. This power of conversion is weak. It reflects capability weakness. This power must be improved to begin with; development and infrastructure projects and action should target this improvement. There is of course an individual aspect to this power of conversion, but at all levels progress depends on the collective conditions – material (infrastructure, financial resources), institutional (legal and financial systems, forms of governance, procedures giving choice, guarantees of secure living standards) and human (training at all levels, motivation to work) – that are set up. This is the complete opposite of charity, even charity given in the name of European citizenship that would keep poor people where they are. The challenge is to start with development needs and create a virtuous circle in which effective participation of all where they are moves forward hand in hand with economic development.[19] The imperative precondition is that material, social and institutional environment be renewed in order to rebuild such spaces for choice and start an upward movement. Collective financing and investment must be guided and designed with this in mind. From the viewpoint of public action (local, national, European) the situations to be treated fall within the purview of a capability approach, in the dynamic and reflexive meaning as illustrated by the diagram below, developed by our own from Amartya Sen, 1985.[20]

Diagram

Improving the power of conversion of means into achievement of valuable outcomes

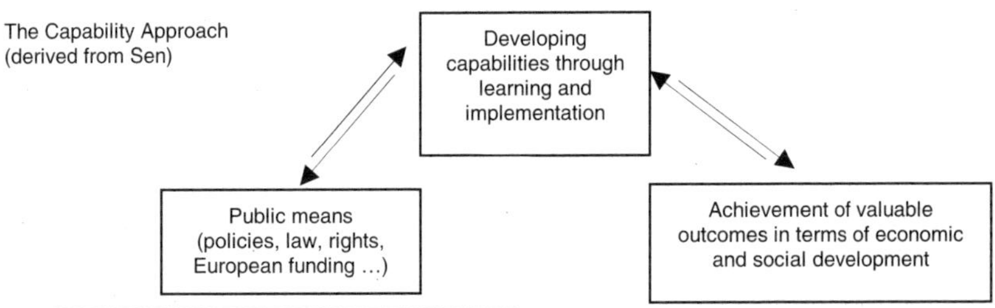

19 Sen 1999.

20 For comments, see Salais, 2004.

In practice, money is not totally lacking, from European structural funds in particular, even if the effort made by the EU is far smaller than for the first enlargement.[21] But this money can be multiplied if it is used to leverage other aide and to obtain loans guaranteed by the EU. There are also European procedures that encourage participation and could improve efficiency: European social dialogue mechanisms (that require active trade unions and employers' organisations, and apprenticeship of negotiation); European works councils (which could be forums for debating corporate strategy of job localisation within Europe and outside of Europe); incentives, albeit embryonic, for corporate social responsibility. Enlargement of social dialogue to a territorial dialogue including local authorities and non-governmental organisations would be favourable in an economic context where restructuring requires modernisation and creation of new activities. As we will see, to finish with the example of services in the general interest (water, transport, energy, environment, education, healthcare, etc.) seeking positive trade-offs between the general interest and the market, in real-life situations, is crucial for a social capability approach. Needs to be satisfied are enormous at a local level. For transportation and environment only, the Commission has estimated costs between 140 and 190 billions euros for the ten acceding countries. From 2004 to 2006, 22 billions euros will be provided for the local levels by the EU.

Some examples of such trade-offs in services at the local level are available. For example, in Gdansk (Poland)[22] a private French corporate group has invested in the modernisation of water supply services, which were initially extremely dilapidated (systematic interruption of supply, poor water quality). For the purpose of managing infrastructures the group and the city have created a joint company. The contributions of both parties have been defined, as well as remuneration and long-term return on investment. Water quality has been brought up to standard, and the price remains lower than the average price in Poland. By rebuilding a social dialogue a number of employees were trained in plant maintenance. These employees have been given incentives to create small businesses qualified as sub-contractors. These beginnings of a fabric of local small and medium enterprises (SME) will at term be active in the services market and contribute to its development. Significantly, this experience encountered some roadblocks due to the conception of European regulations. These regulations ignore intermediate situations: they hold the dogma of the market as sole reference, to the detriment of the inventiveness of private and public actors of the country.

---

21 The net cost of enlargement is very modest for European countries. For instance, it represents 15 Euros per capita and per year for France (Source: Foundation Robert Schuman).

22 Testimonials presented at the Confrontations colloquium held 6-7 November 2003 in Warsaw.

Conclusion

For social citizenship to become a reality in an enlarged Europe, priority must be given to the dynamics of economic development and progress towards social capability. Linking rights and duties in the exercise of effective freedoms must be a prime objective. This progress would in turn provide a key means to economic development. This requires, not political formulas or social gadgets, but a *political method*. The capability approach could be this method.[23] This approach implies to combine available instruments, to create deliberative structures that foster effective and verifiable commitment of all the actors in the field. Solutions must grow out of local situations so as to learn how to adequately harness available resources at different levels (European, national, local). The enlargement as it proceeds calls into question the foundations of European regulatory policy. It cannot be taken as synonymous with the transfer of the "Community *acquis*", or with pinning down the local population to prevent social dumping. The concept and effectiveness of the "Community *acquis*" presuppose a social background (as it has been established in EU countries since a long time) that did not exist in the new Member States at the required level and quality. The priority in these countries is to create such a social background via national and local initiatives of development, supported by the EU. A fine and collectively deliberated assessment should be made of all the projects already financed by European funds of their effectiveness, with regards to the provision of social capability to the people, not to speak of assessing what foreign investment has truly achieved or missed on that respect. An assessment, made not by experts using the European "novlangue", but through the active implication of all actors involved, local, national and European.

If European regulations are to seriously address situations as they are, they cannot be limited to create a single market governed by the competitive principle. To enter into an approach based on social capability, regulations must on the contrary integrate and mobilise a political principle of economic subsidiarity.[24] Subsidiarity should not be confused with the disengagement of the responsibility for Europe in social and economic development of these countries, but as a learning process for their national and local actors to do better with the resources they have or are provided with. The responsibility for pooling resources, project by project, should continue to be assumed at the lowest level of public action (and network of actors) in position to efficiently handle the decision-making processes. This level would act as the executive authority. This condition should hold regardless of the institutional level at which fund is sourced and distributed. If, for instance, for some type

23 For arguments, see Salais and Villeneuve, 2004.

24 Storper and Salais, 1997.

of projects, national governments demonstrate that they are the best suited to take responsibility they should be given the floor. For other projects, the best-suited level of decision would be local, and so on. However, local authorities remain very dependant from the central state level in these countries. A social capability approach should require a hard process of political learning, of local management and autonomy, and of effective participation in decision-making.

Such a social capability approach does not disregard the absolute right to life security, quite the contrary. It includes the right to basic income in last resort as well as effective access to minimum welfare standards. But this approach refuses to consider them as a panacea. Social policy is not window-dressing to cover up the holes of poverty, nor an instrument to grease the wheels of optimal market function. Its goals must integrate active participation and inclusion as the means and the ends of economic development. Only in this way can social citizenship come to life in Europe.

References

Abrahamson, P. (2000): The Active Turn in Scandinavian Social Policy: the Case of Denmark. Contribution in Colloque "Comparer les systèmes de protection sociale en Europe", Paris.

Bean, C., Betolial, S., Bertola, G. & Dolado, J. (1998): Social Europe: One for All?. Centre for Economic Policy Research (CEPR), London.

Bertola, G., Jimeno, J., Marimon, R. & Pissarides, C. (1999): Welfare Systems and Labour Markets in Europe: What Convergence before and after the EMU? Fondazione R. De Benedetti Report, Milano.

Carrera, S. (2005): What Does Free Movement Mean in Theory and Practice in an Enlarged EU. European Law Journal, 11, 699-721.

Economic Policy Initiative (EPI) (1997): Fiscal Policy in Transition. EPI, 3, CEPR and IEWS.

European Commission (EC) (1999): Enlargement Report. Part A Analysis and Part B Strategy.

European Commission (EC) (2003): The Draft Joint Report on Social Inclusion. COM, 773 final.

European Commission (EC) (2006): Enlargement, two years after: an economic evaluation. EC Occasional Paper.

Esping-Andersen, G. (1990): The Three Worlds of Welfare Capitalism. Cambridge.

Hedi Bchir, M. & Maurel, M. (2002) Impacts économiques et sociaux de l'élargissement pour l'Union Européenne et la France. CEPII, Paris.

Giddens, A. (1998): The Third Way. The Renewal of Social Democracy. Cambridge.

Joerges, C. & Rödl, F. (2008): On the 'Social Deficit' of the European Integration Project and its Perpetuation through the ECJ Judgements in Viking and Laval. RECON Online Working Paper.

Kenner, J. (2003): EU Employment Law. From Rome to Amsterdam and Beyond. Oxford.

Kochenov, D. (2003): The European Citizenship Concept and Enlargement of the Union. Romanian Journal of Political Science, 3, 2, 71-97, accessible on http://papers.ssrn.com.

Kochenov, D. (2006): Why the Promotion of the Acquis is not the Same as the Promotion of Democracy and What Can Be Done in Order to also Promote Democracy Instead Just Promoting the Acquis. Hanse Law Review, 2, 2, 171-195, accessible on http://papers.ssrn.com.

Maas, W. (2005): Citizenship, Free Movement, and EU Enlargement. Jean Monnet/Robert Schuman Paper Series, University of Miami, 5, 34.

Magnusson, L. & Stråth, B. (Eds.) (2004): A European Social Citizenship? Preconditions for Future Policies in Historical Light, Bruxelles.

Mansfield, M., Salais, R. & Whiteside, N. (Eds.) (1994) : Aux sources du chômage (1880-1914). Une comparaison interdisciplinaire France-Grande-Bretagne, Paris, Berlin.

Marshall, T.H. (1950): Citizenship and Social Class. In: Shafir, G. (Ed.) (1998): The Citizenship Debates: A Reader, Minneapolis, 93-112.

Milgrom, P. & Roberts, J. (1982): Predation, Reputation, and Entry Deterrence. Journal of Economic Theory, 27, 280-312.

Polanyi, K. (2001): The Great Transformation. London, [first edition 1944].

Reich, N. (2001): Union Citizenship – Metaphor or Source of Rights? European Law Journal, 7, 1, 4-23.

Reich, N. (2005): The Constitutional Relevance of Citizenship and Free Movement in an Enlarged Union. European Law Journal, 11, 6, 675-698.

Salais, R. (2003): Work and Welfare. Toward a Capability Approach. In: Zeitlin, J. & Trubek, D. (Eds.): Governing Work and Welfare in a New Economy. European and American Experiments, Oxford, 317-344.

Salais, R. (2004): Incorporating the capability approach into social and employment policies. In: Salais, R. & Villeneuve, R. (Eds.): Europe and the politics of capabilities. Cambridge, 283-300.

Salais, R. & Villeneuve, R. (Eds.) (2004): Europe and the politics of capabilities. Cambridge.

Sen, A. (1985): Commodities and Capabilities. North-Holland Lectures in Economics, 7, Amsterdam, North Holland.

Sen, A. (1999): Development as Freedom, Oxford.

Stewart, A. (1995): Two conceptions of citizenship. The British Journal of Sociology, 46, 1, 63-78.

Storper, M. & Salais, R. (1997): Worlds of Production. The Action Frameworks of the Economy. Cambridge MA.

Annex

Graph 1: Deflated value of a welfare potential recipient by country in 1995

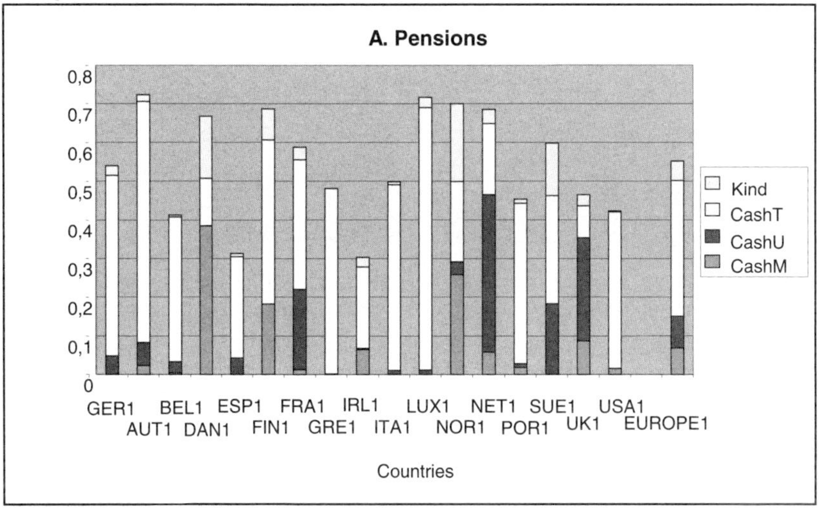

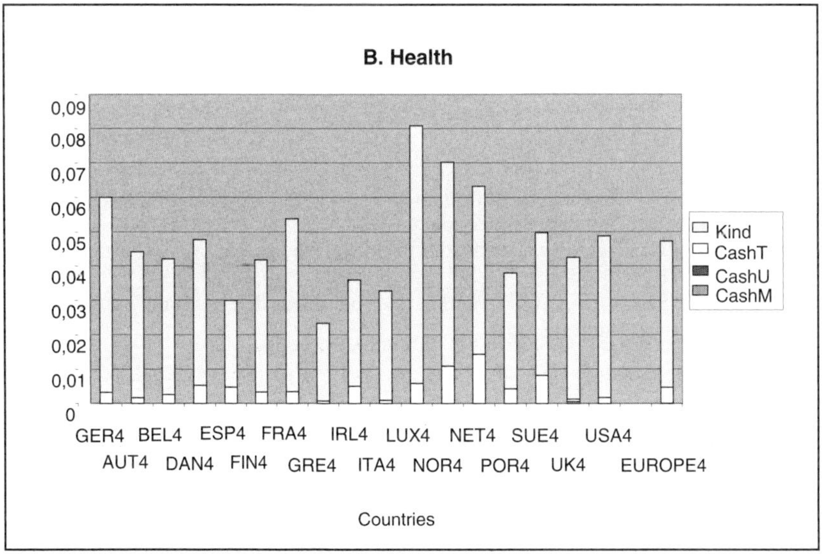

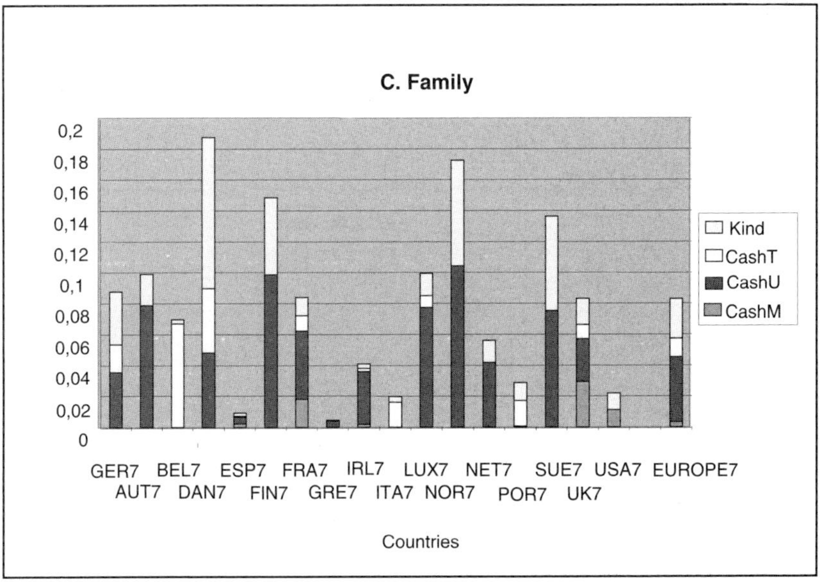

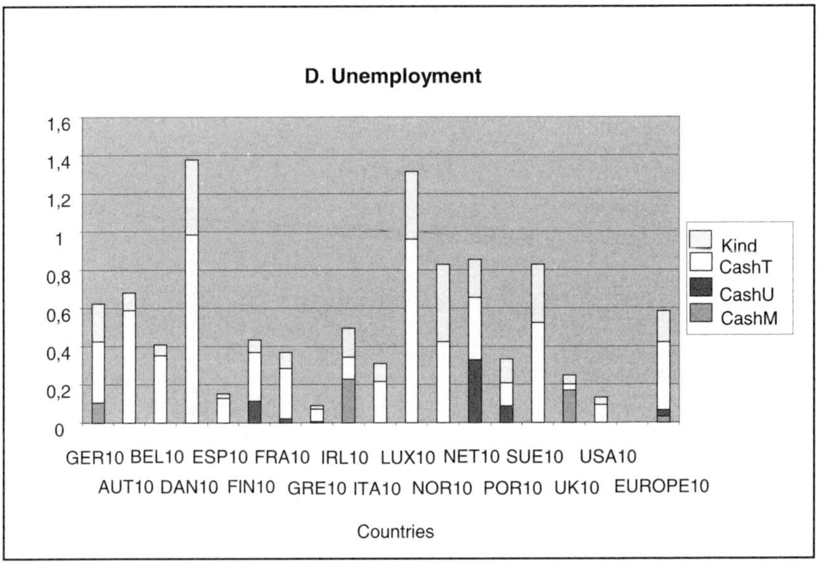

In Graph 1, the values are expressed as the expenditure per potential recipient divided by the mean workers' remuneration of the country.

Hartley Dean[1]

The Capability Approach: A Sufficient Foundation for Welfare Reform?[2]

This chapter offers a constructive critique of the capability approach; a critique informed, in part, from a socialist perspective. I shall first acknowledge that as a potential foundation for welfare reform and for promoting social justice for young people the capabilities approach has advantages over the currently favoured social inclusion approach. But I shall also contend that the capabilities approach, founded as it is on essentially liberal-individualist premises, suffers from three limitations in its understanding of human need:

- it does not question the extent to which the meeting of needs under capitalism rests upon the exploitation of human labour;
- it implicitly invalidates the extent to which human needs can only be satisfied in the context of human interdependency;
- it neglects the importance of parity of participation in the processes by which we name and claim our needs.

In relation to each of these failings, I shall present radical but admittedly speculative alternatives. Elements of these alternative ideas, I suggest, might inform a critical, but strategic, application of the capabilities approach, with specific consequences, for example, for young people's education and democratic participation.

Social inclusion *versus* human capabilities

The concept of capabilities associated with Nobel laureate, Amartya Sen, has played a significant role in debates about social development in the global South – not least upon the framing of the Millennium Development Goals (United Nations Development Programme 2003; United Nations General Assembly 2000), but it has had rather less impact in debates about welfare reform in the global North. At the European level, the capabilities concept has

1 Reader in Social Policy, London School of Economics and Political Science.

2 The chapter draws on other recent publications by the author, namely Dean, H. (2009): Critiquing capabilities: The distractions of a beguiling concept. Critical Social Policy, 29, 2 and Dean, H. (2010): Understanding Human Need, Bristol.

provided a focus for debate under the auspices of the CAPRIGHT (*Resources Rights and Capabilities: In search of social foundations for Europe*) integrated project of the EU Sixth Framework programme (and see, for example, Salais & Villeneuve 2004). Much of that debate, however, appears to have been focussed rather narrowly on issues of labour market activation. In Europe, perhaps, the dominant concept in social policy in recent years has been that of social exclusion, or rather its obverse, *social inclusion*.

A pledge to fight social exclusion had been incorporated as long ago as 1977 in the Amsterdam Treaty, and found expression during the 1980s through the *European Social Agenda* (European Commission 1994). The term "social exclusion" was accepted into policy making discourse in the UK in the 1990s, initially as a synonym for "poverty" (Burchardt, Le Grand & Piachaud 2002), but more particularly under the 'New' Labour government that assumed control in 1997 as a "short hand label" for a range of intractable social problems that were to be addressed by a new cross-departmental Social Exclusion Unit (Social Exclusion Unit 1997). By the year 2000, the Lisbon European Council was ready to announce the European Union Social Inclusion Strategy, which pledged to eradicate poverty in Europe by 2010. To this end, priority was given to the development of "a competitive and dynamic knowledge-based economy" across the whole of Europe, with priority given to maximising labour market participation, but with attention also given to the risks faced by the most vulnerable social groups (Marlier, Atkinson, Cantillon & Nolan 2007). The Social Inclusion Strategy is widely regarded as the central component of EU social policy, through which the policies and the outcomes of member states are periodically monitored. The monitoring processes generate a great deal of valuable social data, but the strategy is built on economistic assumptions.

As a foundation for welfare reform, the social inclusion approach starts from the premise that the causes of poverty and the obstacles to maximum economic performance lie in the exclusion experienced by some people from such resources and opportunities as they are assumed to need. The capabilities approach by contrast is concerned with the freedom of the individual to meet her needs as she might choose. Certainly, the concept of social exclusion, invites us to consider not only from what people are excluded, but who does the excluding (e.g. Barry 2002). But there is a deeper question: if people were truly free to live as they would wish, how might they define and fulfil their needs? For Amartya Sen what matters is not equality or inequality of resources or outcomes, but of what he calls "capabilities". Poverty is primarily a deprivation of human capabilities (Sen 1985; Sen 1992; Sen 1999; Sen 2005).

Capabilities are more than mere opportunities. The term refers to a person's capacity to choose and to act. Nor are capabilities the same as abilities. The term refers not to what people are able to do, but to their freedom to lead the kind of lives they value, and have reason to value. The problem Sen addresses is that of how we as human beings are able to convert "commodities" (goods, services and other resources) into "functionings" (the valuable activities that, through what we can be and do characterise our humanity). Between the space of commodities and the space of functionings lies the space of capabilities and it is within that space that, according to Sen, the most essential of human needs may be defined.

The advantages of the capabilities approach

The capabilities approach is important, not least because it appears elegantly to transcend the distinction between absolute and relative needs.

Sen's contention is that while poverty may be relative in the space of commodities, it is always absolute in the space of capabilities. Equal resources do not necessarily give rise to equal achievements because people are not necessarily free to live as they might wish. The utility of commodities and the well-being to be obtained from their resultant functionings are determined or mediated by a host of intervening socio-economic, cultural, historical, geographical and climatic factors; but human capability is an absolute imperative. The specific distinction between absolute and relative poverty was debated between Sen and Townsend in the 1980s (see Townsend 1993 for a reprise). Sen claimed that Townsend's concept of relative deprivation conflated poverty with inequality. Townsend claimed that Sen's insistence on identifying an "absolutist core" of poverty perpetuated a narrow subsistence-standard conception of poverty. Neither claim stands up, but the debate is instructive. Townsend, whose work has been critically important to the scientific measurement of poverty, was seeking to define the point at which 'relative' deprivation leads to a person's objective exclusion from social participation. Sen, rather as Adam Smith had done (1776: 691), was seeking to identify the circumstances in which a person is "absolutely" deprived of the ability to function "without shame". Both Sen (a social liberal) and Townsend (a Fabian socialist) were adopting different understandings of "absolute" and "relative", but they each in their way recognised the social context of needs.

What is distinctive about Sen's capabilities approach is that it attempts to provide a single all subsuming criterion of need: namely, whether a human being is substantively free to live as she would choose. As such, it offers an advance on other progressive liberal stances (e.g. Rawls 1972) which advocate an equal opportunities approach on the one hand and a positive rights approach to basic necessities on the other. The capabilities approach, by focusing on the substantive freedom of the individual to do or to be that which she values, is better able to accommodate the diversity of human beings and the complexity of their circumstances (see Burchardt 2006).

The drawbacks of the capabilities approach

Despite its advantages, the capabilities concept has its own inherent limitations. Capability remains, fundamentally, an abstract liberal-individualist concept. It is possible to outline three potential criticisms:

- Despite its emphasis on individual freedom it is does not question the extent to which capitalist societies are sustained through the exploitation of individual human labour.
- Despite its awareness of the social context of individual existence, it evades the reality that individuals' being and identity is constituted through human interdependency.
- Despite its concern for individual empowerment, it neglects the importance of parity of participation in the processes by which individuals must name and claim their needs.

The first of these criticisms relates to the silence of the capabilities approach regarding the systemic impediments to human freedom that are associated with capitalism. Sen is clear that hunger and poverty result from human not natural failures (1999) but he is not a critic of the capitalist mode of production. It may be argued that insofar as the capabilities approach would promote "truly human functioning" (Nussbaum 2006: 85) it fits with the Marxist idea that work is constitutive of our "species being" (Marx 1844: 328) (and see Markus 1978: 37-41). But thc capability approach clearly departs from the understanding of capitalism to be found in Marx's later writings (Marx 1887) and is silent regarding the extent to which wage labour – as the dominant form that work takes under capitalism – may alienate us from our social humanity. The implication of the capabilities approach appears to be that human development and capitalist economic development are – potentially, at least – commensurable.

Whereas Marx's vision of communism was of a society in which there would be a unity of humanity and nature, Malcolm Bull (2007) has suggested that the capabilities approach has an equivalent vision of a path to human development, albeit one in which "moving from bare capability to fully human functioning" will not necessarily be universal. Sen (1999: 6) is anxious to defend the principles of free and fair market exchange, and markets for the exchange of goods and services clearly can serve human ends. The Marxist objection is that a market-driven economy necessarily violates the principles of social justice because under capitalism people "do not have equal access to advantage" (Callinicos 2003: 117). On the one hand, necessary and valuable functionings such as caring for children or for disabled relatives, studying, voluntary work or community participation have no marketable value and are not rewarded by the market (e.g. Mooney 2004). On the other, the global market economy though it may not in any obviously sense constrain the capabilities of the comfortable middle classes of the global North, it can compromise them, since our ability to function as we choose may necessarily be achieved at the expense of others' freedom – sometimes in distant parts of the world.

Defenders of the capability approach will argue that it acknowledges the "value" of functionings that are not marketable. Nussbaum's list of central human functional capabilities includes, for example, "Being able to use the senses, to imagine, think and reason .... to laugh, to play, to enjoy recreational activities" (2000b: 79-78). Once again, however, the individual is constructed as an abstract bearer of freedoms and the capabilities that should ideally flow from these. The capability approach may demand substantive freedoms to choose, and offer an uplifting vision of what valuable capabilities might consist of, but it is an approach that must be accommodated with the imperatives of the market economy. Peter Townsend's original objection to the capabilities concept (see above) reflected a fear that it could be used to justify a minimalist rather than an expansive conception of human need. The objection may not have done justice to the logic of Sen's arguments, but the fear it reflected remains legitimate since there is nothing in the capabilities concept itself to challenge the ways in which a capitalist market economy can drive inequalities and impair as much as provide for the satisfaction of human need.

The second objection to the capabilities approach lies in the fact that its liberal foundations frame the individual as an independent entity. Individualistic responses to human need tend to "problematise" dependency: that is they tend to regard the person as if axiomatically she were an individual actor functioning independently from others on life's stage; as an isolated atom unaffected by the gravitational forces of other particles or bodies around her. As a consequence, liberal attitudes tend towards ambiguity towards the ways in which people depend on each other. They find certain kinds of dependency (such as "free-riding") morally objectionable, but perversely regard the dependency of individuals upon their employers for the means of subsistence or upon their families for everyday care as a form of "independence". Independence is equated, or rather conflated, with self-sufficiency. Contemporary Western societies are so imbued with the individualistic ethic that they become strangely blind to human interdependency, despite the inevitable dependencies associated with different stages of the human life-course and despite the extensive social interactions that are essential to human survival. There is a tendency for people to condemn dependency on the part of others and to deny that they are themselves dependent; albeit that – paradoxically –

they may celebrate their own *dependability*, especially for loved ones, neighbours or friends (Dean & Rodgers 2004; Dean & Taylor-Gooby 1992).

The consequences of this for the capability approach have been identified by Deneulin & Stewart (2000), who contend that social structures matter not only because they may enable or constrain what Sen calls "capabilities", but because they are constitutive of our individual identities and the frameworks of meaning by which we value what Sen calls "functionings". A social being cannot wholly be free from others because the terms on which she belongs within a family, a community or a society will matter as much as her freedom to do or to be. Feminist supporters of the capability approach, in fairness, do not necessarily focus exclusively on the self-sufficient individual subject. For example, Nussbaum in her list of central human functional capabilities includes affiliation, which encompasses "being able to live with and towards others" (2000b: 79). She is clearly mindful of people's "need for care in times of extreme dependency" (2000a: 48) and that being wholly dependent on another need not subserve one's moral personality. To this end, she argues, the goal should be to create "a space" within which even the most impaired and dependent individual can give and receive love and respect. In her list of central human capabilities, therefore, Nussbaum stipulates that a person should "be able to imagine the situation of another and have compassion for that situation" (2000b: 79). However, it seems that both the person and "the other" are constituted as the abstract bearers of capabilities, not as what Selma Sevenhuijsen, for example, would term "selves-in-relationship" (2000: 10). To be capable of "imagination" and "compassion" for the situation of another implies disconnection as a starting point, not a substantive connection. The person and "the other" interact in a metaphorical "space of capabilities". Human identity or moral personality depend in a very immediate and substantive sense upon human association. In the final analysis an autonomous self existing within an abstract space of capabilities must remain a conceptual illusion. Insofar as our humanity defines us it places boundaries on our freedoms.

The third objection to the capabilities approach is that just as the space of capabilities remains a metaphorical abstraction, so too must the forum of public deliberation in which we might agree what our capabilities should be. Sen has acknowledged the role that "public reasoning" must play in evolving definitions of capabilities (2005). The capabilities concept rests on the idea that there are things to do and be that the individual values and has reason to value. By implication, the individual must have "good" reason to value such things. But who determines what constitutes good reason? How can recognition be afforded to the value that people may place on them? Such judgements are necessarily contingent and relative. If the capabilities concept is to inform public policy the liberal ideal requires that there should be a public forum in which to deliberate upon the things we should value and to operationalise our capabilities. In the ancient democracies of Athens and Rome the public forum was quite literally a venue for debate. In modern liberal thought it is a metaphorical realm. Habermas (1962) has argued that the public realm as a liberal ideal justifies a social order in which the state is supposedly disengaged from the functioning of a "free" market, yet made accountable before the metaphorical court of public opinion.

Sen himself has been reluctant to engage in the listing of essential capabilities. Certain of his followers (Nussbaum (2000b), Alkire (2002) and Burchardt & Vizard (2007)), however, insist that by public deliberative processes it is possible to determine what a list of central human capabilities should look like. Indeed, they include participation in public deliberation as a core capability. Nussbaum's list of central human functional capabilities includes "Being able to participate effectively in political choices that govern one's life" (2000b: 80). Yet, some would claim that we are witnessing a "dissolution" of the public realm (Clarke 2004). Even the most "democratic" consensual agreements achieved in the process of public deliberation – through public consultations, citizens' juries, participative poverty assessments or focus groups – may elide fundamental social conflicts and hidden forms of oppression. Such deliberative processes seldom if ever achieve effective "parity of participation" (Fraser 1997). They may do nothing more than reflect prevailing hegemonic assumptions about what kind of a life any of us should value and what kinds of need should therefore be recognised.

For these reasons, though the capabilities approach might provide an alternative foundation for social policy to that currently provided in Europe by the social inclusion approach, it is not I would argue a sufficient foundation.

Radical alternatives?

Is it therefore possible to envisage an alternative approach? I can suggest three candidates, each of which – albeit only in theory – might address the objections to the capability approach that I have outlined above:

- First, the acquiescence of the capabilities approach to capitalism's exploitative potential may be countered through a social policy founded on a Marxian "politics of need".
- Second, the ambivalence of the capabilities approach to the realities of human interdependency may be countered through social policy founded on a feminist ethic of care approach and/or an ecologically informed "convivial sustainability" approach.

- Third, the inability of the capabilities approach to achieve effective public deliberation of needs claims may be countered through a social policy founded on what Nancy Fraser has termed a "politics of needs interpretation" (Fraser 1997).

Marx had advanced a concept of "radical" needs; an elusive yet pertinent notion that Agnes Heller has sought to capture. Radical need can be defined as the expression of humanity's ultimate potential; something that is denied to us by capitalism and can only be realised through revolutionary action. Human beings need to work, but in the sense that they should be free to perform labour for its own sake; they need free time, in the sense that they should be free to be truly human; they need universality, in the sense that they should be universally free to develop as individuals (Heller 1974: 88-95). Central to the Marxist project is the concept of praxis: the synthesis between theory and action. The theory of which Marx spoke "is actualised in a people only insofar as it actualises their needs … A deep-going revolution can only be a revolution in basic needs" (cited in Heller 1974: 89). The satisfaction of radical needs, therefore, requires the revolutionary overthrow of capitalism.

One and a quarter centuries since Marx's demise we might suppose that the revolutionary overthrow of capitalism is now a forlorn hope. Nonetheless, Kate Soper (1981) has attempted to address what a "politics of need" might consist of. At the heart of Marxist theory lies the distinction between use value and exchange value. In a capitalist society we observe the relationships between the goods we consume and between the different sorts of work we perform not so much in terms of the extent to which they satisfy our needs, as in terms of notions of their relative value as commodities. Marx's celebrated aphorism – "from each according to his ability, to each according to his need" (cited by Soper 1981: 188) – was an attempt to imagine a society without commodities; in which need would replace value as the measure of things; in which work would be an expression of our species being and not an exchange of labour power. Marx had contended that "only then can the narrow horizon of bourgeois rights be crossed in its entirety" (see Soper 1981: 188). His point was that the basis of rights under capitalism lies in the ownership and exchange of commodities. If human society were organised with a view to satisfying universal need, we would have no need of rights; at least not the kind of citizenship based rights associated with capitalist liberal democracies.

Rights, nevertheless, could still provide an effective discursive resource in the event of an evolutionary as opposed to a revolutionary transition to socialism.

Might we yet conceive of some utopian form of cosmopolitan citizenship (Held 1995) or "deep" citizenship (Clarke 1996) in which social rights and human needs become increasingly synonymous? And down at the quotidian level of the nation state transitions to socialism, according to Soper, require a politics that seeks to plan for the meeting of needs. Soper argues that a society that reads its needs from what it consumes is evading the question of needs (1981: 215-216). The implication here is that the capitalist welfare state did not and does not go far enough in addressing human need. A politics of needs entails decisions about what is needed and this requires *information* upon which to base such decisions and mechanisms for social *participation* in the making of those decisions (1981: 210-211). This is an interpretation of social justice that prioritises the social identification of need above the private production of value and therefore poses an ongoing challenge to the capitalist world order.

Our second alternative has two distinct but not necessarily incompatible strands. One of these stems from the feminist ethic of care debate which began with Carol Gilligan's (1982) claim that feminine moral codes of care are consistently subordinated to masculine codes of moral reasoning (see, for example, Ellis 2004). Moral codes of care, she contended, are rooted in mutual responsibility and relationships, not rights and rules; in everyday reality, not abstract principles of justice and equality. Subsequent commentators (Clement 1998; Friedman 1993) expressed concern that in attempting to revalorise an ethic of care one should not omit to embrace the interdependency of strangers as well as intimates. Principles of justice and equality are necessary if we are to have rights and rules by which to accord recognition and respect to distant others. Nonetheless, individuals can only exist through and with others within networks of care (Sevenhuijsen 1998; Tronto 1994). The meeting of human needs depends not just on how societies organise their means of production, but also how its members care for and about each other (Kittay et al. 2005; Parker 1981). The insight is not necessarily new since it resonates with the premises of *Ubuntu*, the ancient pan-African philosophy (Ramose 2003). Nonetheless it reminds us of the concrete substance of human lives in which everyday relationships can entail conflict, negotiation and struggle. The ways in which we care for and about each other are, as often as not, socially negotiated within such relationships, across the generations and over time (e.g. Finch & Mason 1993). Substantive relations of care must be negotiated on the basis of mutual recognition between needy subjects with shared vulnerabilities. The task, as Fiona Williams has put it "is less one of arguing against autonomy as a liberal concept than one of redefining the concept of autonomy to fit with a notion of interdependence" (2001: 481).

The other strand to the second alternative is to be found in the work of thinkers, such as Freire (1972) and Illich (1977), whose writings continue to inform critical social ecological thinking. Illich's approach, for example, grew out of his own account of "the history of needs". Illich railed on the one hand against the way in which advanced industrial societies – both capitalist and communist – either manufactured or imputed the needs of their citizens; on the other against the way in which modern professionals dictate and disable their clients' understanding of needs.

„... life without addictive access to commodities is rendered either impossible or criminal. Making do without consumption becomes impossible, not just for the average consumer but even for the poor. All forms of welfare ... are of no help. The liberty to design and craft one's own distinctive dwelling is abolished in favor of the bureaucratic provision of standardized housing ... The organization of employment, skills, building resources, rules, and credit favor shelter as a commodity rather than as an activity. Whether the product is provided by an entrepreneur or an apparatchik, the effective result is the same: citizen impotence, our specifically modern experience of poverty" (Illich 1977: vii-ix).

The need for housing, employment, healthcare and education is fashioned by market forces, state planning and/or the ministrations of professionals. The way forward, according to Illich, is to revert to a form of "convivial austerity", the object of which would be "to protect personal use value against disabling enrichment" (1977: 16). It is a "back to the future" prescription that is consonant, for example, with claims by ecologists that "demand must be reduced, not expanded" (Porritt 1984: 136) or with Jordan's (2008) aim of restoring the notion of "social value" to the public policy making process. More fundamentally, however, a social policy approach based on what Illich calls conviviality would require new tools by which to reclaim the practical knowledge that would empower ordinary people to name and claim their own needs (Illich 1971; Illich 1973) (and cf. Freire 1972). Illich's is an essentially anarchistic and romantic quest. Elements of his analysis, however, – especially his assertion that "needs have become almost exclusively coterminous with commodities" (1977: 13) – are strongly redolent of Marxist thinking, albeit that Marx sought not to retreat from the effects of capitalist modernity, but to transcend it. Other elements of the analysis are consonant with an ethic of care approach, since the emphasis is on valorising the quotidian foundations of our human interdependency. What is implied is an eco-socialist/ feminist synthesis informed by a concept of „sustainable conviviality".

In many ways, our third alternative, though still quite abstractly conceived, brings together and breaths additional life into each of the other two. Nancy Fraser's "politics of need interpretation", I believe, provides a glimpse of how Soper's "politics of need" might be combined with feminised and "convivial" forms of participation in order to provide an effective foundation for welfare reform. Fraser starts from the premise that „in late capitalist welfare state societies, talk about people's needs is an important species of political discourse" (1989: 161). She proceeds to explore the ways in which needs are discursively interpreted and communicated. In doing so, she adopts what she later comes to defend as a pragmatic approach to the study of discourse and communicative action (see Fraser 1997: chap. 6). The resulting account provides a distinctive perspective on social policy.

Fraser (1989: ch. 8) identifies three culturally constructed spheres of life or enclaves: the political, the economic and the domestic. She argues that for needs talk to enter the political sphere, it must be „publicised"; projected from the private sphere of commodities and market relations on the one hand and family and personal relations on the other into the public forum of political debate. Everyday livelihoods and personal needs are political, but private: a politics of needs interpretation might serve to democratise them. Social policy theorists, such as Esping-Andersen (1999), have discussed the extent to which capitalist welfare states may both "decommodify" and "defamilialise" (or may subsequently "recommodify" and "refamilialise") their citizens and/or the means by which the needs of citizens are met. Fraser discusses converse processes by which certain kinds of needs and needs talk can remain systemically depoliticised and confined to the economic or domestic spheres. But she also points to the circumstances in which the „runaway needs" of, for example, exploited migrant workers or physically abused women can on occasions leak out of their enclaves and become politicised through "oppositional" forms of discourse. Oppositional discourses may be met with „reprivatisation" discourses that seek to "(re)depoliticise" such needs. In addition to oppositional and reprivatisation discourses, Fraser identifies a third kind of needs discourse; "expert" discourses. These are the discourses of the professional problem solvers who, as "the politics of needs interpretation devolves into the administration of needs satisfaction" (1989: 177), seek to colonise the definition of needs. Fraser's argument here is strikingly similar to that of Illich (see above). The implication is that a more effective and enduring politics of needs interpretation might require, as Illich and Soper each suggest, some means for the democratisation of information and of expert knowledge.

However, Fraser acknowledges two unresolved issues. First, how are we to decide between competing needs claims? This, she says, must involve „balancing democracy and equality" (1989: 182). In later essays (1997: chs. 1 and 3), she casts more light on what this might mean. In her critique of the liberal democratic public sphere she calls for "parity of participation": for steps to ensure that silent and oppressed groups or "publics" should be enabled to access the political sphere on equal terms with more vocal and powerful publics. Fundamentally connected with this call is a wider demand that a politics of recognition should go hand in hand with a politics of redistribution (Fraser & Honneth 2003). A politics of need interpretation must recognise and include everybody's claims in order to negotiate a just distribution of resources. The intention here would seem to go some way to fulfilling Soper's participation requirement.

The second unresolved issue is the relationship between needs claims and rights. We have seen both in this chapter and the last that this is an ambiguous and contested relationship. Fraser for her part decides to align herself „with those who favour translating justified needs into social rights" (1989: 183).

Conclusion

I have argued elsewhere that a discourse of social rights provides a more immediate strategic terrain for a politics of needs interpretation than a discourse of capabilities. Capabilities are construed at one stage removed from the context in which social rights are in practice negotiated (Dean 2009). The strengths and limitations of a rights-based approach are well understood (e.g. Dean 2002). Nonetheless, bearing in mind the theme of this book, I would acknowledge that the capability approach is, potentially, another strategic vehicle through which to contend for welfare reform, provided the reservations I have expressed can be addressed.

Accordingly, it is first necessary to resist the tendency for the capability approach to degenerate into a human capital approach. Sen, in fairness, has remarked upon the limitations of the term human capital on the grounds that „human beings are not merely means of production, but also the end of the exercise" (1999: 296). Though it may have an application within critical sociological analysis (e.g. Bordieu 1997), as a metaphor in policy discourse the concept of human capital takes on a distinctly reductive economistic meaning: individuals are constituted as actual or potential *economic* actors. It is clear nonetheless that many of those who purport to have adopted the idea of human capabilities regard the term, implicitly or explicitly, as a synonym, for human capital.[3] This is a particular hazard in the case of debates about labour market activation or "welfare-to-work". The function that may be claimed for social policy is that ameliorates the diswelfares of a capitalist market economy (Titmuss 1974): it partially at least de-commodifies the wage labourer (Esping-Andersen 1990) and preserves her/him from unfettered exploitation. Human beings – whether young or adult – are not capital, any more than they are commodities. The object of both training and education systems should be to develop people's personalities, not their future productivity: to enable them to fulfil themselves, not to exploit their potential. Can the capabilities approach promote this argument without ambiguity?

Second, any strategic application of the capabilities approach must be mindful that human beings can never be wholly autonomous, but must achieve their unique identities through interaction with others. The task claimed by Fiona Williams for a new political ethics of care "is less one of arguing against autonomy as a liberal concept than one of redefining the concept of autonomy to fit with a notion of interdependence" (2001: 481). The same, I would suggest applies for the concept of capabilities. Similarly, if the

3 In the context of this particular conference, I shall avoid confrontation and refrain from citing specific examples. However, clear instances may readily be found at a supra-European level in the publications of the World Bank and the United Nations Development Programme.

capabilities approach were to open itself to the idea of "convivial sustainability", then the basis of human capabilities could be apprehended less in the context of individualised competitiveness and more in the context of collaborative self-empowerment. This is especially relevant in the sphere of education policy. Freire (1972), in particular, argued that education should be constituted as an essentially dialogical and liberating pedagogical process. I am not sure, but I wonder whether this is an idea that might help ground the capabilities concept in specific form of every day practice.

Finally, I believe, a strategic application of the capabilities approach should acknowledge that the processes of public reasoning by which societies determine the capabilities acknowledged to be "valuable" have to be radically inclusive in a way that existing liberal democracies are not. The abstract nature of the capabilities concept does not readily lend itself to a popular politics of needs interpretation. Supporters of the capabilities approach must nonetheless find ways to link private space of capabilities to the public space of political deliberation. Thinking specifically about young people, ways must be found for their authentic voices to be heard; for their understanding of capabilities to be articulated. Here I would agree with Jean-Michel Bonvin that this is a major challenge faced by the capabilities approach.

It might be supposed that economic globalisation has brought us to a pass where post-materialism (Inglehart 1990) and individualisation (Beck & Beck-Gernsheim 2001) have extinguished the possibility of socialist alternatives, especially for youthful generations inured to the fanciful idea that with the ascendancy of global capitalism human history may now have ended (Fukuyama 1992). Nonetheless, there is some evidence, for example, that neo-liberal moral repertoires have not yet wholly eclipsed the social democratic repertoires that continue to reside within popular discourse (Dean 2004), just as they continue to survive at the margins of political discourse. Certainly, there is a vacuum that the capabilities approach is seeking to fulfil, but the radicalism of the capabilities approach is deceptive and there is scope if not for a deeper radicalism, for at least a more critical debate about what kind of social justice we seek for young people.

References

Alkire, S. (2002): Valuing Freedoms: Sen's capability approach and poverty reduction. New York: World Bank.

Barry, B. (2002): Social exclusion, social isolation and the distribution of income. In: Hills, J., Le Grand, J. & Piachaud, D. (Eds.): Understanding Social Exclusion. Oxford.

Beck, U. & Beck-Gernsheim, E. (2001): Individualization. London.

Bourdieu, P. (1997): The forms of capital. In: Halsey, A., Lauder, H., Brown, P. & Wells, A. (Eds.): Education, Culture, Economy, Society. Oxford.
Bull, M. (2007): Vectors of the biopolitical. New Left Review 45.
Burchardt, T. (2006): Foundations for Measuring Equality: A discussion paper for the Equalities Review - CASEpaper 111. London.
Burchardt, T., Le Grand, J. & Piachaud, D. (2002): Introduction. In: Hills, J., Le Grand, J. & Piachaud, D. (Eds.): Understanding Social Exclusion. Oxford.
Burchardt, T. & Vizard, P. (2007): Definition of Equality and Framework for Measurement: Final recommendations of the Equalities Review Steering Group on Measurement - CASEpaper 120. London.
Callinicos, A. (2003): An Anti-Capitalist Manifesto. Cambridge.
Clarke, J. (2004): Dissolving the public realm? The logics and limits of neo-liberalism. Journal of Social Policy 33, 27-48.
Clarke, P. (1996): Deep Citizenship. London.
Clement, G. (1998): Care, Autonomy and Justice: Feminism and the ethic of care. Boulder.
Dean, H. (2002): Welfare Rights and Social Policy. Harlow.
Dean, H. (2004): Popular discourse and the ethical deficiency of 'Third Way' conceptions of citizenship. Citizenship Studies 8, 65-82.
Dean, H. (2009): Critiquing capabilities: The distractions of a beguiling concept. Critical Social Policy 29.
Dean, H & Rodgers, R. (2004): Popular discourses of dependency, responsibility and rights. In: Dean, H. (Ed.): The Ethics of Welfare. Bristol.
Dean, H & Taylor-Gooby, P. (1992): Dependency Culture: The explosion of a myth. Hemel Hempstead.
Deneulin, S. & Stewart, F. (2000): A capability approach for people living together. In: VHI conference – Justice and Poverty: Examining Sen's capability approach. St Edmunds College, Cambridge.
Ellis, K. (2004): Dependency, justice and the ethic of care. In: Dean, H. (Ed.): The Ethics of welfare: Human rights, dependency and responsibility. Bristol.
Esping-Andersen, G. (1990): The Three Worlds of Welfare Capitalism. Cambridge.
Esping-Andersen, G. (1999): The Social Foundations of Post-Industrial Economies. Oxford.
European Commission (1994): European Social Policy: A way forward for the Union. Luxembourg: OOPEC.
Finch, J. & Mason, J. (1993): Negotiating Family Responsibilities. London.
Fraser, N. (1989): Unruly Practices: Power, discourse and gender in contemporary social theory. Minneapolis.
Fraser, N. (1997): Justice Interruptus: Critical reflections on the 'postsocialist' condition. London.
Fraser, N. & Honneth, A. (2003): Redistribution or Recognition? London.
Freire, P. (1972): Pedagogy of the Oppressed. Harmondsworth.
Friedman, M. (1993): Beyond caring: The de-moralisation of gender. In: Larabee, M. (Ed.): An Ethic of Care: Feminist and interdisciplinary perspectives. New York.
Fukuyama, F. (1992): The End of History and the Last Man. New York.
Gilligan, C. (1982): In a Different Voice: Psychological theory and women's development. Cambridge.

Habermas, J. (1962): The Structural Transformation of the Public Sphere. Cambridge, Mass.

Held, D. (1995): Democracy and the Global Order: From the modern state to cosmopolitan governance. Cambridge.

Heller, A. (1974): The Theory of Need in Marx. London.

Illich, I. (1971): Deschooling Society. London.

Illich, I. (1973): Tools for Conviviality. London.

Illich, I. (1977): Towards a History of Needs. New York.

Inglehart, R. (1990): Culture Shift in Advanced Industrial Society. Princeton NJ.

Jordan, B. (2008): Welfare and Well-Being: Social value in public policy. Bristol.

Kittay, E., Jennings, B. & Wasunna, A. (2005): Dependency, difference and the global ethic of longterm care. The Journal of Political Philosophy 13, 443-469.

Markus, G. (1978): Marxism and Anthopology. Assen, The Netherlands.

Marlier, E., Atkinson, A., Cantillon, B. & Nolan, B. (2007): The EU and Social Inclusion: Facing the challenges. Bristol.

Marx, K. (1844): Economic and Philosophical Manuscripts. In: Colletti, L. (1975 edition): Early Writings. Harmondsworth.

Marx, K. (1887): Capital. Vol. I, II, III. London.

Mooney, G. (2004): Work: Personal lives and social policy. Bristol.

Nussbaum, M. (2000a): The future of feminist liberalism. Proceedings and Addresses of the American Philosophical Association 74, 47-49.

Nussbaum, M. (2000b): Women and Human Development: The capabilities approach. Cambridge.

Nussbaum, M. (2006): Frontiers of Justice: Disability, nationality, species membership. Cambridge.

Parker, R. (1981): Tending and Social Policy. In: Goldberg, E. & Hatch, S. (Eds.): A New Look at the Personal Social Services. London.

Porritt, J. (1984): Seeing Green. Oxford.

Ramose, M. (2003): Globalisation and ubuntu. In: Coetzee, P. & Roux, A. (Eds.): The African Philosophy Reader. London.

Rawls, J. (1972): A Theory of Justice. Oxford.

Salais, R. & Villeneuve, R. (2004): Europe and the Politics of Capabilities. Cambridge.

Sen, A. (1985): Commodities and Capabilities. Amsterdam.

Sen, A. (1992): Inequality Re-examined. Oxford.

Sen, A. (1999): Development as Freedom. Oxford.

Sen, A. (2005): Human rights and capabilities. Journal of Human Development 6, 151-166.

Sevenhuijsen, S. (1998): Citizenship and the Ethics of Care. London.

Sevenhuijsen, S. (2000): Caring in the third way: The relation between obligation, responsibility and care in 'Third Way' discourse. Critical Social Policy 20, 5-37.

Smith, A. (1776): An Inquiry into the Nature and Causes of the Wealth of Nations. London.

Social Exclusion Unit (1997): Social Exclusion Unit: Purpose, work priorities and working methods, briefing document. Cabinet Office, London.

Soper, K. (1981): On Human Needs. Brighton.

Titmuss, R. (1974): Social Policy. London.

Townsend, P. (1993): The International Analysis of Poverty. Hemel Hempstead.

Tronto, J. (1994): Moral Boundaries: A political argument for an ethic of care. New York.
United Nations Development Programme (2003): Human Development Report 2003 - Millennium Development Goals: A compact among nations to end human poverty. New York.
United Nations General Assembly (2000): United Nations Millennium Declaration (Resolution 2 Session 55). New York, UN.
Williams, F. (2001): In and beyond New Labour: Towards a new political ethics of care. Critical Social Policy 21, 467-493.

René Büttner

Thinking in a Capability Language

The popularity currently enjoyed by the capability approach is reflected by an abundant use of its terminology. It shall be argued that this popularity is brought about by the timeliness of its propositions, and the inviting breadth of its applicability. However, these trump cards are also dangerous to the capability approach, as its usage is not always backed by a comprehensive understanding of its implications and its potential. To make matters worse, by jumping on the capability-bandwagon, one can gain attention and acceptance for ideas which have been developed elsewhere. This makes the approach sometimes look like a mere phrasing assistance. As the present text seeks to point out, the capability approach is more than that. It can even be taken beyond the possibilities of an evaluative framework. When employed as a "sensitizing concept" (Bartelheimer et al. 2009: 35; Bartelheimer 2008: 22), it can be used as a source of ideas and its unique perspective conveys new insights. By using its conceptual richness, awareness can be created for dangers lying in societal developments, and for potentials, as well. The present text will produce some evidence for this. It will illustrate how the approach is already used as a perception tool, giving examples from the field of social policy research. Before doing this, the text will investigate some reasons for the approach's frequent usage at present.[1]

Why is everybody talking about capabilities?

The first and most simple reason is that the breadth of the capability approach makes a great number of studies eligible to be associated with the capability approach. Many studies derive their insights from a comparative heuristic method, and the CA offers them a space of comparison which is not limited to a specific kind of society or domain of interest. Being created by an author familiar with the conditions both in developing and industrialized countries, the approach is open to diverse kinds of societies, no matter their state of economic development or their values, at least as long as some basic premises of the approach are not hurt. The space for comparison and evaluation is constituted by capabilities, which are defined as the things a person can be or do

1 I would like to thank Jürgen Kädtler, Tanja Schmidt and Sibylle Jane Kalz for their advice.

and which are considered valuable both by the individual itself and by its society. The capability approach in the understanding of Sen[2] leaves it up to every society to decide upon the very capabilities that constitute the arena in which inequality has to be addressed.

Furthermore it does not prescribe how the respective capabilities must be created. While capabilities are seen in an absolute way (a capability is available or is not available) their production is relative, which means that they can be derived from different kinds of means. For example, at the basis of the capability not to starve, it does not matter whether there is rice or noodles, or whether the food has been bought on the market or grown in ones own production. It doesn't even matter how much a person eats, as long as she has the absolute capability of satisfying her hunger. Of course, this openness permits comparisons also between countries, even if they are very different from each other.[3]

Comparison is not necessarily limited to the level of the country, but to whatever group of people happens to be of interest. Equally, comparison is not confined to specific topics, or forced to treat all topics simultaneously. The capability approach can be applied to various domains of reflection, like education, labor market policy, or gender equality, as long as human capabilities are dealt with. Another point is the following: The CA's proposition of a capability space does not imply whatever claim on the distribution of capabilities among people. Politically, the approach is situated in a liberal philosophical tradition, but it is neither left nor right (Robeyns 2005: 95), and it comes "*without presupposing* any particular economic model or policy programme" (Browne et al. 2004: 212). To make it clearer: By defining what a capability space is, the capability approach gives us a notion about what equality looks like, and even what development looks like (extension of capabilities). The fact that a normative decision is implied in such a definition is highlighted by the capability approach, and the fact that defining a specific capability space requires normative assumptions is equally revealed[4]. But this does not mean that the approach might take the normative stance that equality between one person and another person should actually exist in the defined space. This means that users with different normative backgrounds can work with the CA.

Apart from breadth of applicability, timeliness is an important aspect in explaining the spread of the capability approach. This means that the premises and values characterizing the capability approach are pertinent in the con-

---

2 Martha Nussbaum is following a different path in this respect.

3 Following Beck (2009: 315), there is a growing need for comparing societies among each other. Globalization made it inadmissible to continue skirting this task by simply declaring them incomparable.

4 See "IBJ" below.

text of current societal questions and modes of perception. Firstly, there is the notion of *ethical individualism* (cp. Robeyns 2005: 107), which makes the individual the unit of evaluation. Well-being can not be aggregated over several people, a direct consequence of which is that the well-being of a person can not be traded against the well-being of another person or a group of persons to which the individual belongs. For example, the fact that a household has a car does not imply that all members of the household are allowed to use it, i.e. that the capability of being mobile is equally distributed among them. This perspective is very useful for example in the field of gender equality. Another example is the relationship between the individual and society as a whole. Lessenich (2008) currently sees a fundamental shift in this relationship. Drawing on observations by Boltanski and Chiappello (ibid.: 76), his claim is that the individual is currently increasingly obliged to function for the benefit of the collective.[5] The concept of ethical individualism gets straight to the point of this problem. It is an element of the CA helping to take a well-balanced account of the individual and the collective at the same time.

Secondly, there is the *concept of freedom*, which is specified by the capability approach in a rather complex way. Freedom is placed at the centre of what the capability approach is aiming at. There are two types of freedom considered, opportunity-freedom and process-freedom. The former means that an individual has the real possibility of choosing between several real options of leading its life, and that these options be valuable to her and substantively different among themselves. This conception of freedom is quite relevant in the context of pluralistic societies, as it allows comparing the well-being potential of people with completely different lifestyles. The support of a range of alternatives is also a prerequisite for self-fulfillment, a goal cherished by most people in modern societies, but by definition realized in an individual manner. The second aspect of freedom, process-freedom, is no less topical. It addresses the possibility of influencing the decision processes in one's society, a possibility which each individual should have. The CA therewith subscribes to a democratic ideal, without, however, committing to a specific mechanism by which it should be attained (cp. Robeyns 2005: 110).

Closely connected to the outlined concept of freedom is the *notion of "agency"*. To consider human beings as "agents" means taking into account that they will follow self-defined goals in a self-defined manner. This is an image allowing for non-maximizing and even for truly altruistic behavior. People's actions are not predictable from this perspective, which is a drawback vis-à-vis the pretension, but not the reality, of many neo-classical expla-

5 He goes on to argue that individuals who cannot live up to the high demands of their society risk more and more being left behind, i.e. without collective support. I'd like to suggest that using the capability concept would allow the cited analysis to formulate even more clearly the dangers identified in these developments, but also to see some promises linked to activity (cp. Salais 2003).

nations. At the same time, the concept does not have to ignore people's actual engagements in family or community life or awkwardly reduce it to self-interest.

This section has tried to give some explanation for the popularity of the capability approach, arguing that it is rooted in the broadness of its applicability and the topicality of its concepts and values.[6] I deem it possible that the Nobel Prize of Amartya Sen and the fact that the capability approach is English-speaking[7] has also helped to spread the word. If this should be true, it would not, however, reduce its merits. Yet, as argued above, the popularity of a concept should not prevent taking its aspects seriously and using their potential fully. In the following section, I will reiterate the meaning of some further notions of the CA and show how fruitfully they can be made use of by looking at examples from the literature.

Sparking ideas with the capability approach

Shared concepts can facilitate communication about known issues, as they contain a common pattern of perceiving and denominating, but if newly applied to a thematic field, they can also have the effect of making neglected aspects visible or of letting what is already familiar appear in a new light. In the following, we will look at such cases, clustered around the respective aspect of the capability approach which is relevant.

To begin with the "*informational basis of judgement*" (IBJ), Sen draws our attention to the fact that a prerequisite for any judgement is clarity about the categories of facts that are or are not allowed to influence the judgement (Sen 1992: 73). This decision, a normative one as argued above, is not neutral with respect to the outcome of the judgement. At the core of the capability approach as an evaluative framework is the capability space. In consequence, using the capability approach may lead to judgements which are substantially different from those based on information about resources or utilities. An exemplary case has been made by Sen (1985), and the human development index (HDI), which is inspired by the capability approach, uses the very insight that for evaluating a country's general well-being, the IBJ should not be confined to the GDP. Instead, the HDI also comprises information on life expectancy, literacy and school enrolment. The fact that GDP is kept as one of the indicators of the HDI stems from the assumption that money is a proxy for capabilities requiring consumption, and that money has a great versatility itself. It goes without saying that the ranking of countries is substantially dif-

6 Broadness of applicability, on the other hand, is "up-to-date" itself.

7 Unlike the "Lebenslagenansatz", see below.

ferent according to whether pure GDP per capita or the HDI is used. Alkire (2002) demonstrates the tangible effects of a shift in the IBJ in the evaluation of competing developmental projects: a judgment based on a traditional cost-benefit analysis may opt against the realization of projects which are highly beneficial from a capability point of view, taking into account side-effects like education or self-confidence of the project participants, seen not only as investments, but as values *per se*. If money is not the measure of the target function, aspects that may have an impact on monetary wealth do not have to vanish behind this instrumental value, but can be credited an intrinsic value, too. Sehnbruch (2004: 3) undertakes a similar shift in the informational base, not away from money, but away from a purely quantitative measure: "applying the capability approach to the labor market [...] obliges us to look at the quality of employment rather than merely at the quantity of employment, to wit the unemployment rate" (cp. also Salais 2007: 341). Taking into account a greater variety of indicators, she draws a picture of the Chilean labor market which is much more appropriate to reality in a country where unemployment is something that people can simply not afford. However, besides informational pluralism, there is another important aspect to the IBJ of the capability space: instead of analyzing functionings, which actually have been realized, one can also raise the question about what might be or might have been. An interesting application is to ask whether observable differences in the well-being of people are due to differences in capabilities, or to differences in preferences, i.e. autonomous choice. Bartelheimer (2008: 11) highlights the growing necessity in social policy to discern this in the context of increasingly pluralistic societies in order to keep track of relevant inequalities. For instance, there may be an important difference between two persons who do not have a standard employment contract. One may have been offered such a contract and turned it down, arguing that this would stifle his creativity, the other one might strive in vain for such a contract in order to gain the necessary security for his private life. The field of employment activity is researched by Burchard and Le Grand (2002) with an imaginative empirical implementation of the question about how to discern voluntary from involuntary non-employment. Unfortunately, the results fail to be robust.

While focusing mainly on the ends of human development as described, the capability approach is not completely silent about the means. Let us look at the model for a moment: The capability set of a person can be imagined as all the possible ways in which she can use the resources and rights endowed to her. While capabilities are *potential* usages of endowments, functionings are *actual* usages of endowments. The act of choosing a capability does *not* mean turning the capability into a functioning, but turning one's endowments into a functioning by applying a certain treatment to these endowments. The variety of treatments one can actually perform are determined by a *conversion* function, whose characteristics are dependent on what Robeyns (2005: 99) has classified as individual, collective and environmental conversion factors. The two decisive aspects about this model are, firstly, that the mere existence of endowments does not guarantee that a person can actually benefit from them, and secondly, that their usability does not only depend on the person herself but also on external factors, namely the society. The thought which is the most fruitful about this aspect of the capability approach is the following: If the presence of suitable conversion factors can enable the conversion of resources, their lack can equally represent an obstacle. Applying this logic to the issue of activating labor market policy has led researchers to questioning the rhetoric of the employability discourse with the means of the capability approach (Bonvin; Moachon 2007: 20; Bartelheimer 2007). If the right to work is a resource for the job-seeker, the convertibility of this resource into the capabilities provided by employment depend both on individual factors like health and on societal factors like for example the demand for labor on the labor market. Activating labor market policy, especially of the coercive type, is of no use if the resource of labor demand is just not given due to the condition of the economy. An activating labor market policy truthful to the capability perspective would not consist of eliminating alternatives to participation in the labor market, but of providing the necessary means in order to create capabilities for employment participation valued by the job-seeker. Bartelheimer (2008) critically comments on the German HARTZ-reforms, arguing that the reduction of the formal rights possessed by job-seekers has led to a loss of effective freedom of looking for 'good' work. In the same vein, Salais (2007: 335) points out, "[i]n a capability approach, social expenditure is viewed above all as a collective investment in people's capabilities". Ignoring the stake of the collective in the interactive process eventually leading to the functioning of employment would lead to negative individualism, i.e. making the individual liable for things beyond its influence. This applies also to the situation where an individual conversion condition is not met, with the individual being unable to restore it without the support of the collective (cp. Salais 2003: 13). Quite generally, Salais (2007: 318 et seq.) argues the need to pass "from freedom from want to freedom to act". He also discusses possible beneficial economic implications of such a view in the context of a knowledge economy. Browne et al. (2004: 220) join in: "A capability approach makes it possible to see that social rights, in common with civil and political rights, underpin market access and facilitate an extension of the division of labour and knowledge upon which, in the final analysis, a market depends". So, 'empowering' people, a value in itself, can have the instrumental value of stimulating also their economic activity.

Still, the economy is to the capability approach no more than a means, the ends always being people's capabilities. The *distinction between means and ends* is indeed made very rigorously. "[T]he parameters that policy or social change can influence are the means of the capabilities, and hardly ever the capabilities directly" (Robeyns 2005: 110). But the actual target, capabilities, has to be born in mind when designing or evaluating the means of public policy. "By defining capabilities as the space of comparison, [the CA] asks what the means are that we need to foster in order to achieve certain ends" (Sehnbruch 2004: 21). In order to create the same capabilities, the necessary means will be different depending on the situation, but what is clear is that political intervention always has to tackle either resources or conversion conditions or both in order to alter a capability set. Taking employment as an example again, the distinction between means and ends would imply to stop thinking of employment as an end in itself, but to consider the "capabilities and functionings generated by a job" (ibid.). The relevance of a job for certain capabilities depends on a variety of factors: the features of the person, the quality of the job, the alternatives to this job both inside and outside the labor market, etc. Another occasion for thinking about the relativity of means would be imagining a future characterized by a general lack of natural resources or by a new economic system. How could capabilities enjoyed today be sustained on a completely different material basis or by another mode of organizing production and distribution? Being absolute about what concerns the output (beings and doings), the CA takes a relative stance towards inputs (endowments and conversion factors). But also today and in a country like Germany, the capability approach can be used for reflecting on how to achieve an equivalent living standard between regions which are unequally endowed with infrastructure and economic prosperity (Bartelheimer, forthcoming). Adopting a perspective which stresses freedoms instead of means would equal what could be termed a 'capability-mainstreaming' of policy, i.e. verifying for each political measure how it will affect certain core capabilities. Following Robeyns (2005: 110), "Social structures and institutions can (and generally do) have an important effect on people's capability sets. [...] There is a potential to use the capability approach more in relation with an analysis of institutions". As suggested by Browne et al. (2002: 212), regulation has both a direct and an indirect impact. Rights act as a resource, but also as a norm-giving power, transforming societal conversion factors: "[T]he very existence of social rights can contribute to the development of a different social ethos or set of norms which may enhance individuals' functionings or potential functionings". This should be taken into account when following Sehnbruch (2004: 3), who proposes "to analyze a situation according to the capability approach and then form public policies based on these results".

Closely connected to the aforementioned principles of ethical individualism, agency and informational pluralism, and in a way resulting from them, is the principle of *situated evaluation* (Alkire 2005: 124). It means taking account of "the relevant features of the personal situation to deal with" (Salais 2003: 12), including the interaction of persons with their environment, like the way the person perceives the situation from her point of view. This is not to be interpreted as methodological individualism, but as an attempt to do justice to the (subjective) reality of people's situations, i.e. a refinement of the IBJ. A multitude of informational sources can be used for this, like "idiosyncratic knowledge of the person, its past, character, problems and projects and so on" (ibid.). Of course, situatedness is a major help for identifying opportunities and threats on the individual level, resulting from public policy. This also applies to the experience made by individuals when faced with public authority itself. For Bartelheimer (2008: 13), it follows from the CA that individuals must not be seen as mere objects of welfare state action, but as subjects who actively experience this encounter. Thus, not only the result, but also the production of welfare becomes a field of analysis, so social reporting is extended to welfare state observation. In this regard, the difference between a welfare state functioning on a "logic of insurance" differs from one working with a "ministration logic" (cp. Bartelheimer 2007) not primarily in the amount and conditionality of benefits, but in the relationship between the beneficiary and the State, and their impact on the personality of the former.

However, politics can not just be experienced, but also conditioned by people. At least in Sen's own version of the CA, everything which includes value judgments is left to the discretion of *public deliberation*[8], to begin with the definition of the capabilities which people have "reason-to-value" in a given society and which are therefore eligible for public support, but also the tolerable degree of inequality, and, one should add, the way to deal with calamities resulting from "bad choices" which individuals have made in the past. The fact that all individuals, no matter their position in the community, are invited to participate "as actively as possible in the process of development, implementation and evaluation of public policies" (Bonvin; Moachon 2007: 12, my translation) is an expression of the principle of process freedom, as described above. This does not mean that everybody is obliged to engage in each and every policy issue, the CA acknowledges the need and the possibility for representative democracy. "Freedom includes "a person's ability to get systematically what he would choose no matter who actually controls the levers of operation"" (Sen in Alkire 2005: 121). However, process freedom remains an ambitious aim, which can guide research on social policy. Two questions which can be derived from those previously mentioned are, firstly, to ask whether and where public deliberation actually takes place, and secondly, whether or not the current orientation of social policy follow what comes out or would come out of such deliberations. The European Employment Strategy could be one of the subjects of such scrutiny. As Salais (2007: 342) suggests: "A public debate should develop on indicators and benchmarking that follows a capability path in employment and social poli-

8 Martha Nussbaum, arguing with the dangers of adaptive preferences, proposes an alternative with the definition of a comprehensive list of capabilities which everybody should possess (2000).

cies". There is a case for assuming that such an exercise of process freedom would in the end benefit opportunity freedom, the freedom to do and be what people value and have reason to value.

Conclusion

As this text has tried to demonstrate, the capability approach is a body composed of a number of distinct concepts. Like organs, these concepts have their precise functions. Therefore, research using the capability approach should take their implications and potentials seriously and not just take the wording. Additionally, some normative preconditions have been shown to be inscribed in these concepts. These positions, woven into the structure of the CA, limit in a way its general broadness of applicability. As has been further argued, the concepts gathered in the capability approach allow going beyond the tasks of an evaluatory framework. By detecting dangers, but also potentials lying in situations, it can also be used for creating ideas about future possibilities, which has been shown for social policy by way of example for other fields of analysis. Of course, these insights could potentially have been made without the outlined concepts, this is only normal if they contain some substantial truth. Moreover, similar concepts have been in use before Amartya Sen introduced the capability approach.[9] But the contrary is also true: many analyses and many policies lack the inspiration of a capability perspective.

References

Alkire, S. (2005): Why the Capability Approach? Journal of Human Development 6: 115-133.

Alkire, S. (2002): Valuing Freedoms: Sen's Capability Approach and Poverty Reduction. Economics and Philosophy.

Bartelheimer, P., Moncel, N., Verd Pericàs, J.M. & Vero, J. (2009): Towards Analysing Individual Working Lives in a Resources/Capabilities Perspective. In: Sensitising life course research? Exploring Amartya Sen's capability concept in comparative research on individual working lives, ed. by Bartelheimer, P., Büttner, R. & Moncel, N., Céreq and SOFI.

9 Compare Leßmann (2007), who outlines the striking parallels between the CA and the German "Lebenslagenansatz", or the French tradition of social rights, of which Salais says that "they share the same "capability intuition"" (Salais 2003: 12).

Bartelheimer, P. (2008): Wie man an seiner Eingliederung mitwirkt. Arbeitsmarktdienstleistungen nach SGB II zwischen institutionellem und persönlichem Auftrag. Zeitschrift für Sozialreform.

Bartelheimer, P. (2007): Politik der Teilhabe. Ein soziologischer Beipackzettel. Fachforum Nr. 1, Projekt gesellschaftliche Integration der Friedrich-Ebert-Stiftung, Berlin.

Beck, U. (2009): Jenseits von Klasse und Nation: Individualisierung und Transnationalisierung sozialer Ungleichheiten" Soziale Welt, 59.

Bonvin, J.-M. & Moachon, E. (2005): L'activation et son potentiel de subversion de l'Etat social. In: L'Etat social actif, ed. by Pochet, P., Vielle, Ph., Cassiers, I., Brüssel: P.I.E., 62-92.

Browne, J., Deakin, S. & Wilkinson, F. (2004): Capabilities, social rights and European market integration. In: Salais, R. & Villeneuve, R. (eds.): Towards a European Politics of Capabilities. Cambridge, 293-316.

Burchardt, T. & Le Grand, J. (2002) : Constraint and Opportunity: Identifying Voluntary Non-Employment. Centre for Analysis of Social Exclusion, LSE.

Lessenich, S. (2008): Die Neuerfindung des Sozialen. Bielefeld, Transcript.

Leßmann, O. (2007): Konzeption und Erfassung von Armut. Vergleich des Lebenslage-Ansatzes mit Sens "Capability"-Ansatz. Universität Oldenburg.

Nussbaum, M. (2000): Women and Human Development. The Capabilities Approach. Cambridge.

Robeyns, I. (2005): The Capability Approach: a theoretical survey. Journal of Human Development, 6, 93-114.

Salais, R. (2007): Work and Welfare: Toward a Capability Approach. In: Work and Welfare in a New Economy. Ed. by Zeitlin, J. & Trubek, D., Oxford.

Salais, R. (2003): Social exclusion and capability. In: Marginalization and Social Exclusion, ed. by Heggen, K., Bergen, R., Hoydal, R. & Kvalsund, R.. Volda, 21-36.

Sehnbruch, K. (2004): From the Quantity to the Quality of Employment: An Application of the Capability Approach to the Chilean Labour Market.

Sen, A.K. (1992): Inequality Reexamined. Oxford.

Sen, A.K. (1985): Commodities and Capabilities. Amsterdam.

Wulf Gaertner

Measuring the Extension of Capability Sets

Introduction and Background

Amartya Sen's capability approach (1985) has proved to be a very stimulating and productive concept, both in economics, in particular in welfare and development economics, and in other areas such as philosophy, sociology and, as the present proceedings volume clearly documents, in education. Capabilities refer to what an individual can do or be. A person's capability set represents the set of alternative functioning vectors from which she can choose. The "freedom of choice" approach (see the seminal paper by Pattanaik and Xu 1990) would argue that the more an agent can choose, i.e., the richer the choice set, the better for him or her. The capability approach can be viewed as an attempt to broaden the informational basis of both individual and social choice, to go beyond the narrow focus of "utility" or the somewhat broader concept of "primary goods" (Rawls 1971).

For a long time in economics proper, the measuring rod for economic development were the gross domestic product (GDP) and the growth rate of GDP. So "everything" was reduced to a measure of output (of goods and services) expressed in monetary units. The human development index (HDI) the construction of which was heavily influenced by Sen's capability concept, *par contre* considers very basic functionings, viz., to lead a long and healthy life, to be knowledgeable and to have access to income. These three indicators which are considered to represent elementary dimensions of human development, are turned into one numerical index. An index is a real number. In this sense the HDI is a very handy tool which made it widely applied in international comparisons of living standards. Due to its structure, it established a complete ordering over all nations for which data are available so that an HDI can be formed.

The HDI has its critics. One criticism refers to the equal weighting of the three components listed above. Another criticism raises the question whether it makes sense to use the same index both for highly industrialized societies and agrarian societies, in other words for OECD countries and less developed countries. Life expectancy at birth which enters the component of "a long and healthy life" is not a big issue in the Western world any more but it is a problem in large parts of Africa. Therefore, more specific indexes have been proposed, among others an HDI for developing countries and a gender-related development index.

We do not want to pursue this issue any further since our own approach is quite different. We start from the idea that the income which is available to a particular person buys commodities and these commodities carry certain features. Lancaster (1966) to whom we owe this idea calls these features characteristics. So purchasing fruit and vegetables provides a range of vitamins, milk and eggs, for example, provide proteins, etc. A person who has regular access to these food products and their characteristics can be assumed to lead a healthier life than another person who cannot afford these items and lives on cheap bread and fat meat, let's say. A person who is able to invest in education will become more knowledgeable than an individual who is unable to do so. And an individual who can invest in a good school education with excellent teachers will become even more knowledgeable. Which means that the number of alternative functionings available to a particular person will increase with the quality of education. The ability to structure and solve difficult problems is a requirement for more demanding jobs. These abilities are "honoured" on the labour market in terms of higher incomes which again induce larger sets of characteristics.

After these remarks it should be clear that there is a direct relationship between the purchase of commodities and services on the one hand and the bundle of functionings on the other. The midpoint in this relationship is the set of acquired characteristics. To make the theoretical analysis a bit easier, we shall assume that there is a linear "input-output" relationship both between commodities and characteristics (as in Lancaster) and between characteristics and achievable functionings that constitute a person's capability set. As our examples above hopefully showed, characteristics bring about and invigorate different functionings such as literacy, health, longevity and other basic properties. Note that the conversion from characteristics to functionings can be donc at various levels of efficiency. Imagine that the child of a wealthy couple is sent to an excellent private school but he or she indulgcs in *dolce far niente*. Or think of a student who managed to enter a prestigious university but later on minimizes on effort and involvement. As should be clear from these examples, the size of capability sets will be substantially different at varying levels of effort.

Outline of the Approach

Our aim in this paper is to measure and compare different capability sets that offer alternative sets of functionings. How can this be done? Due to the assumption of a linear technology, our sets of possible functionings will be convex sets. This makes life easier but the question of how to measure and compare capability sets of different sizes is not yet answered. The answer is easy for cases where one set, say *B*, is completely contained in another set *A*. Then, obviously, for any point in *B*, there is a point in *A* that offers at least as much in terms of $n-1$ functionings and contains strictly more in the n-th functioning. This is a rather simple situation. More often will it be the case that, using terminology from set theory, there is a non-empty intersection but no set inclusion between two sets *A* and *B*, let's say. What can be done in such a case? Traditional economics would argue in terms of preferences and sets of nonintersecting indifference curves. Indifference curves or indifference classes contain objects that are deemed to be equivalent for the evaluating subject. Points or objects on a higher indifference curve are preferred to objects on a lower curve. If according to the preferences, the best point in set *A* is better than any point in *B*, then, if this best point in *A* is feasible, set *A* should be preferred to set *B*. Figure 1 depicts such a situation where *x* is the best point in set *A*. Point *x* is better than every point in set *B*, in particular better than the best point in set *B* which is *y*.

Figure 1: Sets A and B have a non-empty intersection

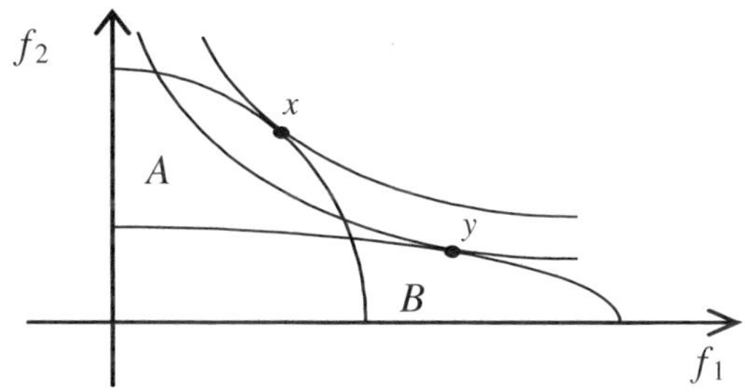

The real issue in this approach is, apart from the question whether such preferences really exist, whose preferences and what type of preferences should count. Is it the myopic or the long-range preferences of the person concerned or rather the preferences of a benevolent dictator who "knows better"?

These are interesting questions undoubtedly. We shall, however, pursue a different approach in this paper. We shall start from some status quo that the agent or country has already achieved or from some point of orientation of the person or country, in other words, from some reference level. Since the functionings that we consider will be assumed to be desirable functionings the individual or country will try to improve upon her situation as much as possible, given her economic resources, i.e. her available income and wealth. The direction of improvement will be north-east, to higher levels of all functionings. Since the precise path that the person or country would like to pursue is not fully clear to her, due perhaps to a certain degree of uneasiness as to the exact combination of different functionings, we assume in a first step that all proportions north-east are equally desirable. In other words, we consider the maximal expansion north-east along a "quarter-ball", i.e., we propose that the radius of a ball with the reference level as its centre be blown up as much as possible such that its north-east part, the quarter-ball, is still fully lying in the capability sets to be considered. Figure 2 in Section 3 below will make this argument much clearer. What we need to assume for our analysis is that the individual functionings are quantifiable and that we are able to measure distances in the functioning space. These assumptions are by no means innocuous but they are, admittedly, necessary requirements for the present analysis.

Basic Notation and Definitions

In order to render our approach as precise as possible, we need a minimal amount of notation. Let IR_+ be the set of all non-negative real numbers, IR_{++} be the set of all positive numbers, IR^n_+ be the n-fold Cartesian product of IR_+ and IR^n_{++} be the n-fold Cartesian product of IR_{++}. Vectors in IR^n_+ will be denoted by $x, y, a, b, \ldots$ and are interpreted as functioning vectors (Sen 1985, 1987). For all $x = (x_1, \ldots, x_n)$, $y = (y_1, \ldots, y_n) \in IR^n_+$, we define $x \geq y$ as $x_i \geq y_i$ for all $i \in \{1, \ldots, n\}$, $x > y$ when $x_i \geq y_i$ for all $i \in \{1, \ldots, n\}$ and $x_j > y_j$ for some $j \in \{1, \ldots, n\}$, and $x >> y$ when $x_i > y_i$ for all $i \in \{1, \ldots, n\}$.

There are several ways to measure the progress that an individual makes when moving from one functioning vector x to another functioning vector y. In the present paper, we shall use the Euclidean distance function to capture the progress made by an agent. The formal definition of this distance function, given any two vectors x and y, is as follows:

$$|x-y| = \sqrt{\sum_{i=1}^{n}(x_i - y_i)^2}.$$

Other distance functions could be used as well but we abstain from giving further details (see Gaertner & Xu 2008).

At any given point of time, the set of all vectors that may be available to the individual is a subset of IR^n_+. Such a set will be called the individual's capability set. We shall use A, B, C etc. to denote the capability sets.

Our endeavour in this paper is to rank different capability sets in terms of the opportunities that they provide and offer to the agent considered. In particular, we confine our attention to opportunity sets that are compact, convex, and contain the origin. The latter two properties are due to the assumption of linear input-output relationships that we briefly discussed in section 1. Our capability sets are star-shaped. We say that a set $A \subseteq IR^n_+$ is star-shaped if and only if for all $x \in IR^n_+$ and all $t \in [0,1]$, if $x \in A$, then $t\,x \in A$. In other words, for any point x lying in set A, all the points on a line between x and the origin also belong to A.

Let K be the set of all capability sets that are compact, convex and star-shaped. For all A, $B \in K$, we write $A \subseteq B$ for "A being a subset of B" and $A \subset B$ for "A being a proper subset of B". For all A, $B \in K$, $A > B$ denotes that [for all $b \in B$ with $b >> 0$, there exists a neighbourhood $N(b,\varepsilon) = \{x \in IR^n_+ : x \geq b\,,\, |x-b| \leq \varepsilon\}$ where $\varepsilon > 0$ of b such that $N(b,\varepsilon) \subseteq A$] and [for all $b \in B$, there exists $a \in A$ such that $a >> b$]. This latter property is being used in one of our axioms where we consider two sets A and B in the following way. If B is a proper subset of A, we claim that in such cases a third set C is lying in between A and B.

Let $x^0 \in IR^n_{++}$ be the status quo point or reference level from which alternative capability sets are evaluated. It is a point in the n-dimensional space of functionings. In this paper, we shall assume that the point is fixed. This point is person-specific or country-specific. Different persons or countries will have differing status-quo points or differing points of orientation. Germany and France have similar status-quo points, but Germany's status-quo point and that of the Ivory Coast or of South-Africa are definitely different.

We now define, for all $t > 0$,

$$X(x^0, t) = \{x \in IR^n_+ : x > x^0, |x-x^0| \leq t\} \ .$$

Geometrically speaking, $X(x^0, t)$ is the north-east part of a ball (quarter-ball) with centre x^0 and radial extension t. It describes functioning possibilities that are better than x^0. In other words, it is a space of richer functionings. The underlying assumption is that "more" is considered to be better than "less", since as emphasized before, what is at stake are very basic functionings that are valuable. Because of a certain degree of uncertainty or incertitude, all combinations of functionings north-east of x^0 are equally desirable a priori. Scalar t measures the Euclidean distance between two vectors in the functioning space.

For all $A \in K$, let

$$r(A) = \begin{cases} -1, & \text{if } x^0 \notin A, \\ \max_t \{t \in IR_+ : \{x \in IR^n_+ : x \geq x^0, | x - x^0 | \leq t\} \subseteq A\}, & \text{if } x^0 \in A. \end{cases}$$

Clearly, $r(A)$ is the maximal radial extension north-east when x^0 lies in A. If x^0 is outside the considered capability set, $r(A) = -1$. Figure 2 depicts the maximal $t \in IR_+$ for two capability sets A and B when $x^0 \in A \cap B$.

Figure 2: Comparison of two capability sets A and B

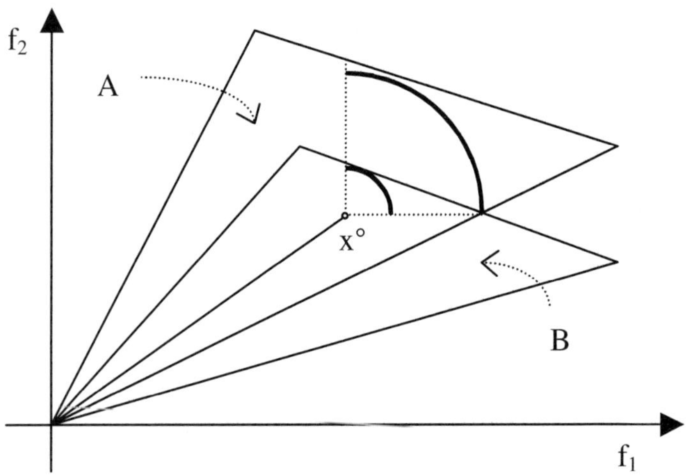

Let $\succeq$ be a binary relation over K that satisfies reflexivity [for all $A \in K$, $A \succeq A$], transitivity [for all $A,B,C \in K$, if $A \succeq B$ and $B \succeq C$, then $A \succeq C$], and completeness [for all $A,B \in K$ with $A \neq B$, $A \succeq B$ or $B \succeq A$]. Thus, $\succeq$ is an ordering. The intended interpretation of $\succeq$ is as follows: for all A, $B \in K$, $A \succeq B$ will be interpreted as "the degree of opportunities offered by A is at least as large as the degree of opportunities offered by B. $\succ$ and $\sim$, respectively, are the asymmetric and symmetric parts of $\succeq$.

Four Axioms and a Theorem

Define the following ordering:

$$\text{For all } A, B \in \mathcal{K}, A \succeq^{r} B \Leftrightarrow \mathrm{r}(A) \geq r(B).$$

Definition 4.1. $\succeq$ over $\mathcal{K}$ satisfies

4.1.1 Monotonicity iff, for all $A, B \in \mathcal{K}$, if $B \subseteq A$ then $A \succeq B$.

4.1.2 Betweenness iff, for all $A, B \in \mathcal{K}$, if $A \succ B$ with $x^0 \in A \cap B$, then there exists $C \in \mathcal{K}$ such that $C > B$ and $A \succ C \succ B$.

4.1.3 Dominance iff, for all $A, B \in \mathcal{K}$, if $x^0 \notin B$, then $A \succeq B$, and furthermore, if $x^0 \in A$, then $A \succ B$.

4.1.4 Domination in terms of uncertainty iff, for all A, B $\in \mathcal{K}$, if there exists $t > 0$ such that $X(x^0, t) \cap A = X(x^0, t)$, and $B \cap X(x^0, t) \subset X(x^0, t)$, then $A \succ B$.

The intuition behind the first axiom is easy to explain. It requires that if set B is a subset of A, then set A is ranked at least as high as B in terms of the opportunities that both sets offer. A offers as much as B and possibly more. Betweenness says that if set A offers more opportunities than B relative to the reference point x^0, there must exist another set C which lies between A and B such that A offers more opportunities than C which offers more than set B. Dominance requires that if the reference level x^0 is not contained in set B, then A is ranked at least as high as B. If furthermore, the reference point x^0 lies in A, then A is strictly better than B in terms of opportunities. The fourth axiom requires that, for two capability sets A and B, whenever A results from achievements made in north-east direction, i.e., achievements in all dimensions of functioning vectors, while B does not offer this particular degree of "progress", the opportunities available under A are judged to be higher than those offered by B.

One can now prove the following theorem (Gaertner & Xu 2008):

Theorem. Suppose that $\succeq$ over $\mathcal{K}$ is an ordering. Then, $\succeq$ satisfies Monotonicity, Betweenness, Dominance and Domination in Terms of Uncertainty if and only if $\succeq = \succeq^{r}$.

We omit the proof. It is given in the reference mentioned above.

Refinements and Some Concluding Remarks

We have assumed so far that every expansion north-east of x^0 is exactly as desirable as every other expansion north-east of the same length. This makes perfect sense in a first approach, particularly in the case of elementary functionings which are vital for subsistence. However we believe that there are situations where characteristics in certain proportions and thence, functionings in certain proportions are viewed as more appropriate than other combinations. Take, for example, being knowledgeable and being healthy as basic functionings. In developed countries such as Germany or France, access to clean water is almost everywhere guaranteed. Also, the density of medical centres and available doctors is relatively high. Education among young people, however, is a problem, particularly among low income groups and immigrants. In such a situation, one may consider a development according to a particular proportion between the two functionings with an emphasis on education as more appropriate than the full 90 degree angle. Of course, in certain countries in Sub-Saharan Africa, priorities will be quite different. There, the provision with clean water and with basic medical care still is an acute problem. Therefore, in these regions, a development according to a different proportion between the levels of knowledge and health may be warranted.

Technically speaking, this modification can be dealt with in a way similar to our basic approach. Let $X(x^0, \delta)$ be a right cone with angle δ and vertex x^0. Note that if $\delta = 0$, there is a unique direction. The width of angle δ can be due to an uncertainty about the right proportion among the functionings. Also, an angle of non-zero degree allows for a certain amount of flexibility. The following figure provides some intuition.

Figure 3: Two alternative sectors of desirable proportions

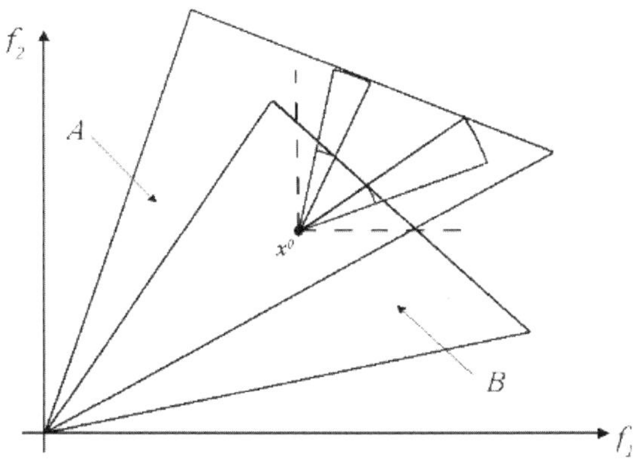

An axiomatic analysis for this and some other cases is given in Gaertner & Xu (2009), though in a different context. Once the approach presented in this paper is accepted, other situations can be dealt with in a straightforward manner. In Gaertner & Xu (2006) we have analyzed a situation where the level of reference falls outside the available capability sets. In such a case a measure analogous to the present one is needed, the latter having the property that the capability set which is nearest to the reference point is chosen. Again, the Euclidean distance or some other measure can be used. Satiation is another phenomenon that can be dealt with in the present framework. Imagine that a particular agent has the feeling that the current state of health is more than satisfactory so that this functioning does not need any further amelioration. However, the functionings of being educated and of engaging in social contacts should be further improved. In such a situation, a three-dimensional cone would shrink to a two-dimensional plane. In the case of only two dimensions, cones such as those in Figure 3 would shrink to a line, being either horizontal or vertical to x^0.

Let us finally go one step beyond the case of satiation. We just said that in the course of time, with an increasing income, let's say, one or several of the functionings may have been realized to such a degree that the agent is no longer interested in achieving any higher level of these. However, it can also be the case that at some point, i.e., given a particular x^0, the agent wishes to reduce the extent of one or several of the functionings while increasing one or several others at the same time. Figure 4 depicts such a situation. It shows two cases. One of these represents the initial case of monotonicity in north-east direction, the other case depicts the situation just mentioned. The agent is monotone with respect to functioning 2 but "anti-monotone'' in relation to f_1. If the latter represents social activities, an agent may wish to reduce his or her social involvement to a lower level while upholding and further extending f_2. The reader will realize that the "tools" to deal with a combination of monotonicity and anti-monotonicity are not much different from the initial ones with overall monotonicity.

Figure 4: A case of monotonicity and anti-monotonicity

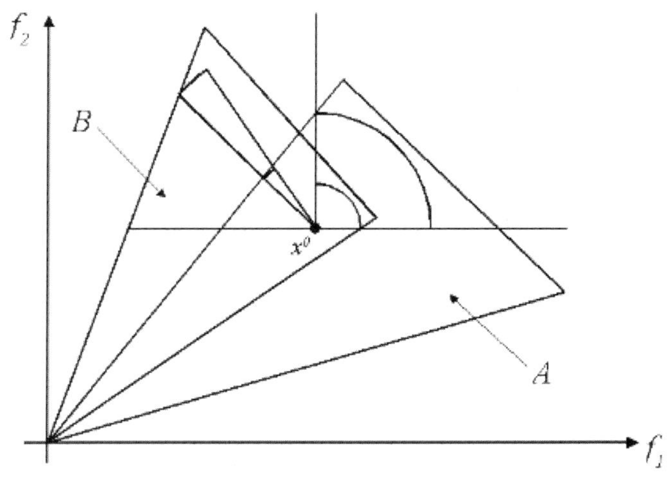

We hope that we were able to show in the present paper that Lancaster's idea of characteristics generated by purchases of commodities can be applied to the creation of different spaces of functionings. These spaces differ in the amount of opportunities that they provide to the individual. Our goal was to present a measure that can reflect the richness of alternative capability sets.

References

Gaertner, W. & Xu, Y. (2006): Capability sets as the basis of a new measure of human development. Journal of Human Development 7, 311-321.

Gaertner W. & Xu, Y. (2008): A new class of measures of the standard of living based on functionings. Economic Theory 35, 201-215.
Gaertner, W. & Xu, Y. (2009): Reference-dependent rankings of sets in characteristics space. Social Choice and Welfare, forthcoming.
Lancaster, K. (1966): A new approach to consumer theory. Journal of Political Economy 74, 132-157.
Pattanaik, P.K. & Xu, Y. (1990): On ranking opportunity sets in terms of freedom of choice. Recherches Economiques de Louvain 56, 383-390.
Rawls, J. (1971): A Theory of Justice. Harvard University Press, Cambridge, Ma.
Sen, A.K. (1985): Commodities and Capabilities. North-Holland, Amsterdam.
Sen, A.K. (1987): The Standard of Living. Cambridge University Press, Cambridge.

Mirtha R. Muñiz Castillo

Human Autonomy and Development Effectiveness: Introducing a People-Centred Framework for Project Assessment[1]

Introduction

Evaluation usually focuses on intended and tangible outputs and their direct impacts. A linear causal logic already specified for a project or programme, such as in a 'logical framework', holds that the achievement of such outputs and purposes leads to particular positive outcomes or development goals. Nevertheless, projects may influence people's lives more broadly and in the longer term.

This chapter proposes to focus on individuals, their goals and values, rather than on projects as designed to directly produce changes for people. It presents a conception of autonomy that requires relatedness, and suggests a new criterion of development effectiveness called 'human autonomy effect-tiveness', for which the expansion of individual autonomy is considered a priority goal.

Promoting individual autonomy contributes to sustainable human development. The more autonomous people have more options and are better able to choose the life they value and take action to achieve it. They are also more likely to expand the potentials or capabilities that they most value (Sen 1993, 1999; etc.). Therefore, development initiatives should focus on *whether* and *how* these initiatives influence individual autonomy.

In the context of project aid, the chapter introduces a people-centred framework for project assessment. The framework looks at how projects can positively influence certain factors that determine individual autonomy and how they favour the exercise of autonomy by part of project recipients. It draws on a study of four infrastructure projects in Nicaragua and El Salvador that were supported by Luxembourg's aid agency between 1999 and 2005 (Muñiz Castillo 2009).

Evidence from one water project illustrates the general argument. The project reached about 500 households in a rural village in the East of El Sal-

---

1 This chapter is based on Muñiz Castillo, M.R. & Gasper, D. (2009), work presented before audiences at the University of Antwerp, the University of Bielefeld and the Pontifical Catholic University of Peru.

vador. It aimed at improving the health and living conditions of the residents through the provision of stable access to drinking water service and sanitation and environmental protection actions.

A conceptual model of individual autonomy

Individual autonomy is a person's capability to make choices in significant matters, authentically motivated, and achieve positive results in his or her life. To develop and realise this capability, individuals require resources, relations and certain conditions.

At a conceptual level, autonomy can be defined as a combined capability (Nussbaum 2000) to distinguish between (a) an internal element, which corresponds to *agency* in the sense of the capacity to make reasoned choices and act accordingly, and (b) an external element, the context that promotes or restricts opportunities for the exercise of agency.

Looking at agency as an internal capacity[2], autonomy can be understood as qualified effective agency. It is effective because individuals can take action to advance their goals, if they so decide, given that the influence of contexts is already taken into account – this is the idea of capability as possible reachable outcomes. It is qualified because autonomy concerns decisions on significant aspects of life (Taylor 1979; Doyal & Gough 1991; Kabeer 1999), decisions which cohere with one's own values and personality and for which one is self- motivated.

At a practical level, autonomy can be analysed in terms of three determinants: entitlements, agency and multilevel structural contexts, which are to be studied individually and in interaction (see Figure 1).

2 The definition of agency here is different from the one used by Sen (1985b, 1993) when he refers to wellbeing and agency as two dimensions how the situation of an individual could be assessed.

Figure 1: A conceptual model of autonomy

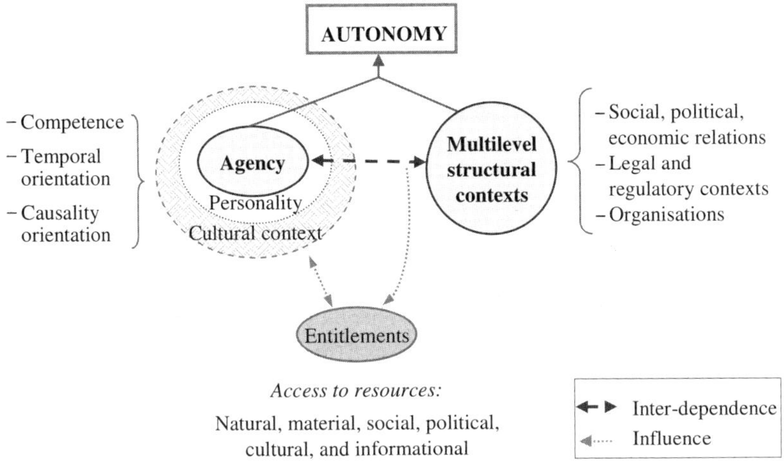

Source: Muñiz Castillo (2009, Fig. 2-6: 36)

Entitlements represent the access to resources. People are entitled to certain resources to promote their goals when they own or can get these resources from market or non-market channels (e.g. public goods, social transfers, relationships). Entitlements are negotiated in multilevel structural contexts and their meaning is given by the use that individuals make of resources, which is culturally influenced.

Agency depends on several elements. Competence is the capacity to perform well, to be able to use personal abilities to reach goals. These abilities can be physical, intellectual or emotional. Self-confidence is essential for autonomy because how individuals regard themselves and their efficacy will partially influence their objectives, aspirations, and perceptions about the opportunities and risks in the external environment (Bandura 2000). Self-perceived competence is influenced by contexts and fuels intentional action.

Moreover, agency is influenced by two forms of *internal orientation*: temporal orientation (Emirbayer & Mische 1995) and causality orientation (Deci & Ryan 1985; 2000).

Temporal orientation is the tendency of individuals to give more weight to the past, the present or the future when they analyse possible actions, that is, if they act following past patterns of thought or habits, make their judgements in response to events in the evolving situations, or imaginatively generate possible future trajectories of action. The latter element is related to the 'capacity to aspire' (Appadurai 2004) that, when ex-pressed in voice and participation, can stimulate development.

Causality orientation refers to what are the reasons to act in a certain way, as the agent perceives them. Individuals can consider that: (i) they are originators of events, (ii) they behave as they must (due to external reasons), or (iii) whatever happens is independent of their intentions. An orientation of the first type is called 'autonomy' orientation. It implies more than being 'in control' of events or contexts. For instance, in our water project, a resident could feel competent to build a home sanitation system to dispose of grey water (from kitchens, lavatories and bathrooms) and actually build it, so feeling in control of this specific process and satisfied with the outcome. However, if he or she did not value the system and only built it because project staff required it, this person would not have an autonomy causality orientation.

The model includes two *internal contexts* (Alexander 1992): personality and cultural context. Figure 1 presents them as concentric circles around agency to indicate that these contexts influence agency. The cultural context (larger circle) is filtered by the personality of each individual that gives meaning to the cultural and external contexts.

The structural contexts are the environments in which individuals negotiate their roles, meaning systems and entitlements (cf. Alexander 1993). They comprise all sets of social relations (economic, political and associational) coordinated with stable or sporadic, formal or informal rules. Contexts can be analysed at several levels. In fact, projects take place in specific national and local contexts that imprint their character on what happens, and are influenced by policies and practices in international contexts.

It is worth stressing that, although contexts shape values and opportunities, autonomy is an individual feature of unique human beings with their own biographies, emotions, aspirations and commitments. As Christman (1998: 387) affirms, "the autonomous person is one who acts, chooses, and judges for herself (however complex, embedded and interconnected with others that self turns out to be)".

Individuals exhibit different degrees of autonomy. For analysis purposes, autonomy can be classified into basic and critical autonomy. *Basic autonomy* requires a certain level of competence and satisfaction of human needs so that people can effectively participate in social life. For instance, adequate health, housing and education must be secured. The required level of competence depends on the particular cultural setting.

Critical autonomy (Doyal & Gough 1991) requires a higher level of competence, intercultural knowledge and political freedom so that individuals can realise the capabilities that they choose, in structural contexts that may support or restrict their goals. Individuals may require joining efforts with others to promote significant change in their lives.

A criterion of development effectiveness: human autonomy effectiveness

Foreign development aid usually fills the gaps that poor countries face in terms of resources, skills and systems (Riddell 2007: 180) to improve the wellbeing of their citizens. There are customary evaluation criteria and tools to evaluate their fulfilment. A basic criterion is *effectiveness*, which refers to the extent to which objectives are achieved, taking into account their relative importance (OECD 2002). However, several development objectives are difficult to quantify, the causal assumptions used in the design often do not hold, and several external and country specific structural factors affect outcomes. Correspondingly, the section introduces a new and arguably more relevant interpretation of development effectiveness, called 'human autonomy effecttiveness'.

In the case of projects, this criterion indicates that effectiveness should be assessed in relation to whether and how individual autonomy has been expanded – in addition to, and indeed as more important than (other) formal project goals. This criterion is different from:

- Operational effectiveness, which refers to the achievement of operational results that can be relatively secured by project staff;
- Intended impact, which refers to the achievement of higher-level project goals, outside the relative control of project staff; and
- Economic effectiveness, focused on objectives expressible in monetary terms.

Project beneficiaries could have diverse goals (different from pre-defined project goals), on which they evaluate effectiveness and, furthermore, some of these goals could be opposite or normatively contestable. The criterion of human autonomy effectiveness refers to the promotion of autonomy that supports human development[3], but not to the achievement of particular goals; not all personal goals are important for human development.

In addition, this evaluation criterion requires that the expansion of autonomy does not contract other priority capabilities (Alkire 2002: 180). For instance, project participants may develop their competence by working in self-construction activities and attending workshops, but these actions should not prevent them from working in their farm to sustain themselves. It is neces-

3 'Human development refers to (i) a sustainable improvement in well-being or a positive change in the actual lives that people lead – that include objective and subjective aspects, and (ii) the expansion of valuable human potentials (capabilities) that secure a life with dignity for everyone in interaction with others' (Muñiz Castillo 2009: 24).

sary to discuss and agree on a capability hierarchy so that secondary goals that would constrain valuable capabilities are not pursued.[4]

It is also crucial to reflect on which objectives are defined, by whom, and who shares them. The analysis proposed here focuses on the experiences of social actors during the change process *supported by* a project (cf. Crawford et al. 2005). This means that the change is not directed by outsiders but initiated by local people so that the project supports ongoing or self-motivated change; only such a change is sustainable (Ellerman 2006).

In contrast, a pseudo-motivated change, visible during a project timeframe, could be result of an extrinsic motivation; aid recipients could behave as project staff expects and play as 'good beneficiaries' in order to secure what they perceive the project can offer (cf. Wood 2003). Traditional ex-post evaluations could wrongly consider this change as sustainable. So, impact should instead be assessed over a term that exceeds the usual timeframe of an aid project.

Human autonomy effectiveness refers to a long run perspective, including what comes after the end of a project. Whatever may be its direct contributions to human development during its duration (e.g., improved health, learned construction skills), a project that fails to build persons' autonomy during and through its processes will fail to lead on to sustained and continuing post-project contributions to human development.

Introducing a framework for project assessment

Judging whether a project is effective in terms of human autonomy is challenging given that the target is complex and not easily quantifiable. First, individual autonomy as a capability (feasible to be exercised) can be expanded through improvements in its determinants: agency, entitlements and structural contexts. A project could be seen as human-autonomy effective if these determinants improve.

Nevertheless, a project might have *different effects* on each determinant. Projects might affect the access to resources, individual skills, and power relations, but each in a *different way*. For instance, if people are induced to work long hours to secure the prompt delivery of outputs but they are mistreated, their entitlements would expand but their self-confidence and agency would be undermined. This highlights that it is crucial to identify the synergic

4 Several scholars have developed lists of such capabilities (see Alkire 2002). Different qualitative and participatory methods can help to identify priority capabilities in particular contexts (White & Pettit 2004). There are also mixed approaches based on explicit normative theories (see Robeyns 2003).

satisfiers (Max-Neef et al. 1991) that support more than one relevant factor contributing to individual autonomy, without restricting others.

Second, the exercise of autonomy (i.e., the functioning) and the effectiveness of the decisions made are also relevant because people are aware of and develop their capability when they exercise it. This refers to empowerment[5], which should be of priority because it supports the capacity of people to effect change in their own lives. If people consider that their actions have real positive outcomes, their self-confidence to initiate actions will improve. The degree of this positive effect on autonomy depends on the role of project participants and their motivations to participate (Muñiz Castillo 2009).

Returning to our example, the residents who built the sanitation system had control on the process (their community leaders even supervised the works) and reached the expected outcomes. However, for some of them, building the system was not a decision based on the conviction that it was useful for their health. They will be less interested than others in using and maintaining such systems well because their action did not reflect an exercise of autonomy.

Hence, it is relevant to look at whether people have the opportunity and act to pursue their goals, with autonomy *causality orientation* (in contrast to control orientation led by expectations of rewards or punishments) with respect to valued matters. A second step would be to analyse whether they were able to bring their goals about, most likely through collective action in the case of people with (relative) lack of entitlements.

The analysis requires looking explicitly at local goals, values and capacities. It is necessary to identify which project processes (systemic series of activities leading to a defined goal) were valued by project participants, and whether they could be involved and were effectively involved. *Involvement* is a high-quality participation that means that beneficiaries are reasonably informed, are able to speak out and share in relevant decision-making. Participation leads to empowerment when people are self-motivated and involved in valued processes of a project that achieves valued outcomes.

In our water case, the design included the construction of a reservoir to water livestock. However, during the project execution, community leaders planned and started a business of raising tilapias. They connected the reservoir to a pre-existing gravity water system, bought fry and obtained donations as well. In this way, they planned to support their local economy. This flexibility to adapt the original design to the local needs was evidenced in a matter that was important for residents, in which leaders (in representation of other

5 Empowerment has been broadly discussed (e.g., Narayan 2002; Alsop et al. 2006) although sometimes overused given its relatively imprecise meaning. In this model, empowerment refers to the exercise of autonomy, considering the effectiveness of decisions. It refers to both process freedom (self-motivated and relevant decision-making) and opportunity freedom (achievement of valued outcomes).

community members) exercised autonomy and enrolled project staff in their 'project'. Unfortunately, external factors harmed its sustainability.

Understanding complex influences on individual autonomy

Returning to the first perspective to analyse individual autonomy, i.e. in function to its determinants, how can we analyse the different effects that a project could have?

The logical framework approach, operational through the logframe matrix (see Eggers 1998), is the most used tool in project design. It defines a series of causal links between a project and its objectives, establishing an explicit hierarchy. It reflects the prevailing project theory (Rossi, Lipsey & Freeman 2004) and expresses the explicit logic of a project. However, change can be influenced by non-project factors, unintended interactions of a project with other factors, unintended routes and unforeseen effects (Conway & Maxwell 1999; Gasper 1999). This array of possible influences, pathways and effects is not captured by a logframe.

Moreover, a project is not only about what is written and expected, but also about *what* is done and *how* that is done. Practices reflect its *implicit* logic. Practices are forms of interaction and practical strategies carried out by social actors that evolve from their actions in specific contexts and are manifested in several ways (Long & van der Ploeg 1994). Practices are not rigidly linked to particular events or project activities. The same activity can have different meanings for individuals in the same locality and can stimulate different (and sometimes opposite) responses, depending on each person's specific capacities, cultural context and personality.

It is worth noting that a project brings its organisational culture and functional structure. Project staff (not necessarily from only one organisation) may hold values and promote social practices different from the local ones, with different effects on local participants. Practices will reflect the power relations in specific communities and between local stakeholders and project staffs. For example, a practice of hierarchical project management may reflect assumptions that project participants will do as they are told, and that they have no independent objectives or no 'exit' options. Such practice is more dangerous when institutional contexts are uncertain and stakeholders have competing interests. In our water case, this resulted in the 'alignment' of community leaders around project staff and the separation of the municipality mayor from project activities.

Identifying project practices helps us to understand how a project works, how different it is from others, and what makes it work in a given way (Pawson & Tilley 1997). Practices signal the mechanisms behind certain effects, and can explain the emergence of unintended or unexpected effects, whose analysis escapes the scope of logical frameworks as traditionally used.

Following the criterion of human autonomy effectiveness, the focus here is on individuals as agents of change, not on projects designed to produce change for people. Then, evaluators should look at changes in the determinants of individual autonomy and examine whether these changes were primarily driven by the project or other factors, by analysing thoroughly the 'full' project logic (the explicit and the implicit logic).

Three steps help identifying the full project logic:

1. Knowing the project logic stated in the logical framework and other project documents;
2. Identifying the specific activities carried out during the project cycle, who decided about changes to the original design, why and under which circumstances; and
3. Investigating the practices that evolved over time, as result of the interaction of individuals with project staff and other actors in the multilevel structural contexts.

The logical framework makes project design and implementation transparent conceptually and can be adapted to place autonomy as an overall goal; however, it is not well suited for describing complex causation. Change will be explained not only by project outputs (which may or may not translate into the foreseen and intended impacts), but also by project practices and relations that affect project participants in different ways, and are influenced by structural contexts. Then, it might be more accurate to speak of project influences than project effects, as many other factors will contribute to explain human development outcomes.

An assessment matrix (see Table 1) can assist the analysis of project influences on the determinants of autonomy. It requires not only that project practices are identified and their implications analysed, but also that their processes of formation are understood.

Table 1: Assessment matrix of project influences on individual autonomy

	PROJECT LOGIC		ACTUAL EFFECTS	
(i) Determinants of autonomy	(ii) Hypotheses on effects	(iii) Expected conditions	(iv) Actual situation	(v) Assessment of effect
- Entitlements - Agency (inc. self-confidence) - Structural contexts (e.g., communal organisation, social capital)	Intended and unintended impacts based on the project 'full' logic.	Assumptions and outputs that are explicit and implicit in project logic.	Actual conditions or change in conditions (in contrast to expected conditions) related or not to the project.	- Yes/no, partial - Short or long-term - Sustainable, at risk (vs. Hypotheses)

Source: Muñiz Castillo (2009, Table 4-4: 88)

In conceptual terms, a project could have direct effects on entitlements at the individual and the community level. However, the intended positive effect could not occur if, for instance, elites concentrate resources, undermining trust, with a deep negative effect on the causality orientation of other community members. Particular dynamics in structural contexts are also important. For example, access to safe drinking water could be constrained by poor maintenance of the water plant (due to institutional factors) or inadequate setting of the water tariffs (related to coordination practices during the project).

A project could also support agency, primarily individual competence, through an improvement in health conditions, skills, and so on. Moreover, self-confidence (at the individual level) and organisational capacity (at the community level) could be fostered or undermined depending on the quality of the participation and cooperation of individuals within community organisations. In addition, the structural contexts could change, for instance, if power relations are affected as a result of a redistribution of resources and decision-making.

Since the influences are of different nature, a combination of data collection and analysis methods is required. However, causality has to be explored via qualitative analysis methods in order to capture what really matters to beneficiaries and the meanings and interpretations that they form. This is particularly important to explore the subjective elements of autonomy (the feeling of being autonomous). For instance, self-confidence, which supports the initiation of autonomous action, depends on the existence of supportive external contexts and personal factors.

Conclusions

This chapter has proposed the criterion of human autonomy effectiveness to assess the effects of projects on people's lives, which primarily looks at how participants' autonomy is positively influenced by projects, without restricting other priority capabilities. The analytical framework explores two channels how individual autonomy can be promoted, through an improvement in its determinants and through the exercise of autonomy by part of participants during the project cycle.

The focus is on individuals as agents of change, not on projects designed to produce change for individuals. The framework emphasizes practices and relations, not only planned activities and tangible outputs, because a change process is not caused merely by a design. Change is pursued, lived and felt by individuals who negotiate goals, experience conflicts or reach agreements while seeking to exercise their autonomy in their specific circumstances.

The framework requires a careful analysis of the 'full' project logic, which is jointly constructed – by project participants, project staff, formulators and other stakeholders. As such, this logic should be analysed through several channels at different times during the project. This exercise will shed light on different influences on individual autonomy and, indirectly, on opportunities and challenges for the project operational effectiveness.

Guided by the criterion of human autonomy effectives, project planners and managers have to understand the livelihoods and aspirations of local participants, respect their change process, not impose values that are 'accepted' only as result of conditionality, and encourage their efforts to exercise voice. This implies, for instance, that some adaptations to the original design of a project should be possible. Building partnerships with local people in the presence of power imbalances is a sensitive issue. In some cases, project staff could facilitate the participation of otherwise excluded people who already possess a motivation to improve their lives. Its role would be to identify intrinsic motivation and support local efforts.

Participation leads to empowerment when people are self-motivated and involved in valued processes of a project that achieves valued outcomes. The challenge is to identify and promote involvement that implies a certain exercise of autonomy and clearly differentiate it from, for instance, participation as enforced workload. Human-autonomy effective projects could lead to more horizontal relations between aid recipients and funders toward the achievement of valued goals, with thereby greater chance of sustained positive effects on human development.

References

Alexander, J.C. (1992): Recent sociological theory between agency and social structure. Schweizerische Zeitschrift für Soziologie 18, 1, 7-11.

Alexander, J.C. (1993): More notes on the problem of agency: a reply. Schweizerische Zeitschrift für Soziologie, 19, 501-506.

Alkire, S. (2002): Valuing freedoms: Sen's capability approach and poverty reduction. Oxford.

Alsop, R., Bertelsen, M. & Holland, J. (2006): Empowerment in practice: from analysis to implementation. Directions in Development Series. Washington, DC.

Appadurai, A. (2004): The capacity to aspire: culture and the terms of recognition. In: Rao, V. & Walton, M. (Eds.): Culture and public action. Stanford, 59-84.

Bandura, A. (2000): Exercise of human agency through collective efficacy. Current Directions in Psychological Science, 9, 3, 75-78.

Christman, J. (1998): Autonomy, independence, and poverty-related welfare policies. Public Affairs Quarterly, 12, 4, 383-405.

Conway, T. & Maxwell, S. (1999a): Country programme evaluation: synthesis report from the workshop. In: OECD, Evaluating Country Programmes, Vienna Workshop 1999, chapter 1, DAC Working Party on Aid Evaluation.

Crawford, P., Swete Kelly, D., Mitchell, C. & Bryce, P. (2005): Aristotle and Plato at it again? Philosophical divergence within international aid project design and monitoring & evaluation [electronic paper]. Retrieved June 10, 2008, from http://www.aid-at.com.au/Portals/0/Documents/070105_Aristotle%20and%20 Plato%20at%20it%20again.pdf

Deci, E.L. & Ryan, R.M. (1985): The general causality orientations scale: self-determination in personality. Journal in Research on Personality, 19, 109-134.

Deci, E.L. & Ryan, R.M. (2000): The "what" and "why" of goal pursuits: human needs and the self-determination of behaviour. Psychological Inquiry, 11, 4, 227–268.

Doyal, L. & Gough, I. (1991): A theory of human need. London.

Eggers, H.W. (1998): Project cycle management revisited. The Courier, 169, 69-72.

Ellerman, D. (2006): Helping people help themselves: from the World Bank to an alternative philosophy of development assistance. Paperback edition. Ann Arbor.

Emirbayer, M. & Mische, A. (1995): What is agency? American Journal of Sociology, 103, 4, 962-1023.

Gasper, D. (1999): Problems in the logical framework approach and challenges for project cycle management. The Courier, 173, 75-77.

Hirschman, A.O. (1967): Development projects observed. Washington, D.C.: The Brookings Institution (reissued 1995).

Hodgson, G. (2006): What are institutions? Journal of Economic Issues, 40, 1, 1-25.

Kabeer, N. (1999): The conditions and consequences of choice: reflections on the measurement of women's empowerment. UNRISD Discussion Paper 108. Geneva: United Nations Research Institute for Social Development.

Long, N. & van der Ploeg, J.D. (1994): Heterogeneity, actor and structure: towards a reconstitution of the concept of structure. In: Booth, D. (Ed.): Rethinking social development: theory, research and practice. Essex, 62-89.

Max-Neef, M.A., Elizalde, A. & Hopenhayn, M. (1991): Human scale development: conception, application and further reflections. New York.

Muñiz Castillo, M.R. (2009): Human development and autonomy in project aid: Experiences from four bilateral projects in Nicaragua and El Salvador. (Doctoral dissertation, Maastricht University) MGSoG Dissertation Series 4. Maastricht.

Muñiz Castillo, M.R. & Gasper, D. (2009): Looking for long-run development effectiveness: An autonomy-centred framework for project evaluation. MGSoG Working Paper, 2009/005. Maastricht.

Narayan, D. (2002): Empowerment and poverty reduction: a sourcebook. Washington D.C.

Nussbaum, M. (2000): Women and human development. Cambridge.

OECD (Organisation for Economic Co-operation and Development) (2002): Glossary of key terms in evaluation and results based management. Paris: OECD, DAC.

Pawson, R. & Tilley, N. (1997): Realistic evaluation. London, Thousand Oaks, New Delhi, reprinted 2000.

Robeyns, I. (2003): Sen's capability approach and gender inequality: selecting relevant capabilities. Feminist Economics, 9, 2-3, 61-92.

Riddell, R.C. (2007): Does foreign aid really work? Oxford.

Rossi, P.H., Lipsey, M.W. & Freeman H.E. (2004): Evaluation: a systematic approach (7th ed.). Thousand Oaks, CA.

Schischka, J.A. (2006): Putting the capability approach into practice for project development and evaluation. Development Bulletin, 60, 119-122.

Sen, A. (1985): Well-being, agency and freedom: the Dewey lectures 1984. The Journal of Philosophy, 82, 4, 169-221.

Sen, A. (1993): Capability and well-being. In Nussbaum, M. & Sen, A. (Eds.): The quality of life. Oxford, 30-53.

Sen, A. (1999): Development as freedom. New York.

Taylor, C. (1979): What's wrong with negative liberty. In: Ryan, A. (Ed.): The idea of freedom; excerpted in Miller, D. (Ed.) (1999): Liberty. Oxford, 141-162.

White, S. & Pettit, J. (2004): Participatory approaches and the measurement of human well-being. WIDER Research Paper 2004/57.

Wood, G. (2003): Staying secure, staying poor: the ''Faustian bargain''. World Development, 31, 3, 455-471.

John Cameron

Preparing Young People for Eudaimonia: Moving Capabilities across Generations

"And one man in his time plays many parts,
His acts being seven ages. At first the infant.
Mewling and puking in the nurse's arms.
And then the whining schoolboy, with his satchel,
And shining morning face, creeping like snail
Unwilling to school. And then the lover
Sighing like furnace, with a woeful ballad
Made to his mistress' eyebrow. Then a soldier,
Full of strange oaths, and bearded like the pard,
Jealous in honour, sudden and quick in quarrel,
Seeking the bubble reputation
Even in the cannon's mouth. And then the justice,
In fair round belly with good capon lin'd'
With eyes severe, and beard of formal cut,
Full of wise saws and modern instances;
And so he plays his part. The sixth age shifts
Into the lean and slipper'd pantaloon,
With spectacles on nose and pouch on side,
His youthful hose well sav'd, a world too wide
For his shrunk shank; and his big manly voice,
Turning again toward childish treble, pipes
And whistles in his sound. Last scene of all,
That ends this strange eventful history,
Is second childishness and mere oblivion,
Sans teeth, sans eyes, sans taste, sans everything"

William Shakespeare
from *As You Like It*, Act 2, Scene 7

Background

This paper is concerned with a tendency to neglect challenges of intergenerational relationships and the stages of a human life in the capability approach. These challenges can be summarised as:

- A tendency to look at capability as a state of 'preparation' for choice of functionings, de facto concluding at the end of formal education.
- A 'blindness' to ageing – though Nussbaum's concerns with Aristotlean eudaimonia does raise questions of the whole, well lived life and how that can be assessed at different points in that journey.

Aristotle's concept of eudaimonia is central to this paper. For Aristotle, the good life was believed to involve the exercise of deductive reason in decision-making, responsibility for others, plus care for the body in terms of the inductive recognition that moderation in the appetites preserved human capabilities. A central concept in Aristotlean eudaimonia envisages a whole, well lived life in which capabilities are developed and exercised to increase human well-being throughout life and uncertainty and adversity are faced with dignity.

Capability theory is fundamentally concerned with the quality of human life and how it changes as a result of public policy. But the quality of human life changes with age without public policy changes. Despite the fact that human life is fundamentally affected by ageing, the capability discourse has rather neglected this vital dimension of human existence. But it is worth noting that reflecting on our physical fundamental experiences as human beings, such as ageing is a central concern in the post-modern discourse (e.g. Lyotard 1991).

Understandably, driven by concerns for the degrading physical environment and depletion of non-renewable or difficult-to-renew resources, interest in intergenerational relationships has concentrated on depleted inheritance and longer term movements through time as one generation dies and another takes its place.

But the ages of people in any society are not just sequential as in Shakespeare's seven ages, they also co-exist and this paper is primarily concerned with the cross-sectional pattern of intergenerational relationships at a point in time. From infancy to senility, the people (the equivalent poem for women would still distinguish between 'ages') of all Shakespeare's ages have to share space and time, where capabilities are distributed between the ages according to natural forces and social rules. As examples, too many school-boys not developing capabilities at school, or, too many soldiers developing violent capabilities, can have implications for everyone's quality of life in their society at each point in time.

Thus ageing for the purpose of this paper will be treated in the form of discrete "generations". The concept of a "generation" adds explicit demographic, socio-cultural, psychological and psycho-emotional, and, political dimensions to that of ageing. We do not merely grow physically older, we also experience changes in how we feel and think about others and about ourselves as we change our relative position with respect to older and younger people.

To be of a "generation" is an important element of human identity in which the simple chronological process of becoming older is only one, albeit important, dimension. The movement between generations may be associated with formal rites of passage, but the change is more often a prolonged transition. A shift may be only be felt after a great deal of reflection - both on one's image in the eyes of others and physiologically in mirrors.

In Amartya Sen's terms, generational stages of a human life can be seen as involving changing patterns of entitlements capabilities, and functionings (Sen 1985; Sen 1997). A full development discourse needs to recognise these changes, analyse them, and evaluate how well societies meet the needs and aspirations of all generations. This paper approaches these issues from a capabilities perspective applied to intra- and intergenerational relationships.

Therefore, for the purposes here, a "generation" is defined as a group of people possessing a distinctive pattern of capabilities and functionings, effective rights and obligations (often freely and gladly accepted), and, entitlements. From this perspective a generation has no precise meaning in terms of chronological age. People move between generations as their particular patterns change, partially driven by changes in physical capabilities and legal status entitlements.

An individual at one point in time can imagine ideal relationships to other generations as mixtures of rights and obligations. The young child may well imagine its rights as creating obligations on all older generations, unless undesirable circumstances dictate otherwise. The mid-life aged person may recognise the primacy of obligations to older and younger people. The older person may wish to take responsibilities for younger generations, but may be aware that diminishing capabilities are reducing ability to meet those responsibilities and that there is a need to exercise rights as well as express obligations.

But relationships between generations are not only worked out between individuals, but also collectively at a moral distance. The exercise of effective rights and accepted obligations both collectively and at a distance is a particular problem for Western moral philosophy and particularly for development ethics. Attempting to encompass the collective representation of rights and obligations moves the discourse of moral philosophy from models of individual choice towards institutional power. The resulting action at a distance introduces problems of assessing both accuracy of information and confidence in intermediary agencies.

Shakespeare's seven ages are rather too demanding for this paper. Three generations are more manageable – younger, elder and middle-aged. Such a number will be commonly recognised and found at most life-cycle and festival events. Those events are moments in which transfers of capabilities between generations find symbolic expression and apparent balance. In Durkheimian terms, the more frequent such events the more the symbols become the reality of mechanical solidarity. The less frequent such symbolic events, then the more conscious choices are brought into play and the more organic the solidarity between generations.

Generally, processes of change in the world today are breaking mechanical solidarity between the generations. Spatial migration and cultural individualisation mean that generations have organically to decide to meet, rather than mechanically be brought together as a matter of course. The transfer of capabilities that are automatically produced in face to face contact is no longer guaranteed. The generations no longer meet as often in families, but meet in surrogate forms at a societal level. The major implication of such a change is that the transfer of capabilities is no longer a matter of face to face negotiations at the family dining place.

The differing interests of the various generations are weighed within wider political movements that claim to represent all generations. But these movements are lobbied by non-governmental organisations with specific generational concerns. For instance, children have to be saved, aged people attract concern. More subtly, commercial interests target particular generations with goods and services appropriate to different stages of life. Also, the generations are stereotyped in the mass media and given images of themselves behaving badly and (occasionally) well.

Relationships between the generations appear in all aspects of modern existence. Generational concerns and images can be found in all institutions: family, local civil society, NGO institutions between civil society and the state, political party manifestos and bureaucratic division of labour between ministries and departments, and in the manifestations of large-scale markets and mass culture. This very ubiquity of generational concerns means intergenerational relationships are difficult to analyse. The differing moral principles of family life, political lobbying, policy development and implementation, commercial advertising, and the mass media are all present in intergenerational relationships.

Relationships between generations vary greatly between societies and within societies. The model of the extended family meeting for a meal reduces social distance to a minimum. Purchasing a gift for a more distant relative in a different generation is a complex statement not only about that person, but also about socially manufactured perceptions of the needs and desires of that person's generation. A neighbourhood festival decreases the distance between generations. Thinking about contributing to, or receiving assistance from, a NGO concerned with a particular generation or age group can operate at widely varying social and spatial distances. Participating in a national demonstration for pensioners' rights is an act of concern looking to the priorities of government as a distinctive agent. Joining a global movement for abolition of child labour can also be seen as an intergenerational act, though without a clear agency to deliver the goal of that act.

The static image of reciprocal intergenerational kinship relationships sharing capabilities around a common pot may have been over-idealised for many families. So this paper will not assume that families can be relied upon to meet intergenerational needs and it is useful to reflect on intergenerational relationships and capabilities in whole societies and the human species overall. This paper is centrally concerned with more distant expressions of intergenerational relationships beyond kin and neighbourhood.

From entitlements, capabilities and functionings to effective rights and accepted obligations

Entitlements for the purpose of this paper are the collection of actual and potential rights to resources that an individual possesses. These rights are acknowledged and sanctioned by society largely independent of the choices and actions of the individual family. Entitlements will often be conditional in that there may be actions by an individual that will damage rights to entitlements. Therefore entitlements are intimately connected with rights to resources that are qualified by obligations not to act in a manner that breaks explicit and implicit conditions set by society.

Entitlements can rest upon accepted obligations from kin, neighbours, and various levels and programmes of government, or, the expected outcomes of market exchange. The operation of markets may involve ability to trade in terms of quantities of goods and services and/or to exchange at a particular price. The original work on entitlements by Amartya Sen emphasised the loss of economic exchange entitlements, uncompensated by increased social/ political obligations (Sen 1981).

But all forms of entitlement may vary with generational status. Growing older may modify rights to access to all other forms of entitlements as well as change capability to use those entitlements. To change age and generational status may change what may be expected in terms of entitlement rights and obligations from family, civil society, and the state. Elements of these changes will be independent of the capabilities and choices of the individual, but other elements will lie under the control of the individual who can accept or refuse a changing pattern of rights and obligations.

With respect to capability, Sen's own discussion of differing capability frequently draws examples from physical disabilities from natural causes. Though social restrictions on entitlements, notably those related to gender and impairment inequalities for Sen, also produce unequal capability. Sen also claims that unequal capability extend to the incapability of even recognising a right to higher capability. Sen finds an example of this double incapacitation in his analysis of the Bengal famine with the relatively low self-recognition of hardship among widows as compared to widowers of famine victims. In Sen's "free" society, all such differences in capability merit unequal resourcing in favour of those unable to achieve a pattern of activities that they have 'good reason to value' (Sen 1985).

Capability changes with age and generation for natural and social reasons. We physically change with age – arguably initially becoming more capable, latterly less. Though in this paper, it is more appropriate to argue that we become differently capable. We acquire capabilities in social and technical skills when young, which may become more or less useful when older. Ability both to utilise rights and meet obligations depends upon capability. Therefore, if capabilities change with age and generation, then it might be expected that there will be a mapping into changing potential rights and obligations.

Functionings are the choices people make on how to exercise their capabilities. Capabilities are permissive with respect to rights and obligations and enable a choice of functionings. It is the choice of particular functionings from amid all the ways of expressing potential capabilities that concretises rights and obligations. But the determinants of the choice of individual and family functionings are not independent of social norms on good and bad ends in the social order and the means to achieve them. These norms appear as patterns of entitlements, and incentives and disincentives to behaving in certain ways. This can be envisaged as a triangle of rights, obligations and choices linked to entitlements, capabilities and functionings is therefore complete (see Fig. 1).

Figure 1: A Stylised Sen Triangle

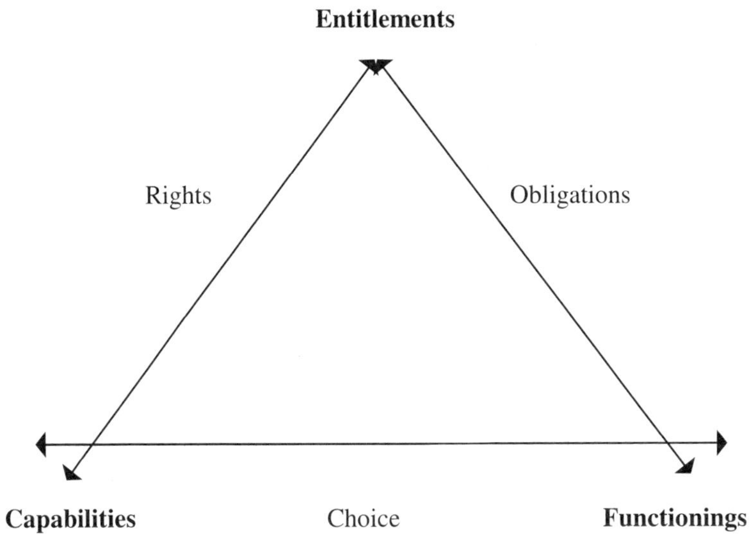

Rights and obligations can be found at all points on the triangle. Entitlements embody social rights and obligations. Capabilities mix individual characteristics and social opportunities to produce a potential set of achievable rights and obligations. Functionings involve choice among the capabilities that link individual expression of rights and obligations to the social pattern embodied in entitlements.

The triangle changes its form with ageing and movement between generations. For the purposes of this paper, the changing form will be discussed in terms of three age groups and generations – childhood, being elderly (which is often associated with being a grandparent and great grandparent), and being in middle age (often associated with being a parent). Thus the continuity of ageing takes on much of its social meaning through discontinuities in the form of shifts between generations.

While a stylisation of human life into three generations is convenient for purposes of exposition, it is not essential to the principle developed here. This principle is that entitlements, capabilities and functionings change with ageing and generational shifts.

In terms of developmental dynamics, this paper is concerned there is no guarantee that aggregate outcomes from tendencies towards more collective and more distant relationships between generations will produce a tidy balance of rights and obligations at any point in time. This has implications for quality of life both at that point in time and for future development. But before discussing those implications, it will be useful to apply the concepts of entitlements, capabilities and functionings and their association with effective rights and accepted obligations to three ages of personhood.

The three ages are the subjects of the following three sections of the paper. The younger and older generations are described before the middle-aged as these two generations are seen as more vulnerable to experiencing capability neglect. All three generations are described with little reference to other important sources of differentiation such as class, ethnicity and gender. This focus is not intended to privilege the category of age above other differences, but to promote greater consideration of age as one, and only one, dimension of intersectional human experience of difference.

The Younger Generation

The new born child can be seen as without obligations. The mass of undeveloped capabilities embodied in the new-born leads to no choice of functionings beyond the instinct to suckle. The entitlement to continue life, the right to life, varies between societies. For example, to be born female in some parts of the world appears to bring less practical entitlement to live than to be born male. Some civil societies do not recognise an entitlement to bodily integrity in terms of genital 'interference'. Entitlements to State care and protection are often weak and passive compared to the power that lies in the hands of kin and local civil society. Infancy is a time of low obligations and uncertain rights.

The process of child development can be seen as a period of rapidly increasing capability, though turning this increased capability into functionings will often be carefully monitored and supervised. Increased practical capability will not necessarily bring commensurate rights to choose how to exercise them. For instance, though capable of productive activity, children are denied the right to work in many societies.

The debate over child work/labour can be illuminated from this direction. From this perspective, the issue is not whether working for money is morally bad in itself for children. The issue is what is happening to the overall development of capabilities and the capacity to choose functionings in childhood or in the future. Obliging children to attend schools in "oppressive conditions" (Mac an Ghaill 1994: 171) is then a complex relative judgement, not an absolute good or bad (Illich 1971). Approaching childhood as a period when rights to develop capabilities and capacity to choose functionings are important gives a different perspective on work/labour/school trade-offs. Resting and associational periods of time then acquire significance as developing capability, independently of whether the child is at school, labouring or working (see CONCERN-Nepal 1997; UNICEF (ICDC) 1993 for examples of working within this framework).

But, arguably, obligations grow at a faster rate than rights through childhood for many children. Formal obligations to attend school may be accompanied by the less formal obligation to work hard at school and, even, to perform well at school. From this perspective, the idealised "western" childhood can appear to be constructed out of proscriptions – obligations not to do this or that – with very few positive rights and little practice in choosing functionings.

Mac an Ghaill captures the sense of restriction in the following terms:

> "The research focuses upon the confusions and contradictions that are constitutive of the students' construction of gendered and sexual identities in relation to major influences, including increasing central and local state regulation, changing family networks, restructured local labour markets, changing sexual patterns of consumption, peer and leisure group practices and media representations." (Mac an Ghaill 1994: 13).

Much of the discussion around children's rights is couched in terms of negative rights, rights not to labour, rights not to be sexually active, rights not to be shouted at or struck. These rights are valuable in themselves. But as the child physically matures, the expansion of capabilities will almost inevitably lead to the demands for positive rights to choose functionings, rather than being barred from some activities.

The capabilities/functionings combined with rights/obligations approach is concerned with the way young people's entitlements are converted from negative to positive rights to choose functionings as childhood progresses towards adulthood. Generally, there may be concern if the tendency for obligations to increase during childhood is not matched by the acquisition of positive rights. If obligations to develop capabilities are not associated with rights to freely choose functionings, then the approach to adulthood may prove unnecessarily bumpy.

The capability approach can be used to analyse processes in which entitlement patterns move from kin and neighbours to become more collective and abstract. Capabilities to function effectively as citizens as well as traders are important in gaining entitlements to sustain livelihoods in adulthood.

But, from a neo-Kantian moral perspective (Cameron 1992), childhood should not be merely a means preparing for adulthood; and even less reduced to the building of human capital to service the economy. The balance of rights and obligations in capability development and functionings choice for young people is of interest in itself, but the balance that can be achieved by young people depends crucially on the room for manoeuvre left by the other generations with whom they co-exist.

Young people's voices are being heard more often as part of the wider debate on rights of the child (e.g. Johnson et al., undated). But there is an element of political tokenism in this and there is a growing global literature on how restricted and tense is the psychological room for manoeuvre for young people moving towards adulthood. For instance, Torres Strait Islanders and other indigenous Australians "have attempted to control external influences on their culture by maintaining their cultural boundaries from 'whitefella business' … Yet schools have been responsible for overlapping the cultural boundaries" (Dawes 1998: 23) with the result that young people developed a "code of conduct based on loyalty to the group [which] allowed it to partially avoid the panoptic gaze of teachers and school administrators" (Dawes 1998: 28). And on the other side of the globe, research suggests for some male teenagers in the UK:

"the future is worrying, uncharted territory replete with large questions – will I get beaten up? Will I pass my exams? Will I get a job? Will I ever afford a house and a car? (and perhaps more immediately) what on earth do I do about girls?" (Walker & Kushner 1999: 49).

The Elderly Generation

Being elderly is attracting greater attention in thinking about social change (HelpAge International 1999). The growing proportion of elderly people in most societies is one obvious reason for this increased interest. More and more people are becoming elderly in the sense of being older than the:

"average age the individual passes the invisible frontier of failure to cope with the expected work load or responsibilities of the indigenous culture" (Messkoub 1997: 3).

Public policy issues arise as being more elderly is frequently associated with loss of some physical capabilities and increased needs for physical care and repair. Loss of mental capabilities may also occur, increasing vulnerability to forms of harm to the individual and discomfort to a wider sense of social well-being.

But the physiological aspect of ageing is only one dimension of the capabilities and functionings change that more elderly people experience. Frequently the elderly lose access to paid work irrespective of their physiological condition and the obligation to maintain oneself becomes doubly onerous as needs increase and income diminishes. The elderly may also be expected to take responsibility for grandchildren, after a considerable period away from child-care. Thus the quantity of obligations may shift, rather than fall and the choice of functionings may narrow for physiological and social reasons.

Rights that come with greater age in society can vary enormously. Some true gerontocracies may exist in which rights increase with age. But for many more elderly people, rights may diminish at a faster rate than obligations. The right to a place by the family hearth for the grand- and great grand-parent becomes more problematic when there are four candidates, rather than the one or two in the previous generation. The right to emotional support may disappear with the death of a partner.

The elderly may be expected by their kin and themselves to be more self-sufficient than in the past. And government may only be able to offer very limited entitlements (Giang & Pfau 2009) – and often only to those who have worked in government itself (Barrientos 1999). The market does offer opportunities to resource consumption and maintain capabilities in old age through turning assets into cash, but often on terms that exclude the majority and cheat the minority. The rights associated with the "grey dollar" are restricted to a privileged few. Generally, the claim to entitlements from the past exercise of capabilities and choice of socially valuable functionings is proving to be a weak rights claim in older age, especially among groups who are additionally vulnerable for reasons of gender, class or ethnicity (Messkoub 1999; Sen 1995).

The elderly as a group are experiencing a global crisis as generational rights, previously found in kin relationships, diminish and are not augmented sufficiently from wider collective civil society, or government or market. But obligations to maintain oneself with social dignity are increasing with growing longevity. Failure to meet this obligation can be de facto confinement in conditions that are likely to hasten death. But, even under such conditions, the right to choose how and when that event will occur is not under the individual's control.

The loss of capabilities and subsequent loss of choice over functionings that occur with becoming elderly do not have to involve gains in obligations and loss of rights. There is no necessary link and societies can choose the trade-off between "hospitality" and "hospitals" in the approach to the elderly (Illich 1992: 42-44). The key element is whether entitlements are sensitive to the changes that ageing inevitably involves and those that are socially constructed. As with the younger generation, the balance of rights and obligations experienced by the generation of elderly depend upon the room for manoeuvre left by the other generations in a society (Messkoub 1999: 232).

The Middle-Aged Generation

Capabilities may continue to grow after the transition from childhood into middle age. But it is in the realm of effective rights that growth accelerates.

The choice of functionings increases with rights to full citizenship and to contract in labour and financial markets. It is this generation that has the greatest choice over the balance of rights and obligations. And this choice has implications for the other two generations co-existing with it, and future generations.

Partially for this reason of wider individual choice, the middle-aged generation is the most difficult to describe as a group. High levels of both capabilities and rights give the capacity to choose very different patterns of obligations. Analysis is frustrated by this relatively high degree of effective agency and consequent heterogeneity.

In addition, the middle aged generation in general is seen as the natural state of humankind and therefore exercising hegemonic control over the discourse on age in which the other generations are only known by their difference from the norm. From this perspective, it is the other generations that have problematic identities, while the middle-aged generation has no problems as it understands itself as the natural state of humankind. From this perspective, childhood is a preparation for joining the middle-aged generation, old age a retreat from that generation.

The middle-aged generation's sense of its own importance can also make it self-obsessed. It is very concerned with its own differentiations. In western society, being a bit younger middle-aged becomes important compared with being slightly older middle-aged – eclipsing the vast difference between being a child or being elderly compared to the differences between human beings in their middle years.

The middle-aged generation sets the parameters for overall economic inequality within society. This inequality not only exists at each point of time, it also applies to inequality in insecurity and uncertainty about the future. Some patterns of entitlements are more vulnerable than others to external shocks. Compared to the middle-aged, the impact of all these forms of inequality is experienced by children and the elderly as victims, not agents.

But many middle-aged people see themselves as overwhelmed by obligations. Feeling responsible for generations on either side of their middle ground, they feel pressure to meet obligations rather than power of exercising rights. But pressure is not the same as compulsion. To feel moral pressure and yet be able to choose not to act on that pressure is an aspect of power since it carries the possibility of refusing the pressure.

A stylised model of the stresses produced by changing intergenerational relationships

The generational model developed in this paper stylises three generations as having distinctive patterns of rights and obligations (see Fig. 2). The younger generation starts from a position of no obligations and very few rights and rapidly accumulates obligations faster than rights. The elderly generation may wish to express rights, but has need of increased obligations to provide new levels and forms of entitlements. In-between is a generation which tends to accumulate rights plus pressure to accept obligations. An indicative gender dimension has been included in the Figure suggesting that women have greater obligations (both imposed and freely accepted) than men in this stylised society.

Figure 2: A Stylised Chart of Changes in Rights and Obligations with Age

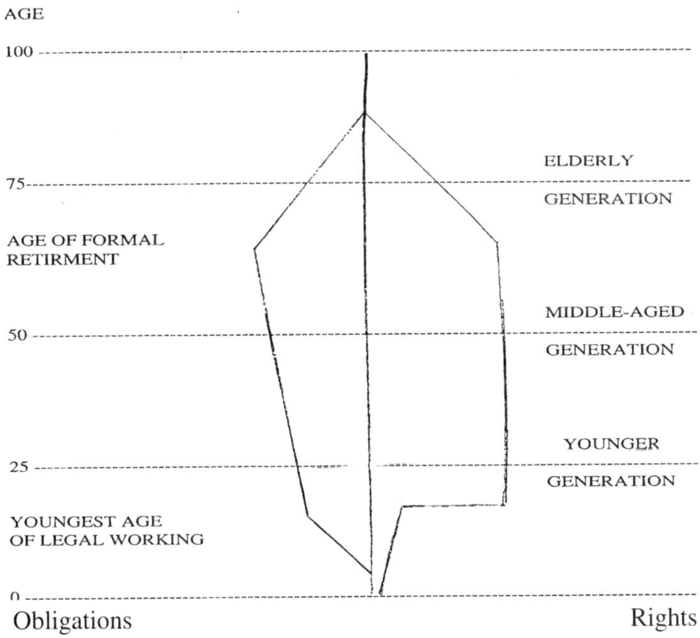

N.B. Rights are closely related to capabilities – with greater capabilities come greater effective rights. Choice of functionings is closely with obligations than others.

The quality of life in a society at any point in time depends on those who have rights to choose obligations. The middle-aged generation has those rights. They can claim they have not been left sufficient from the past or that their children will have opportunities they do not. But, at any moment in time, it is they that largely choose for any society what quality of life people of all ages will have at that point in time.

But this is a choice. There is no necessary balance of rights and obligations for any society. The middle aged can choose to claim rights and reject obligations that displace social pressures onto children and the elderly. A society can serve the middle-aged well and leave children and the elderly with very low qualities of life.

But, in most societies today, many middle-aged people feel they are under pressure from absolute poverty or from relative deprivation with respect to their peer group. This pressure may lead to emphasis on inequality within the middle-aged rather than inequality between generations. But focusing on inequality within the middle-aged as a key dimension of overall social well-being means making strong assumptions about intergenerational relationships, e.g. improving the conditions of life for more deprived middle-aged people will trickle down to deprived older and younger people.

If poverty and inequality among the middle-aged are to reflect the overall welfare of a society, then it must be assumed that the other generations suffer from no more poverty and inequality than the middle aged. This, in turn, means that distributional arrangements protect both other generations from any tendency for them to have fewer rights and more obligations than the middle-aged. Somewhere in the patterns of entitlements from kin, community, neighbourhood, state and markets, there must be safety nets for young and old if they are not to be disproportionally disadvantaged by weaker capabilities.

In much of the development discourse, it is assumed that such multi-dimensional safety nets are present. But there is always a risk that everybody's obligation leads to nobody's action. The State assumes kin will care, kin assumes the State will care, both assume care in the community. And there are always labour or financial market challenges and opportunities that absorb time and energy. Such assumptions may mean many children and the elderly people fall between stools, exposed by their limited capabilities and lack of effective entitlements.

The capabilities and rights of the middle-aged generation give it the power to choose qualities of lives for children and the elderly. There is a considerable element of moral or ethical judgement in this choice. A society can logically exist in which the middle-aged generation does not explicitly, consciously and collectively accept obligations to, and construct entitlements for, the other generations. Such a society will offer a low quality of life to many young and elderly people.

Such a society, in which hedonistic middle-aged people have lives taking full advantage of their rights and accepting no obligations, is an extreme case. 'Natural' human affections may guarantee the children and the elderly will be given secure entitlements, though 'natural' affection between the genders has not guaranteed women their full share of societies' resources (Razavi 2007).

In a less extreme case, the hard-working, middle-aged generation that lives off income from labour and financial markets and works with machine intensive technology may not see an economic self-interest in increasing the relational capabilities of their children, accepting the internet as a major socialising force. And may also see little moral obligation to an elderly generation that "should" have made provision for itself, while it was middle-aged.

Generational relationships and the associated patterns of rights and obligations are becoming more anonymised, more distant, more societal, and more marketised. These processes mean that less can be assumed than in the past about a benign balance of rights and obligations that offer a good quality of life to all three generations. We therefore need to be more conscious of how people of different ages co-exist at any point in time and it is in the power of the middle-aged to choose the mode of that co-existence.

Looking beyond the cross-sectional distribution by age of quality of life as a developmental dimension, we can see implications for developmental dynamics of differing distributions of effective rights and accepted obligations between generations. What happens if the middle-aged generation with highest effective capabilities chooses functionings that reflect a greater concern for its rights than its obligations? Children will find their capabilities neglected and fail to flourish. The elderly will live without dignity. And there will be implications for longer term change.

Neglecting the elderly will probably mean they die earlier with little direct implication for the future of a society. The major future impact of neglecting the elderly will be indirect. In the knowledge of their own probable bleak future, some of the middle-aged may choose to protect themselves by creating emotional and financial obligations on their children. Others will choose to live hedonistic life-styles that reduce the probability of becoming elderly themselves.

Creating emotional obligations on children is becoming more difficult in more mobile societies. But financial markets are encouraging numerous obligations to be created on the next generation. Middle-aged parents may say to their own children that they have no intention of being a burden on them in their old age. But their pension rights create obligations on the wider, global children's generation to work for them. And insofar as those pension rights are invested in profit-maximising companies, their choices implicitly condemn the next generation to reproduce capitalist relations and to work for capital on its terms. And if the companies are trans-national then it will be the children's generation on a global scale who will be so condemned.

But this attempt to create obligations may not succeed. When they themselves become middle-aged, the children's generation may exercise their increased rights to escape or refuse the financial obligations with which they have been burdened. This could be in the form of refusing to work for capital on its terms with resulting bankruptcies and price inflation which can erode the real value of pension funds.

If a middle-aged generation as a whole attempt to escape the fate to which they have condemned the elderly by burdening the next generation with financial obligations, they in turn become vulnerable to neglect as the next generation gains the right to refuse these obligations. It is a rash middle-aged generation that tries to reduce intergenerational relationships to a financial bargain with no moral content.

If neglect of the elderly has implications for future society, what about neglect of children? Surely, self-interest will set limits to such neglect? The capabilities of children need to be developed to increase potential provision for the middle-aged when they become elderly. But does this apply to all capabilities of all children? The limits set by middle-aged self-interest could be very low. Capabilities will be emphasised that fit with working productively – both in terms of skills and attitudes. And the considerable demand for personal services by the middle-aged and the elderly will mean many children's capabilities can be minimally developed in order to function totally satisfactorily as instruments for the pleasures of the middle-aged and needs of the elderly.

A society in which exercising effective rights outpaces meeting obligations means some people's claims to entitlements will not be met. The middle-aged have the power to displace unmet claims on to the younger and older generations in their choices of functionings. In terms of development, the resulting society may be expected to show political and cultural instability as each generation of neglected children reaching middle age exercises its power to deny rights to the other generations and changes the pattern of entitlements in its favour. Distorted development of children's capabilities may make it more likely that the subsequent middle-aged generation will use its power selfishly.

But such a society may grow economically for two reasons. More young and old people will have to seek work - even low productivity work. Also the middle-aged have an interest in developing technology that maximises their own productivity and the possibility that the economy can provide for them when they are themselves elderly. Politically non-sustainable intergenerational entitlements may combine with technological dualism in such a society in which children and the elderly work in a low paid service sector while the middle-aged work with hi-tech machinery.

But, what if accepted obligations tend to outpace claims to rights? In such a situation the middle-aged will use their high capabilities in functionings that ensure provision of entitlements to the younger and older generations before considering themselves. The resulting society will be culturally and politically more stable as people will have confidence in the intergenerational bargain. But the society may not grow fast economically as more middle-aged people will undertake low labour productivity work in providing caring services to children and the elderly. Such a state of society might be characterised as having politically sustainable intergenerational entitlements in an economic low-tech level equilibrium.

Implications for the intergenerational social contract and capability transfer from the older to the younger generations

This exploration of intergenerational relationships has arrived at uncomfortable analytical conclusions. As intergenerational relationships become more organic and less mechanical in terms of solidarity through increasing distances and collectivisation, the interplay of capabilities and functionings, rights and obligations between generations can produce some worrying outcomes. If claims to rights by the generation with highest capabilities outpace acceptance of obligations then the functionings they choose could leave numerous younger and older people suffering from insecure entitlements and low quality of life. Development processes may be unstable and divisive. In terms of currently popular development concepts; human, social and natural sources of wealth will come under pressure and only "hard" produced wealth will benefit (World Bank 1997).

There are several arguments that might seek to qualify this bleak scenario. The first is that the model treats the middle-aged as a relatively homogeneous class of people. Gender is a vital consideration in intergenerational relationships, as social obligations to care are not distributed equally between middle-aged women and men. The degree of choice of functionings within generations also differs by economic class. From this perspective, the middle aged are not a class in themselves. There are parallels with debates about gender as a class relationship. In most societies, generations have not constituted distinctive collective political organisations, but this does not necessarily mean that power is not exercised. Substituting "middle-aged" for "men" and "age" for "gender" in the following quotes brings out the issue:

> "Granted that men collectively do not form committees to ensure their continued domination, and that men themselves are exploited and dominated by other men, we can nevertheless still speak of a set of gender relations in which the power of men is taken for granted" (Brittan 1989: 5/6).

"While we might agree that men do not constitute a class, this is not to say that particular groups of men do not sometimes *act* like a class." (Brittan 1989: 110)

With the implication that a "class" interest finds expression on behalf of all men independent of many of their wills through the actions of particular groups. The representation of a middle-aged interest may be subtle, but it would be wrong to assume therefore it is absent.

A second argument is that human life does not tidily break down demographically into three generations – even Shakespeare's seven might be too few. Also human society is much less tidy in its generational patterns with many people simultaneously being children, parents and, increasingly grandparents. Intergenerational trade-offs take place within many individuals which is a stabilising force and the middle-aged cannot be regarded as a class for this reason, though the tensions of the trade-off may produce psychological stress.

A third is that this exploration understates human affections and empathy. Kin has proved a durable source of care for many younger and older people in all human societies to date. While the assumption cannot be made that kin will cope in many societies today, the fact that we collectively love "our" children and "our" elderly relatives means we quickly create institutions in civil society and the state apparatus to care for them and protect their interests. There may be some institutional transitional costs and delays in moving between care regimes, but natural human affections will re-assert themselves. These set a bottom line to intergenerational neglect – though it is crucially important to understand who are "our" children and "our" elderly on this bottom line.

Accepting all these qualifications must restrict the conclusions of this paper to the language of tendencies rather than predictions. A society moving towards more organic patterns of intergenerational solidary relationships faces a danger of increasing numbers of people being damaged at both ends of the age range and a shift towards a pattern of socio-economic change that is less sustainable. To off-set this tendency requires a conscious moral intergenerational social contract on collective rights and obligations and associated capabilities and entitlements, not just a financial bargain (Lloyd-Sherlock 2004).

As part of this intergenerational social contract, this paper offers an image of connecting the older and younger generations through a transfer of capabilities. The claim is that members of the older generation have learned capabilities in living through the challenges that a 'normal' human life presents. A set of such capabilities is offered in Table 1. The set is dominated by broadly defined relational capabilities and bear a close relationship to several of those capabilities in Martha Nussbaum's list of ten required capabilities for a well lived human life. Of course, not all older people will have developed these capabilities to an equal degree, but all will have had experiences that are relevant to all of these capabilities.

Table 1: Capabilities that could be transferred from older to younger generations

- **Deliberative Decision-Making Skills** – experiences of political processes
- **Self-Confidence** – experiences of life crises and disappointments overcome
- **Manageable Impairments** – experiences of poor health/disabilities
- **Compassion** – understanding the shared fundamentals of the human condition
- **Ethical Judgement** – moral decisions made and lessons learned
- **Emotional Intelligence** – the consequences of expressions of strong emotions
- **Caring Skills** – emotional and physiological opportunities to care
- **Aesthetic Judgement** – criteria for perceiving beauty
- **Relevant Skills for Fulfilling Recreation** – recognising lessons about risk and uncertainty from games of chance and how to win and lose with dignity

Building institutions to create more times and spaces in which these capabilities could be shared with younger people could help meet some of the challenges widely identified with young people and 'youth culture':

- A truncated, short time horizon emphasising hedonistic immediate experiences
- Valued capabilities emphasising 'natural' talents
- Functionings/role models emphasising high income at early age
- 'Adapted preferences' as a reaction to frustration

Thus encouraging recognition of eudaimonia as a set of capabilities for the well lived, whole life may be part of meeting these challenges. If this recognition is less available in intergenerational kin relationships, then arguably it 'should' be made available in wider societal institutions.

Building such institutions requires:

- Learning from ethnographies of cultures where 'healthier' intergenerational relationships exist or have existed in the past
- Researching good practices of intergenerational interactions and identifying gaps – mappings of spaces and times valued by different generations and identifying access difficulties
- Subsequent planning of more times and spaces where all generations feel welcome in schools, workplaces, recreational spaces, shopping spaces
- Creating images and events for developing mutual intergenerational respect as a capability

- Developing facilitating/mentoring capabilities among older people to place their experiences in a capability framework

If these efforts are successful, then there may be positive implications for future society as the young generation take the new capabilities and values they have acquired into middle age.

References

Barrientos, A. (1999): Retirement, household income, and economic vulnerability of older groups. Economics Paper 20, University of Hertfordshire Business School, Hertford.

Brittan, A. (1989): Masculinity and Power. Blackwell, Oxford.

Cameron, J. (1992): Adjusting Structural Adjustment: getting beyond the UNICEF compromise. In: Mosley, P. (Ed.): Development Finance and Policy Reform, St Macmillan, London, 291-309.

CONCERN-Nepal (1997): Burden on Childhood: Child porters in the Kathmandu Valley. CONCERN-Nepal, Kathmandu.

Dawes, G. (1998): The art of the body: aboriginal and Torres Strait Islander youth subcultural practices. Journal of Intercultural Studies, 19, 1, 21-34.

Giang, T.L. & Pfau, W.D. (2009): Ageing, poverty and the role of a social pension in Vietnam. Development and Change, 40, 2, 333-360.

HelpAge International (1999): The Ageing & Development Report. EARTHSCAN, London.

Illich, I. (1971): Deschooling Society. Calder and Boyars, London.

Illich, I. (1992): In the Mirror of the Past. Marian Boyars, London.

Johnson, V., Hill, J. & Ivan-Smith, E. (undated): Listening to Smaller Voices: Children in an environment of change. ACTIONAID, London.

Lloyd Sherlock, P. (2004): Living Longer: Ageing, Development and Social Protection. Zed, London.

Lyotard, J.-F. (1991): Inhuman. Cambridge.

Mac an Ghaill, M. (1994): The Making of Men. Buckingham.

Messkoub, M. (1997): Crisis of ageing in less developed countries, a crisis for whom? ISS Working Paper Series No 254, ISS, The Hague.

Messkoub, M. (1999): Crisis of ageing in less developed countries: too much consumption or too little production? Development and Change, 30, 2, 217-235.

Razavi, S. (2007): The return to social policy and the persistent neglect of unpaid care. Development and Change, 38, 3, 377-400.

Sen, A.K. (1981): Poverty and Famines: an essay on entitlement and deprivation. Oxford.

Sen, A.K. (1985): Commodities and Capabilities. North-Holland, Amsterdam.

Sen, A.K. (1995): Gender, culture and later life. Gender and Development, 3, 3, 36-42.

Sen, A.K. (1997): On Economic Inequality: an expanded edition. Oxford.

UNICEF (ICDC) (1993): Street and Working Children: Summary report on the Innocenti Global Seminar. ICDC, Florence.

Walker, B.M. & Kushner, S. (1999): The building site: an educational approach to masculine identity. Journal of Youth Studies, 2, 1, 45-58.

World Bank (1997): Expanding the Measure of Wealth: indicators of Environmentally Sustainable Development. Environmentally Sustainable Development Studies and Monographs Series No. 17, World Bank, Washington, D.C.

Heinrich W. Schäfer

Capabilities – From a Relationist Viewpoint

"Closing the capability gap", the programmatic lemma of this conference, presupposes that there is a rift between the actual situation of many people and the ideal of seeing them develop their capabilities of – let's say with the famous list of Martha Nussbaum – bodily health, integrity, emotions, social affiliation and much more. The Aristotelian ideal (based on empirical observation, not on metaphysics) of a good, a truly human life that fuels Nussbaum's approach is based upon an 'empirical essentialism' that focuses on equality, not on difference as many of her critics do (Nussbaum 1999b: 179). While these critics end up in cultural relativism, as Nussbaum judges, she searches for universal validity of her criteria. This is an important discussion that the philosopher masters by herself. Nevertheless, the notion of a "gap" connotes difference; and difference connotes relation. The latter is an important category to understand human life, seen from the viewpoint of modern philosophy (e.g. Cassirer) or social sciences (e.g. Bourdieu) or seen from most of the non north-Atlantic cultures in objection of Western individualism. A closer look at Nussbaum's list and her classification of 'combined, internal and basic capabilities' shows that many of her criteria are strongly relational: e.g. bodily health and integrity, emotion, affiliation, other species, control over one's environment. Finally, Nussbaum herself reflects upon social conditions for the realization of capabilities, which means that she takes into account social relations.[1] In terms of philosophical theory this focus is represented in the important (and very Aristotelian) role of experience and a strong concept of a 'good life' in the capability approach, in contrast to an abstract methodological individualism of "rational fools" (Sen) or to an equally abstract liberalism of 'state of nature' or 'original position'.

Taking this into account, the conference triggered my imagination to reflect upon possibilities to fruitfully combine Nussbaum's 'essentialism' of human nature with a strongly relational social and ethic theory – without drifting away into relativism, abstract principles or economic individualism. As my duty in the final panel of the conference was simply to draw some conclusions out of my own perspective – the one of a sociologist and theological ethicist – in the following I will simply sketch some brief ideas in a loose order.

1 This is even more the case for Sen's use of the capability-concept.

Experience, society and power – social theory as a means of ethics

It is crucial for Nussbaum's concept of universal human traits – condensed in her list of capabilities – that these are based upon a non-metaphysical, anti-Platonist, reading of Aristotle. Hence, there is no metaphysical 'backstage' that guarantees the list of capabilities. It is simply empirical observation and the sorting out of the most constant characteristics that allows establishing a list of 'essential' conditions for a truly human life.[2] In this regard, it is the observation of human *praxis* from which the ethical criteria are derived. A person who shares a contextual approach to ethics will have no problems with that (but there will arise some problems when it comes to intercultural relations). A further implication of the empirical approach is that the social context in which the universal human capabilities ought to develop comes into the focus. This is the case when Nussbaum claims an "Aristotelian Social Democracy" (Nussbaum 1990). This normative demand presupposes that a society (and with it the state and the government) is responsible of establishing adequate conditions for the realization of human capabilities. As the social science context of Nussbaum and Sen suggests, Social Democracy is understood as a counter program to neoliberal capitalist globalism and its way to organize societies according to simple economic maximization, to foster injustice, to marginalize the biggest part of the world's population and to reject social responsibility of property or even wealth systematically. From an epistemological point of view, there is something like a *descriptive* social theory[3] presupposed behind normative ethic claims. From a contextualistic point of view this is no problem either. Even more: it can be seen as a chance to develop an ethical hermeneutics that includes normatively identified instruments for the description and analysis of the social conditions in which capabilities can flourish or not. This, of course, is a circular operation. But, reflexively done, such an integration of social science expertise into the interplay of description and norm is far better than letting preconceptions of society exert their influence unconsciously upon ethic deliberations. Furthermore, an explicit and well suited social theory can help to frame all the necessary intents to operationalize the capability approach in developmental politics, education, life course related research, indicators for measurement a.s.f. very well. If this is the case, the question arises, what kind of theory fits best.

Taking into account that the Capability Approach focuses on human conditions, action and axiological orientation, a sociological program would have

2 This is – in a strict sense – no statement of grounds, but can be accused of being based on an error in terms of Hume's 'is-ought problem'. We do not follow this well known line of discussion about contextualistic ethics here.

3 …more developed in the works of Amartya Sen.

to be actor oriented. This – and many more traits in capability-logics – prevent the option for functionalistic grand-theories; especially those without actors. Equally or even more, Rational Choice and any methodological individualism are *per definitionem* excluded from the list of candidates. Praxeological theories, on the other hand, that integrate 'structure' and actor (Giddens, Sahlins, Bourdieu) seem to be capable of providing significant instruments for social analysis as well as for matters of application.

To me, it is especially Bourdieu who provides a sufficiently coherent and, at the same time, flexible framework for Capability interests. First of all, Bourdieu's focus on the actors is counts with a highly developed theory of the interplay of internal and external conditions of action. The concept of 'habitus' in combination with those of 'practical logic', 'strategy', 'sense of the game', 'taste' and 'style' depicts a person as a social being (a *zoon politikón*, to use an Aristotelian term) and not as an exponent of formal reasoning or of rationally calculated maximization (Bourdieu 1977, 1980). The concepts furnish a wide range of ways to understand how perception, judgement and action of human beings are incorporated in deep-rooted affective and cognitive dispositions, influence upon tastes, lead to value ascriptions and communication, regulate strategies in accordance with objective determinants and situations, form styles and social coherence, constitute images of the self and of others, relate individual and collective identities etc. It seems to me quite obvious that these instruments permit, for example, to develop models of how capabilities generate and develop (in processes of socialization) in midst of the tension between dispositions of habitus and the challenges, opportunities and constraints of the social conditions in a given society. Second, the focus on actors is intimately connected with the theories of fields and the social space. Thus, the perspective of subjective disposition and capability (!) of action is framed by a combined theory of the objective conditions of identity formation and (individual as well as collective) action. The concept of 'field' – together with those of 'game', '*conjoncture*', 'power', 'capital', 'investment', 'doxa', 'nomos', 'profit', 'stakes' etc. (see Schäfer 2011) – allows to describe and analyze 'horizontal' social differenciation in a way that closely links to the concepts related to subjective dispositions and action (Bourdieu 1996, 1983). Thus, different fields of social practice can be dealt with in a more dynamic way than it is possible with functionalistic theories (including Systems Theory) and in a more structure-related way than it is possible with Rational Choice individualism. Hereby, chances and restrictions for the development or realization of capabilities in specific fields – like education, law, politics, economics, religion etc. – can be framed and analyzed according to the specific logic of practice in that field. So we can, for example, frame the use of the concept of 'capital' (as in 'social capital', 'educational capital' etc.) within a broader theory of the objective and subjective conditions of human action. Moreover, the concept of 'field' according to Bourdieu is strictly constructivistic, which means that there '*are*' no ontologically given fields, but any object of research can be constructed as a field – so that its logic of action, power-distribution, chances and constraints can systematically be focused on. Finally, the concept of field theorizes relations of power according to specific 'spheres' (Weber) of social reproduction. And power seems to be a crucial category when social support and hindrance to human capabilities are of interest. Third, the theory of social space (Bourdieu 1984) – together with the concepts of economic and cultural capital, style, class, culture, career perspectives etc. – offers another objectivistic means of framing human action by taking power into account. It organizes social inequality according to the vertical *and* horizontal differentiation. Thus, instead of abstractly talking about human conditions – the model permits to locate the actors of interest and their subjective ('internal') conditions within a framework of the distribution of social power. So their subjective chances of realization of capabilities can be seen in a direct relation to their objective opportunities and constraints according to the distribution of – basically – wealth and knowledge.[4] For capability research this means that social inequality comes into focus as a basic condition of the realization of capabilities. And beyond this, inequality is theorized as a condition for and a function of power. Thus, capabilities of given actors can be interpreted within the framework of objective social power relations. So research can clearly name the social reasons – e.g. too big a share of social wealth of some actors, in difference to a very small share of others – for a positive or negative realization of capabilities in different social actors; and it can name causal relations between one and the other.

Beyond these specifically sociological aspects of Bourdieu's theory, there are two more that come along with it. First, it has often been commented that Bourdieu carries quite some axiological load in his social theory, insofar as his focus on power and social struggle is undergirded by an – neo Marxist – option for the lower classes. This is, first of all, an effect of a power-oriented methodology in the perception of an observer. Seen from the viewpoint of the Capability Approach however, there is nothing wrong with it, since one of its basic assumptions is that power relations that go against the realization of a truly human life are ethically disqualified. At this point, there is much more overlap of the Capability Approach with Bourdieuian assumptions than with those of Rational Choice or whatever kind of Functionalism. Second, Bourdieu puts emphasis on a "*Realpolitik* of reason" (Bourdieu 2002; Bourdieu & Wacquant 2006), sociological epistemology of auto-critique. For the social scientist it is important to take into account from what social position and habitual dispositions he or she approaches the object of research. Thus, the researcher does not remain simply objective, but is himself set into his or her

4 There are, of course, other possibilities to construct a model according to other sorts of capital.

social relation with the object. These critical hermeneutics are of some worth for ethicists, since in ethics it is even more important to critically reflect upon the social conditions of judgment.

Human nature – a relational view

Nussbaum puts very much emphasis on 'essentialism' and a substantive theory of the good (Nussbaum 1993, 1999b: 178ff.). I read this as to underscore that there are conditions of a truly human life that can be positively named (and thus form a semantic content) and that each and every human being has a right to – in distinction to theories that emphasize mere procedures and formal maximization and to theories that favour a strict cultural relativism. Now it may seem – according to the impression that render some passages of Nussbaum's writings – that such an empirical essentialism has to be understood in those strong ontological terms of the substance theory in ancient metaphysics – and thus exclude any attempt of a modern, relational understanding of personhood, subjectivity, identity etc. I do not think that this is the case. If it was, however, I would not deem it necessary or even detrimental for a capability oriented ethics, since it would appear as a strong theory of objective grounds and, moreover, it would bind the statement of grounds to an ancient idea of how the physical and the metaphysical world is structured. But Nussbaum does not even claim that her list is closed; instead she explicitly leaves it open to results of new empirical observation. This means that the list of necessary capabilities for a truly human life can (slightly) develop according to varying social relations. Moreover, the way Nussbaum explains the *social* genesis of what is sometimes called the 'female nature' (Nussbaum 1999a: 170ff.) indicates that her concepts of capabilities cannot be understood as metaphysical, but instead as historical and bound to human socialization. In consequence, the concept of 'human nature' does not denote some*thing* self-contained, closed in itself; something that could be depicted as a ball or a sphere – as it would be in classical substance-ontology. If the concept of 'human nature' in the Capability Approach turns out to be historical, then there are two conclusions at hand: First, as the items of Nussbaum's list break down the seeming 'substance' of human nature into different states and practices of human beings which, ontologically, are *not* transcendental (platonic) entities. Instead, they are simply states and practices that make up – as well – items of human self description. This does not seem to be much. However, when a person says 'I am human', (most of) these items are (somehow) present in this description and therefore they are a personal and social reality. To untie the concept of 'human nature' from specific metaphysical preconditions and to historicize it according to human experience facilitates intercultural plausibilization. But on the other hand it transposes the discussion of basic underpinnings and substantiation from metaphysics to anthropology and history. Second and in consequence, the 'substantive' (Nussbaum) content of the list of capabilities has to be confirmed in its morally binding character simply on this basis. Nussbaum substantiates it – following a non-metaphysical reading of Aristotle – simply by stating that virtually every human being in normal conditions is endowed with the listed capabilities. So, the statement of grounds and the claim of universal too, are based on nothing more than empirical experience. The good grounds weaken, the concepts become relative and the items of the list become vague. On the other hand, Capability-people have an interest in strong grounds for their statements. But there is no way back to metaphysics in a pluralist world and finite history does not produce absolute truth. But there is some chance to create stronger plausibility and wider evidence for Capability-claims, I suppose: not fleeing the historicist argument, but deepening it.

The (implicit) anthropology of Capability-thought counters – as far as I see – both simple rationalism and (methodological) individualism. It claims, instead, the importance of bodily, emotional, intellectual and social life of any individual.[5] And it is from here that we can historicize somewhat more. While we keep on ascribing the rights – connoted in the capabilities – to each and any individual, we conceive of individuals as intrinsically social beings in a quite radical way. Richard Rorty (Rorty 1989) – in Wittgensteinian as well as in American pragmatic tradition – develops the idea of the very *self* as a contingent *network* of convictions, knowledge, desires, relationships a.s.f., quite much in the same way as he conceives of language and society as networks, too. The network that constitutes the self is anchored in the experiences of the past, as well as extended to the future by its desires and projections. Such a network is being woven during the process of socialization. Its texture in some regions is dense and strong: stark experiences and reflection upon it have produced deep knowledge, firm convictions and staunch sentiments in certain realms of life; other areas of the tissue are like light and thin gauze: few experience, dim knowledge and little orientation in other realms of life. And the tissue has no rim, but it is open to shed old and to tie up to new threads. And, of course, such a network is finite in a double sense: it never can encompass everything, catch it all; and it is never complete, but its weaving disrupts with death. We can – drawing now on Bourdieu's concept of habitus – think of such a network as the entirety of cognitive, emotional and bodily dispositions of the habitus of a given individual, group, people etc. These dispositions are embodied figurations of the persons' experience of the social world and of the persons' self-experience within the context of social

5 … similar to many Latin American philosophers of liberation in dialogue with Kantian tradition 'Discourse Ethics', e.g. Hinkelammert 1994; see Fornet-Betancourt 1992a, 1992b, 1994; also Schäfer 2004.

world; and they are utterly social since any individual shares almost all of its dispositions with a certain amount of other individuals. So all networks of dispositions are both individual and collective fabric – while any individual stays individual by virtue of its unique combination, integration and processing of its experience. Such a network of the self of course contains all the experiences of a person with his or her own basic needs and capacities, the trained skills and the external relationships – or in other words: with basic, internal and combined capabilities as Nussbaum would say. From such networks, their generation, their interchange etc. it is that a common ethos develops. And of course the network of any person contains notions of what can be called 'human' – even if they are distorted by oppression and misery.

It is important for the habitus-based network model of the self that the dispositions a person embodies during its life can be heavily molded by dominance, violence, injustice, slavery, humiliation etc. – as Bourdieu often points out.[6] Nussbaum (Nussbaum 1999b) – in this line of thought – mentions e.g. poor women in India, who have interiorized their disadvantage in such a way that they accept it as 'natural'. Domination has become part of the cognitive, emotional and bodily dispositions. The networks of a common ethos, thus, are more or less interwoven by the strong threads of domination that exert influence on the shared convictions. In midst of given social power relations we humans weave our common networks of ethos, develop communitarian morals, reflect upon them and construct ethic systems and, finally, principles with universal claims. And, of course, we oppose against oppression, misery a.s.f. in the name of human dignity – reminding one another of what that means, among other ways by referring to the Nussbaum-list.

Networking convictions – thick and thin morals

'Reminding one another' is a communicative act that presupposes social relations, interests of the actors involved, cognition and recognition of situations that call for remembering human dignity etc. – in short: it needs perception, judgment and action on a common social ground. The anthropological considerations in the former section also think of the humans as embedded in a social environment (*politiká*) since the human being is a social being (*zoon politikón*). Then the community has to be taken into account for the generation of moral and ethic orientation. However, it would rather be a short-circuit than a short-cut to opt for a normative edition of communitarianism, as e.g. of Alisdair McIntyre or Samuel Huntington. Instead, I should like to derive from our anthropological considerations what one might call a 'methodological

6 …and as the sociological approach presented above facilitates to detect and to analyze.

communitarianism'. It is methodological in the sense that it makes a specific premise for work. This is different from e.g. the Kantian premise in baroque anthropology (dividing reason from experience), from the liberal premise of an 'original position' (Rawls) or from the axiom of a free, calculating and maximizing individual. The anthropological premise is that humans are social beings and their self can be conceived of as a network, as explained above. What does that imply for an ethics that is competent to communicate convincingly and for everybody alike the normative contents of Nussbaum's list?

I guess that, even if controversial, Michael Walzer's distinction between 'thick' and 'thin' morals can be usefully adopted to the network-idea. If we think of communities of people generating common convictions etc., the local or regional praxis tends to be regulated by a high number of (implicit or explicit) dos and don'ts. Norms, virtues, values, commandments etc. generate in the 'thick' contexts of meaning that dominate the every-day experience (and condenses e.g. in routines etc.). The actors adopt their orientation from traditions, link emotional loyalties, value judgments and self esteem to them. The accompanying ideas mostly have a strong semantic or semiotic content – transmitted by stories, parables, symbols etc. – and are closely associated to the concrete daily life. Thick morals are focused on the regulation of 'life world'-issues; a claim to universal validity normally is made only in a naïve way, if ever. On the other hand, we can visualize thin morals as lighter networks with just some thread which, in turn, are quite strong. Historically, they can be understood as the result of a longer period of reflection upon thick norm, especially when encountering other cultures with different thick morals. Typically 'thin' are formal, procedural principles. These abstract from the networks of thick habitual dispositions and reflexively draw conclusions from the large amount of seemingly unstructured experiences. Hence it is possible to think of Kant's 'Categorical Imperative' as a result of a long standing reflection upon reciprocal relations. Principles recall what historically has been achieved (Rorty 2001: 186), condensing the achievements in formulas. J.B. Schneewind sees an important function of principles – be it the Categorical Imperative or the utilitarian 'Happiness' – as a self-critical 'moral ambulance'. Among others, the claim to universal validity implies that principles can easily be used by others in order to critically examine those who emitted the given principle; they are of reciprocal use. Moreover, to hold on to a principle categorically makes one's own behavior results predictable for others and, thus, produces certainty. Principles generate from the dealings between people of different thick convictions their interest in the universal perspective. Therefore they are most useful in (international) political contexts with highly formalized standards of regulation.

But where are the items of the capability list to be localized, in thick or thin environments? If we examine the distinction between 'thick' and 'thin' morals according to systematic criteria, it seems to me that the items do not fit in either. Nor does it make much sense to divide the items as to ascribe 'life' and 'bodily health' to 'thin' and 'affiliation' or 'control over one's environment' to 'thick'. But we interpreted the distinction between 'thick' and 'thin' morals also in relation to different contexts of practical use: local everyday life and translocal political decision making. It seems to me that Nussbaum's list has a bridging position between both. In its general focus is the human being as such. This is the bridging interest. At the same time there are some items that are more easily related to a universalist and formally political background (life, health …) and other items that invite one to be filled with everyday cultural practices (e.g. emotion, affiliation, environment). As long as this distinction is a practical one and not a categorical, the similarity of certain items to certain types of practices invite one to work with the list, beginning with the items closer to one's own practical context and thus gaining plausibility for the other items. Thus, the list can acquire a kind of 'glocal' (Roberston) character, combining both levels of practice without urging uniformity – and this could turn out to be a little bit more than just specifying the list according to 'local conditions' (Nussbaum 1999b: 213).

Networking between cultures – transversal reason

The theme of thick and thin morals already connotes much of the discussion about the intercultural validity of the list. Nussbaum sees herself in a strong contradiction to cultural relativists (Nussbaum 1999b: 176ff.). On the other hand she warns her critics not to misunderstand her universalistic claims as some kind of 'metaphysical realism' (Nussbaum 1999b: 182). As mentioned above, a non-metaphysical universalism that does not recur on reason in the Kantian sense but highlights the characteristics of a good life ought to be a *historical* and empirical one.[7] As such, it is 'relatively relative': If we imagine a continuum between a strong metaphysical realism on the one end and a strong cultural relativism on the other, then an empirical universalism of the good life falls somewhere in the middle. Its certainty about the truth and validity of its criteria (the list) is being produced by studying constant traits of human life and generating a *consensus* about the results among a certain group of humans (e.g. the Capability-people). What comes to pass is that the criteria are a social reality due to a network of convictions shared by a network of people. Hence, the criteria can neither be implemented by decreeing nor by recurring to a higher form of reason – as evident in a strongly plural but not pluralistic word! As a consequence, a strategy to further the convic-

7 Nussbaum's (Nussbaum 1999b: 178) self definition as 'essentialist' rks!) does not help very much, since it triggers misunderstandings.

tions has no other way than to use the dynamics of the network to produce *plausibility*. As another consequence, especially for the intercultural relations, it might be a good idea to rethink the (Western) concept of reason. This is the only point of interest that I will focus on under the rubric of intercultural relations.

In our context of a culturally plural world many postmodern thinkers tend to criticize formal and universalistic Kantian or utilitarian concepts of reason and counter with a strong relativism. If we, again, imagine a continuum between the 'birds perspective' of reason on the one end and the idea of an 'archipelago' of dispersed rationalities on the other, again an adequate concept of reason for intercultural networks should be placed somewhere in the middle.[8] The metaphor of 'reason as an archipelago of rationalities' serves, according to François Lyotard, to protect particular and plural forms of reason from the uniforming power of capital. Cultural relativity becomes an instrument to serve the powerless. But aren't particular cultures already strongly involved in relations with others on almost all the fields of human life? And isn't it already a universalistic manipulation of the particular, if someone tries to 'save' it by isolating it? On the one hand, it seems that the metaphor of the archipelago of unconnected rationalities produces a performative contradiction. On the other hand, there are deontological ethics, in Kantian liberal tradition, promoting universalistic principles. The interest is to strengthen what is common to everybody, in opposition to particularism. The bird's perspective of these approaches, however, generates serious difficulties for intercultural communication as e.g. Karl-Otto Apel underscores for the Moral Principle of Discourse Ethics (Apel 1994). Moreover, insofar as the cultural background of these rationalistic ethics is based on typical European (and North American) Enlightenment tradition, they also end up in a performative contradiction. A Western principle is not directly evident in any other culture. As any other ethical orientation it has to cnter into dialogue, compete with other ideas and prove its usefulness within a network of coexistence and communication. As a matter of fact, there are many different rationalities, but they are interconnected in very different ways (sometimes violent) and there is also an interest in universally valid orienttation. When it comes to the concept of reason, it seems to me that Wolfgang Welsch proposed an interesting idea: 'transversal reason'.[9] According to this approach, reason is always woven into the cultural practices of different 'lifeworlds'. Reason works as the particular rationality of this praxis, and at the same time as the human capacity to develop concepts of larger units and of the commonly human. Different rationalities are not completely dispersed and different. They are imagined as different regions of a vast landscape of

8 See for the whole argument Welsch 1996.

9 Welsch 1996. For some reading in a similar vein compare Wittgenstein 2009 and the phenomenological works of Bernhard Waldenfels (Waldenfels 1980, 1985, 1990) and others.

human life. Reason, according to this approach, is woven into the fabric of specific cultural rationalities, but its specific use is to build as many bridges as possible from this specific rationality over to different ones: It operates transversally comparing and combining different rationalities with an interest in common traits. Thus, the perspective of the 'commonly human' is present, but it is not connoted with uniformity; and the perspective of the culturally specific is present, but it is not connoted with particularism. However, reason itself does not hold the majestic position anymore that rationalism once gave to it. Reason is simply a (very important) capability among others.

Certainty and solidarity – networking among power relations

The relational approach to Nussbaum's historical 'essentialism' renders obvious that the items of the list do not have the objective strength to *oblige* actors to realize these conditions in their social context – even if we conceived of the items as principles in the strict sense of the word. They need consent to be acknowledged and heeded. Or they need to be codified in international law (on constitutional level) and enforced by transnational organisations like the UN. It is this context that e.g. the relation between the capability-list and Human Rights are discussed in, a context impregnated by power relations. Taking these considerations into account I would like to discuss two more points. First: what helps, in a relational perspective, to generate plausibility for the capability-thought? Second: what about power relations? Both questions can best be answered if we take into account, in a short remark, that both have to do with the specific genesis of the Capability Approach.

The Capability Approach of Amartya Sen originated as a critique of a (neo-)liberal bureaucratic development policy; a critique 'from below', out of the perspective of the Disadvantaged and the Marginalized. This hermeneutics renders the Capability Approach quite similar to Latin American Liberation-Philosophy and -Theology: e.g. Franz Hinkelammert developed in dialog with the Mexican Zapatista-movement and in debate with the German Discourse Ethics the criterion of corporal integrity as the basic condition of any ethical judgment and as criterion of truth of "universalism of the concrete human being" (Hinkelammert 1994: 139). This idea leads to similar results as the "Theology of life" and the "Conciliar Process for Justice, Peace and the Integrity of Creation" of the *World Council of Churches* (Geneva)[10] that employs a hermeneutic from below and integrates worldwide into international institutional resources with local religious-groups fostering social

10 http://www.oikoumene.org/en/who-are-we.html.

justice, conciliating violent conflict, advocating Human Rights a.s.f. This kind of genesis, hermeneutics and practical engagement aligns, up to a certain point, these positions in the field of ethics with the people on the low end of the global stratification and, in consequence, it makes them relatively weak on the field of ethics. This has consequences for the ways in which capability-ethicists generate plausibility and find themselves positioned among the power relations.

Creating *plausibility* for the capabilities and their claim is a communicative process that operates with cognitive contents, emotional states, social relations and reflection on their logics etc. Pointing to cognitive contents, reinforced by their affective connotations, the listed capabilities themselves are of primary importance. To me, they should be evident to anybody and easy to explain[11] – as long as no interests stand against the recognition of their validity in relation to *other people*. Out of a relationist view, however, I think that the convincing power of human 'essentials' can be fostered by taking relational operations into account.

Any communication, according to Habermas (Habermas 1988), goes along with an experience of the intersubjective validity of communicational rules. Communication and its way of operation can hence be useful to create a conscience for interdependency, mutuality and, thus, under good circumstances, for the right of *other people* to realize their capabilities, too. I would like to sketch briefly some axiologically relevant communicational relations on the cognitive and emotional level.

(1) Reciprocity is a type of relation that, for ages, has made moral similitude and human equality a regulating notion for social organization. The exchange of gift and counter-gift is, since Marcel Mauss, recognized as a basic social relation and as a strong means for social coherence.[12] Anthropology of law considers reciprocity as groundwork of legal common sense and organization.[13] Reciprocity is plausible everywhere, even if the gifts as such are different: in one society the valid currency may be money and its symbols, in another it may be honor. In any case, we can state some fundamental points: reciprocity presupposes the recognition that the other person has the right to live a life more or less comparable to one's own life. Reciprocity relies

11 About the universal evidence etc. of capabilities a discussion is going on; it is not object of our considerations out of a relationist perspective.

12 See Mauss 1954 and Malinowski 1922. For economy see Thurnwald 1932. Ceremonial exchange of gifts is simply a special form of exchange. Even modern social theories presuppose reciprocity, even if it is mediated by institutions multiplied by functional differentiation (Luhmann 1995).

13 See Thurnwald 1934. When we are talking about do ut des it is a good idea not to underscore too much the word ut, since this would happen out of a subjectivistic misunderstanding.

on socially shared ideas of what is valuable. And if a given actor recognizes the rules of reciprocity other actors can count on his schemes of behavior as reliable, and social stability is fostered (what, on the other hand, also makes it so easy to gain short hand profit by a calculated rupture of reciprocal logics). Reciprocity can count on practical, almost universal plausibility. From reciprocity stems social recognition, stable conditions and, in the end, universalistic reasoning – it confirms each and any of the capability items.

(2) On the basis of simple reciprocity, many religions developed the so called "Golden Rule". The *Project World Ethos*,[14] initiated by the German theologian Hans Küng, showed clearly that the Golden Rule is a good starting point for intercultural understanding. Moreover, the Golden Rule implies a dynamic of auto-obligation for the actor who commits to it. Jesus pronounced in the Sermon on the Mount: "Therefore all things whatsoever ye would that men should do to you, do ye even so to them: for this is the law and the prophets" (Mt. 7, 12). This obligation to act in favor of the other is valid, independently of the other's response and calculations concerning any counter-gift. This obligation turns the Golden Rule to be strong and weak at the same time. It is strong, since such a way to act it helps actors in a given situation to act counter-intuitively and, thus, e.g. to find a way out of the escalation of a (possible) conflict. It is weak, since it can be exploited by others. Believers might be strong enough in themselves to risk this without any protection. For the general public and even outright selfish people the Golden Rule might still be attractive, if sanctions protect the rule against exploitation.

(3) The experiences of suffering and solidarity are very intimately interwoven into the cognitive and emotional fabric of the most particular cultures (Rorty 1989). At the same time, suffering and solidarity are universal experiences. Especially suffering is very different from the ways in which cultures celebrate themselves. Celebrations often do seem strange to foreigners. Think about Shiite *Ashura*-celebrations in the eyes of Western observers or the *Christopher Street Day* in the eyes of Muslim believers. Both trigger feelings of rejection. In contrast, experiences of suffering, pain or humiliation, the burning of houses, the death of a child, hunger, epidemic sickness a.s.f. invite to identify with the victim. A sentence as "I know what it means to lose a child. What can I do for you?" is an expression of primordial solidarity transcending all boundaries. Here we have the groundwork for a secular ethic of solidarity as Richard Rorty (Rorty 1989) projects. Moreover every religion has some account on suffering and soli-

14 http://www.weltethos.org/dat-english/index.htm. See similar: Parliament of the World Religions 1993.

> darity, richly expressed by symbols and stories as the Biblical account of the Samaritan highlights. All the religions – except their fundamentalist transformations (but up to a certain point even these) – are masters in contradicting the reality of suffering and finally even death. And they know how to mobilize the power of compassion (e.g. Metz 2004). If ethics ties up to experiences of suffering, it gets in touch with the most intimate fabric of feelings and convictions; and at the same time it always is on the brink to universal consensus. And compassion in solidarity is something very different from sentimentality. Acting in solidarity always also means to act out of the threshold of inter-subjective and objective needs and rights. This becomes obvious, if one conceives of the Human Rights as a response to systematically produced experiences of suffering and injustice. In this sense, the universal validity of Human Rights does not stem from Western dogmatism but from the mere universality of human suffering itself – and the social conditions that guarantee the development of human capabilities thus become criteria also for judging a situation according to the Human Rights.[15]

Power, of course, is a relation that withstands in many contexts the thriving for capabilities to be developed. A brief look at the history and the focus of the Human Development and Capability Association shows that there is quite clear conscience of how important social power relations and their political transformation are. The HDCA takes a viewpoint 'from below', and Nussbaum (Nussbaum 1999b: 186) points out that even in Aristotle's ethics the powerless are omitted easily. Identifying with the 'miserables' (or at least with their interests) obliges the ethicist to refer to a social theory in order to justify his or her judgments. Thus, some fields of debate in ethics drift towards empirical, sociological reasoning. There are only some few thoughts that I would like to point out about this drift.

Social science, out of a relationist perspective, can be of some use, when the debate between Nussbaum's (empirical) 'essentialism' and cultural-relativist opinions arises (Nussbaum 1999b: 178ff.). If we do not argue in a metaphysical but historical (stronger: historicist) way, we cannot make a strong stance for 'essentials'; but that does not mean that a naïve relativism has to be the consequence. Individuals cannot be compared without their relations and positions in their social context; cultures cannot be compared without their intercultural, social relations on the regional and global level. Comparison in context presupposes that any social action is embedded in social relations. And these are relations of inequality and power. Hence, to me it seems that it is not so much of interest, if people of a given culture have the right to do this

15 The long complex discussion of the relation between Human Rights and Capabilities, however, is not object of our brief considerations.

or that. The question is, if they exert power relations upon other people that these people dislike. And this is the moment when the oppressed people can claim their rights, for example referring to their right to develop their capabilities. But: this argument still needs to be sharpened. Since there are people who are so accustomed to being oppressed that they habitualize it and would not even complain about it (cf. Nussbaum 1999b: 210). Here, of course, the ethicist would have to act 'enlightening' this person's situation and line up with her in solidarity. But this is nothing more than to fight according to one's own convictions or, in other words, tying up to the network of convictions and action (which is a network of power relations) in order to weave new patterns.

Power relations, in my understanding, need to be addressed with priority. But this does not solve problems of substantiation with one strike. It only transforms them as two gross issues of ethical relevance may illustrate. These are exploitation and exclusion of many human beings by neoliberal economics i.e. economists – beginning with the 'Chicago boys' benefiting from a torturing dictator in Chile and ending with investment bankers causing by their usual business hundreds of millions of people starving (to death). All of this is, of course, a matter of ethics. But it cannot be resolved by ethics alone, as the comparison between torture and banking shows. That torture is unethical, even an investment banker would agree upon (even though Friedrich Hajek and Friedman-followers in the seventies legitimized Pinochet). But he would not agree upon his responsibility whatsoever for starving people. He would – as any neoliberal – more or less say that poor people are themselves responsible for their situation; and he would try to legitimize that with economic and socio-scientific arguments – not with ethics. So, we are caught within a kind of double bind. Without a strong theory of social power relations and inequality behind our interest in justice, we cannot argue the reasons of injustice and the way to justice. And without a strong ethic commitment to human basic needs and/or capabilities we are not able to substantiate our socio-scientific approach. This means that things inevitably become political.

Thus, the action connoted by the lemma of this conference: "Closing the capability gap" turns out to be, finally, political transformation."

References

Apel, K.-O. (1994): Anderssein, ein Menschenrecht? In: Blätter für deutsche und internationale Politik, 9, 1062-1068.

Bourdieu, P. (1977): Outline of a Theory of Practice. Cambridge.

Bourdieu, P. (1980): Le sens pratique. Paris.

Bourdieu, P. (1983): The Field of Cultural Production or the Economic World Reversed. In: Poetics, 12, 4-5, 311-356.
Bourdieu, P. (1984): Distinction. A social critique of the judgement of taste. Reprint. London.
Bourdieu, P. (1996): The Rules of Art. Genesis and Structure of the Literary Field. London.
Bourdieu, P. (2002): Fieldwork in Philosophy. In: Bourdieu, P. (Ed.): Rede und Antwort. Frankfurt a.M., 15-49.
Bourdieu, P. & Wacquant, L.J.D. (2006): Reflexive Anthropologie. 1. Aufl. Frankfurt a.M.
Fornet-Betancourt, R. (Ed.) (1992a): Die Diskursethik und ihre lateinamerikanische Kritik. Aachen.
Fornet-Betancourt, R. (Ed.) (1992b): Diskursethik oder Befreiungsethik? Aachen.
Fornet-Betancourt, R. (Ed.) (1994): Konvergenz oder Divergenz? Eine Bilanz des Gesprächs zwischen Diskursethik und Befreiungsethik. Aachen.
Habermas, J. (1988): On the logic of the social sciences. Cambridge, Mass.
Hinkelammert, F. (1994): Diskursethik und Verantwortungsethik: eine kritische Stellungnahme. In: Fornet-Betancourt, R. (Ed.): Konvergenz oder Divergenz? Eine Bilanz des Gesprächs zwischen Diskursethik und Befreiungsethik. Aachen, 111-149.
Luhmann, N. (1995): Social systems. Stanford, CA.
Malinowski, B. (1922): Argonauts of the Western Pacific. An account of native enterprise and adventure in the Archipelagoes of Melanesian New Guinea. London.
Mauss, M. (1954): The gift. Forms and functions of exchange in archaic societies. London.
Metz, J.B. (2004): Compassion. Das Leid der anderen spüren. In: Was tust du, fragt der Engel, Freiburg, 38-42.
Nussbaum, M. (1990): Aristotelian Social Democracy. In: Douglass, B., Mara, G. & Richardson, H. (Eds.): Liberalism and the Good. New York, 203-252.
Nussbaum, M. (1993): Non Relative Virtues. An Aristotelian Approach. In: Nussbaum, M. & Sen, A. (Eds.): The Quality of Life. Oxford.
Nussbaum, M. (1999a): Gefühle und Fähigkeiten von Frauen. In: Nussbaum, M. (Ed.): Gerechtigkeit oder Das gute Leben. Gender Studies. Frankfurt, 131-175.
Nussbaum, M. (1999b): Menschliche Fähigkeiten, weibliche Menschen. In: Nussbaum, M. (Ed.): Gerechtigkeit oder Das gute Leben. Gender Studies. Frankfurt, 176ff.
Parliament of the World Religions (1993): Declaration Toward a Global Ethic. Online verfügbar unter http://www.parliamentofreligions.org/_includes/FCKcontent/-File/TowardsAGlobalEthic.pdf.
Rorty, R. (1989): Contingency, irony, and solidarity. Cambridge.
Rorty, R. (2001): Gefangen zwischen Kant und Dewey. Die gegenwärtige Lage der Moralphilosophie. In: Deutsche Zeitschrift für Philosophie, 49, 2, 179-196.
Schäfer, H. (2004): Globalisierung und topische Ethik. Zur interkulturellen Plausibilisierung universaler Humanität. In: Schäfer, H. (Ed.): Praxis - Theologie – Religion. Frankfurt, 369-402.
Schäfer, H. (2011): Identity politics and the political field – a theoretical approach to modelling a 'field of identity politics'. In: Raab, J., Thies, S. & Kaltmeier, O.

(Eds.): Ethnicities under Construction: Inter-American Perspectives on Identity Politics.
Thurnwald, R. (1932): Werden, Wandel und Gestaltung der Wirtschaft. Berlin.
Thurnwald, R. (1934): Werden, Wandel und Gestaltung des Rechtes im Lichte der Völkerforschung. Berlin, Leipzig.
Waldenfels, B. (1980): Der Spielraum des Verhaltens. Frankfurt.
Waldenfels, B. (1985): In den Netzen der Lebenswelt. Frankfurt.
Waldenfels, B. (1990): Der Stachel des Fremden. Frankfurt.
Welsch, W. (1996): Vernunft. Die zeitgenössische Vernunftkritik und das Konzept der transversalen Vernunft. Frankfurt.
Wittgenstein, L. (2009): Philosophical Investigations. 4. Aufl. New York.

Part II – Capability Gaps of the Young

Peter Bartelheimer, René Büttner & Tanja Schmidt

Dynamic Capabilities – A Capability Approach to Life Courses and the Case of Young Adults[1]

1. Individualisation and inequality – two stories on social transformation

When called upon to assess the general direction of societal change in Western capitalist societies over the past decades, social scientists tend to tell two contrasting stories – one about increasing individualisation, the other about growing inequality. Individualisation implies that a person's place within the employment and production system, his or her educational achievements and life pattern are at present far less predetermined and fixed by social class, by institutional constraints or by collective identities than they were in the "fordist" post-war period. By contrast, the inequality story features a widening stratification of education and employment opportunities and of resulting incomes, a sharpened difference between the primary and secondary sectors of segmented labour markets against the background of tougher international economic competition and eroding protections provided by social rights. While an increasing number of people experience new forms of collective precariousness, other social groups, being less affected, continue to attain higher education, to maintain secure jobs and comfortable incomes and living standards.

In discussing these scenarios, most social scientists will agree that today's life patterns tend to differ more, both within and between national socio-economic regimes (Heinz 2003). The hitherto "normal" timing of education and training, labour market entrance, family formation and parenthood, career development, "older worker" phase, labour market exit and retirement is becoming less "linear" and increasingly "disorderly": states can be combined in more ways and may follow each other in more sequence patterns than before. Findings on growing diversity of life patterns rank high in both stories

1 This contribution is based on two conference papers. The first paper, "The capability to be of age – applied Sen for life courses of young adults", was delivered at the international conference "Closing the Capability Gap – Renegotiating Social Justice" at Bielefeld University, 15th/16th May 2009. The second paper, "Multidimensional Trajectories to Adulthood and Capabilities", was presented at the Cambridge Workshop on "Capabilities and Work Lives" held within the framework of the European integrated project "Resources, Rights and Capabilities (CAPRIGHT), at Cambridge, 29th -1st October 2009.

on social change, but in the "optimistic" version increasing mobility and uncertainty are "a price of progress toward greater personal freedom" whereas in the "pessimistic" narrative deviations from mainstream life patterns are imposed by economic pressures of "globalization" and "marketization" rather than sought by individuals (Streeck 2008: 9 sq.; cf. Mayer 2009).

Possibly, both stories tell partial yet related truths. As the "fordist" post-war economies and the social institutions which used to standardise life patterns undergo profound transformation, the very same changes may offer some segments of society new freedoms of choice between possible life patterns while restricting opportunities for others. Advantage or disadvantage accumulate over time, and one approach to measuring inequality could well be to look at the cumulative effects of options or constraints in individual trajectories. For example, the assessment of a given labour force status, a standard or non-standard form of employment or the quality of a work situation at some point in time largely depends on the upward or downward gradient of the professional trajectory they are situated in. That is why both the individualisation and the inequality narrative of social change should better be tested against biographical evidence, the research question being how to distinguish between voluntary and involuntary turbulence in individual life courses.

2. Agency and structure in life course research and welfare economics

2.1 Social change and individual development in life course research

The object of sociological life course studies is to identify and to explain changes in social structure by looking at the social positions individuals hold over time, both over their life time and at different points in historical time. The life course[2] can be defined as the sequence of states and transitions relating "to participation of individuals in different life domains, mainly education, work, family and welfare" (Heinz 2003). Researchers agree on at least four qualities of the life course that have to be taken into account (Mayer 2008, 2004; Schmidt 2007):

- Individual biographies are constructed both socially and individually (Klammer et al. 2007: 9) in a *multi-level* process: Individuals build their life history through choices and actions that make use of

2 The differences between the terms "life course" and "life cycle" (cf. Elliott 2005: 73) as well as "life span" (cf. Diewald/Mayer 2008) have to be neglected in this paper.

options a society offers at a given historical time. Their individual lives are embedded in age cohorts and social groups and shaped by socio-economic regimes (Mayer 2001, 2005) that are subject to change. Since the relative importance of collective units such as families, households, partnerships, social status groups for individual lives varies from country to country and between historical periods, different levels of aggregation may serve as units of analysis for life course research.

- Individual trajectories are *multidimensional*: They comprise and combine biological events and social events in the various life domains of family, household, training, employment and professional development. Research has to account for interdependence and causal relations between separate yet linked time patterns in each of these domains.
- As individual life histories follow an internal, endogenous dynamic, events, phases, transitions and life-phases cannot be examined in isolation from each other. Life patterns are *self-referential* systems in which "future states and events are always dependent on the prior life history in the sense of experiences, resource allocation, choices, and turning points" (Diewald & Mayer 2008: 5). Therefore, life course studies always have to reckon with "path-dependency", i.e. with the influence of earlier life phases on transitions and events.
- By constructing their life histories, individuals also *reproduce* social structures.[3] Personal actions and choices are not completely determined by the life course regime predominant in society at a given point in historical time. "When many people in the same cohort behave in concert, they can produce social change" (Naegele et al. 2003: 17). Thus, individual agency can effect social innovation and cause institutions and organisations to adapt their rules to new and divergent life course patterns – either by the sheer weight of aggregate individual behaviour or by organised political expression of needs that arise from changed new temporal patterns.

Consequently, life course research is about "the potential interplay of social change with individual development" (Elder et al. 2004: 11). One strand of research has emphasised the institutionalisation of life patterns, i.e. the standardising effects of informal and legal norms, especially the welfare state regulations, that enforce a sequence of participation patterns in various life domains (Diewald & Mayer 2008: 5). Other strands have rather focussed on the individual life course and on individual development on the micro level,

3 The reproductive aspect of the life course obviously refers to what Giddens (1988) called the "dualism of structure": While people make use of routines and societal conventions so as to act efficiently, they can also act against conventions and thus create new structures.

paying less attention to socio-economic context. Individual life histories at the micro-level, temporal patterns of households, groups or cohorts at the meso-level, or life course institutions (Kohli 1992) at the macro-level of societies can serve as different "points of entry for study" (Elder et al. 2004: 15), but all these entry points will lead to the "intersection between individual agency and historical and cultural context" (Elliot 2005: 72). Micro-level analysis may rely more on qualitative methods like case histories while macro-level analysis may benefit from the increasing availability of prospective longitudinal datasets for individuals and households, but the traditional distinctions between quantitative and qualitative research "becomes blurred" as "statistical models increasingly have a temporal or chronological dimension that gives them a certain narrative quality" (ibid: 1).

Five different concepts (Brückner & Mayer 2005) are presently being used in discussing the effects of social change on diversity and turbulence in life patterns:

- Life courses can be more or less institutionalised. *De-institutionalisation* would imply that age-graded institutions and welfare state policies lose some of their power to define states and transitions in individual lives.
- The degree in which life courses are standardised can vary. *De-standardisation* would mean that hitherto typical states or sequences become less prevalent in a population or that their timing (e.g. the ages at which a transition is experienced) is now less uniform.
- *Differentiation* stands for an increase in the number of separately defined states (e.g. jobs held with different firms) that follow each other over time.
- *Pluralisation,* by contrast, refers to an increase in the number of states that may occur simultaneously at the same life stage, either across a population (e.g. family forms) or in individual lives (e.g. jobs and training).
- While the other concepts describe different aspects of diversity in trajectories, the concept of *individualisation* implies that this diversity results from more individual control over lives, expressing "autonomous" achievement rather than "unwanted adaptation to insurmountable barriers and anomy" (Diewald & Mayer 2008: 9).

Technically, a number of measurements can be used in testing these concepts of biographical diversity:

- Prevalence: how often does a state or transition occur?
- Age variance: how often does a state or transition occur at specific ages?
- Duration variance: how often do people spend a similar amount of time in a state?

- Inter-event dependency: to what extent is one state associated with another?
- Sequence uniformity: to what extent are events and states uniformly timed and ordered?

In line with assumptions on de-institutionalisation and individualisation, recent life course research has somewhat shifted its attention from structural to individual effects. While life span psychologists have argued "that in times of sudden social change and less rigid institutions, the impact of personality may rise" (Heckhausen 1999, quoted in Diewald & Mayer 2008: 8), sociologists assume that "modern institutions have to rely on psychic capabilities and dispositions to work in a satisfying manner" (Meyer 1986, quoted ibid.).

In the analytical tool set, this shift of focus may be associated with the distinction between transitions and key points. Any change in state that takes place in a short time span throughout a person's biographical pathway is a transition. Some role transitions are age-graded and some are not; many transitions are also institutionally defined, e.g. moves from school to work or from employment to unpaid care work/parenting. Transitions can usually be identified in quantitative longitudinal data. Key points, by contrast, are those transitions that imply a fundamental change in a person's life and can have a decisive influence on the choices that a person makes, e.g. with regard to labour market participation. Thus, this concept rather refers to personal significance. While "potential" key points can be found in quantitative or register data, they can only be actually defined by recourse to qualitative data based on biographical interviews.

Diewald and Mayer (2008: 7) see the sociology of the life course on the move from "structure without agency" or "agency without agents", leaving individuality "below the sociological radar", towards the notion of 'agency within structure'" (Settersten 1999, quoted ibid.). They propose looking at the agents more closely to distinguish between role sets and social positions "with the resources and constraints linked to it, and the person who occupies this position and brings his specific capabilities and orientations with him" (ibid.). This is where Sen might come in.

2.2 Enter Sen – life courses as cumulative capabilities

Whereas for life course research the distinction between voluntary and imposed turbulence remains rather analytical, in Amartya Sen's concept of measuring well-being it acquires a more normative meaning.

Sen proposes capabilities as a "broad and comprehensive" (Leßmann 2009: 1) measure both of well-being and of inequality. Instead of comparing social positions by looking only at resources – monetary incomes, items of living standards and entitlements – or by subjective utility measures like life satisfaction, he proposes to target the degree of real freedom individuals have to choose the way of life they value (cp. Sen 1999: 4). A full description of a social position, according to Sen, should include not only "who did what" but also "what options each person had" (Sen 2002: 593). In his terminology, while life 'functionings' stand for actual achievements of a person, the combination of everything a person is or does, capabilities represent the potential combinations of achievements, including alternatives that were available but not chosen (ibid). "Sen's answer to the question 'equality of what' introduces two basic notions. What matters to define well-being are the functionings of a person, i.e. her achievements: what she manages to do or to be (being well-nourished, well-clothed, mobile, taking part in the life of the community). According to him, however, more important than well-being is the advantage of the person, i.e. her real opportunities. These are called capabilities." (Schokkaert 2008: 2). In formal economic language, life functionings make up a multidimensional vector (or "bundle") of outcomes that constitute a person's way of life, whereas her capabilities constitute all the vectors of opportunities within her reach.

Diagram 1: From resources and functionings to capabilities

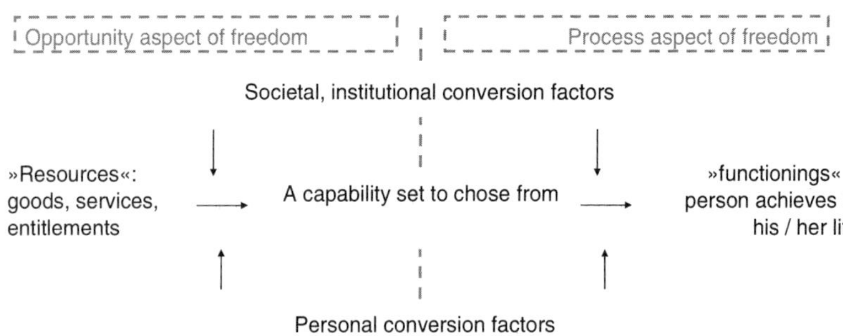

Diagram 1 presents the reading of Sen used within the European research network Resources, Rights and Capabilities (CAPRIGHT)[4] in a formalised way. A person's capability set, i.e. the different combinations of functionings she can choose from, depends on resources (goods, services and entitlements, whether exchanged on the market or not) and on the person's ability to transform these resources into functionings valuable to herself. As for these "conversion factors" that make up an individual's utilisation function, Robeyns (2003) has proposed to distinguish personal abilities from social and environmental factors. The functionings a person achieves reflect the degree of freedom to choose, conditioned both by the number of options available ("opportunity aspect") and by the procedure by which choices are made ("process aspect").

The capability approach as advocated by Sen offers a very sophisticated analytical and normative model of individual choice that in itself can be seen as a theoretical reflection of a more individualised society. Analytically, the model obviously revolves around the issue of agency, and normatively it takes the individual for its "ultimate unit of moral concern" (Leßmann 2009: 11). Yet, even without entering into the problems of operationalising the capability concept, two shortcomings of this approach to measuring well-being stand out.

Firstly, Sen has not concerned himself much with linking the capability concept with socio-economic regimes, social structures and social stratification. As is obvious from diagram 1, both individual opportunities and freedom of choice largely depend upon collective supports, both in the form of resources and of social conversion factors – supports that cannot be provided by the market alone but have to be assured by "capability friendly" political regulation and intervention. As Sen himself (1999: 283 sq.) acknowledges, individual agency is realised within a socially constructed context. But until today capability research is putting more effort into measurements of "what" constitutes inequality in present societies while rather neglecting the crucial sociological question of "who" is unequal to whom. As Leßmann (2009: 2) puts it, "the interplay between social groups or social stratification and individual agency is not modelled in much detail". While life course research is still struggling with the issue of individual agency, the capability approach needs to give more attention to the institutions that attribute resources and define conversion factors.

Secondly, as was equally emphasised by Leßmann (2009a: 1), the theoretical model that constructs the capability set of a person at a given point in time so far does not account for "the impact current choices have on the future capabilities, nor does it make clear how a person's ability to choose

4 For a more detailed presentation see Bartelheimer et al. (2009: 24 sq.).

may change over time". This is the shortcoming specifically addressed in this paper.

Both the resources and conversion factors that determine opportunity and the values that condition choice can be seen as variant over time. Introducing time into the model of capabilities would bring the approach closer to 'real life' but also raises a multitude of questions.[5] As argued by Bartelheimer et al. (2009: 35), the capability 'school' should consider the tools developed by life course research in order to deal with the changes capability sets and functioning vectors undergo over time.

Individual lives can be seen as a long chain of countless decisions involving both biographically important key points and sequences of states between them. Re-stating the already familiar self-referential quality of trajectories in capability language, Comim (2004: 18)[6] points out that „functionings in t-1 can be understood as capabilities in time t", and that "from this perspective, they could be understood as potentials", i.e. as the base for future resources and conversion factors.

Evidently, path-dependence does not imply determinism but rather "agency within structure" (see above). On the one hand, the agent should be aware that "choosing from a capability set always involves choosing a bundle of functionings in combination with a future capability set" (Leßmann 2009: 3).[7] On the other hand, the available alternatives are determined not only by the chooser, but rather co-produced by the individual and the collective. By choosing a functioning in time t, an individual can influence who it will be in time t+1 and what resources it will be able to use. Conversely, society can extend or restrict a person's capabilities in time t+1 by providing or not providing resources and creating or altering societal conversion factors. Capability sets are interdependent and sequentially ordered over time, and inequality of resources and conversion factors can exclude one person from valuable functions in the future, resulting in a trajectory of cumulative disadvantage while enabling another one to accumulate biographical advantage over time. Life course sensitive or life course relevant public action can intervene in the chain of successive options available to an individual.

Diagram 2 expands the basic theoretical model of the capability space (see Diagram 1 above) by accounting for successive states over time. Functioning bundles, beings and doings, have two kinds of qualities: firstly they determine a person's current well-being ('consumption'), and secondly they condition the capability space from which the functionings of the following period can be chosen ('investment'). As the diagram shows, therefore both

5 For some of the recent efforts to add "becoming" to "doing" and "being" within the capability informational space see the sources given in Bartelheimer et al. 2009: 26.

6 The authors thank Flavio Comim for kindly permitting to cite this draft paper.

7 The authors thank Ortrud Leßmann for kindly permitting this citation from an unpublished paper.

functioning bundle and respective capability space are jointly presented at the same time slot.[8] In the diagram, the two qualities in which functioning bundles differ are visualised by their size (big circles symbolizing high, small circles symbolizing low 'consumption') and by their surface (plain circles indicating high, hatched circles indicating low 'investment'). In the diagram for instance, the first period is characterized by a functioning bundle which yields not only high current well-being, but also opens up a large array of options for the future. The latter is due to the positive impact of the present beings and doings on resources and conversion factors. The person might for example be a student at time t. From there on, the trajectory depends on the choices made by the person. From the multitude of possible trajectories, the diagram shows one possible outcome that is paradigmatic for the argument presented in this paper.

Diagram 2: Path dependency and institutional intervention in successive capability sets

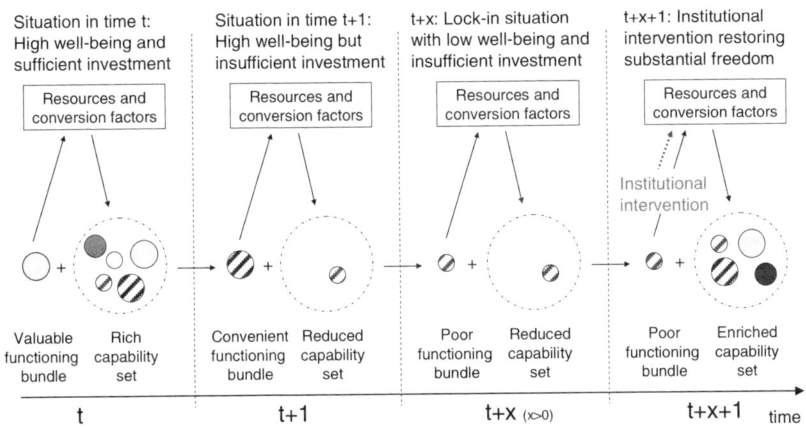

After a favourable start, a 'risky' choice leads through successive path-dependent stages to a situation in which the person is locked in a disadvantageous state. In the last period of the diagram, institutional intervention, positively affecting resources and/or conversion factors, restores substantial freedom. In our example, the student may have chosen to neglect his education, enjoying

8 The authors are indebted to Ortrud Leßmann (2009) for the idea of presenting functionings and capabilities simultaneously. Whereas her paper discusses how people learn to choose, emphasising individual ability to make good choices, this paper is more concerned with collective supports, i.e. with interventions providing sufficient resources and appropriate collective conversion factors that enlarge a person's opportunity set.

many liberties in period t+1, but without finally attaining any certificate. After some periods of subsequent low-paid jobs, a scheme of further education is proposed to him by the employment service. While not all of her initial capabilities could be reproduced, new capabilities now figure in her capability set. Whether a path change will actually take place depends on the functionings which the person will choose for period t+x+2. As before, different kinds of functionings are eligible, some of them involving a trade-off between current and future well-being. The sequence shown in the diagram suggests the possibility that institutional intervention introduces some degree of fault tolerance into people's trajectories.

3. Cumulative Functionings – The case of young adults

The passage to adulthood is marked by some important "key transitions" (Aassve et al. 2007) in private and professional development. In the life span from the age of 17 to 30, young adults may have a first partner, may or may not move out of the parent's household, may or may not form a family of their own, while also graduating from school and possibly entering the labour market. While most professional transition markers are age-graded and institutionally defined, some of these transitions constitute biographical key points[9] in a young person's life. Using prospective monthly observations from the German Socio-economic panel GSOEP[10] for two cohorts born 1968 to 1971 and 1973 to 1976, six distinctly different pathways to adult life were identified by applying a variant of sequence analysis.[11]

The first resulting trajectory type[12] (1) may be characterized as "long and recurrent education and late household formation". Among a wide variance in the successions of different states within both professional and private life, the pattern "training followed by employment followed by training and followed again by employment" is the most common. Concerning private life the succession of "living with parents, not married, no kids" followed by "living independent, not married, no kids" up to the age of 30 is most common. These successions are additionally underpinned by the result that 52.2% of the young adults have two and more transitions from training into gainful employment. Over 40% have transitions from employment to training. This

9 For the distinction between transitions and key points, see above.

10 Wagner et al. (2007).

11 To compare all multidimensional sequences of all young adults between their 17 and 30 year of age the optimal matching technique of Lesnard (2006) was applied (see also Aisenbrey & Fasang 2007). Afterwards the distance results were clustered by a multistage clustering method.

12 Some of the following results are also shown in Table 1.

shows the importance of training within this group, all in all they spend 63.1% of the observed time within the education system. Combining with the private life, young adults of this type spend 62.8% of the period between the 17th and 30th year of their lives within the parents' household, are not married, have no child and are in training. This type of trajectory is predominantly lived by young men.

In the second cluster (2) of „stable labour market integration and late household formation", the sequences are more uniformly structured: they start with "training" and are followed by "employment" up to the age of 30. In the private life these young adults, mainly males, typically live in the parental household during all of the observed period, are not married and have no kids. For almost 70% of this life phase, their are in gainful employment and have the highest portion of unique transitions of training in employment as well as nearly no changes of employment to unemployment. They thereby make proof of stable job market integration. The predominant private life pattern is similar to that of the 1st cluster: nearly 86% of the observed life span they stay with their parents, are not married and have no kids, accordingly they have the lowest share of transitions from the parental household to independent living.

The 3rd cluster (3), "labour market integration and household formation" consists of women and men in nearly equal portions. As in cluster 2, the main succession in professional life is "training followed by employment". Also, at the personal level, the most common sequence pattern is "living with parents, not married, no kids", followed by "living independently, not married and no kids". Yet these young adults spend a smaller share of the observed life span in the parental household and by the age of 30 all of them (100%) have moved out. Within this trajectory a very high portion of unique transitions of training into gainful employment take place and the young adults of this type are employed for 72.5% of the observed period. At the same time, this group has the most frequent transitions to unemployment and also back from unemployment into gainful employment.

The young adults of the fourth cluster (4) "training and employment, late family formation" have a high portion (44.2%) of repeated transitions between training and employment. This is underpinned by the succession of alternating times in training and employment. In total they are in training just under 40% of the time and in gainful employment about 50% of the time. In addition they are, compared with the other clusters, the longest time in unemployment (6.8%). Concerning private life, the succession: "living with parents, not married, no kids" followed by "living independent, not married, no kids" is dominant. They spend about 60% of the entire time in the parental household, but at the age of 30 almost all (96%) live independently in their own household. This type of trajectory is lived by nearly the same portion of women and men.

Cluster five (5), characterized by „training and employment with early family formation“, is the largest and mainly female cluster. There are many different sequences of different states but it shows a quite high portion of 30% transitions of employment into education and/or non-employment as well as the highest portion of all clusters with transitions from training in unemployment (almost 20%). Concerning private life, this cluster also shows many different successions of the different states: in the beginning they live "with parents, not married, no kids" followed by times "within the parental household, married, no kids", furthermore followed by times of "independent living, married, no kids" and followed by "living independently, married and with a child" at the end of time span. Young adults of this cluster have the highest portion of transitions to married life and to having the first child; accordingly the young adults of this cluster live to nearly 30% of the time together with children and are gainfully employed for almost half of the time.

Table 1: Selected aspects of types of trajectories to adulthood

Cluster	1	2	3	4	5	6
Distribution male population	26,3	23,3	12,7	18,0	18,8	0,9
Distribution female population	15,4	7,9	11,3	19,4	25,5	20,5
Cumulative times in						
Parents, single, no child, training	62,8	25,4	19,2	34,5	20,5	9,0
Parents, single, no child, employed	14,5	59,9	24,3	20,7	14,4	3,1
Independent, single, no child, employed	5,6	3,9	40,0	19,9	6,9	0,9
Independent, married, child, employed	0,6	2,8	2,0	5,1	15,0	12,3
Independent, married, child, domestic	0,2	0,6	0,2	1,1	10,2	28,2
Transitions						
Transitions: training → employment more than 2	52,2	27,7	22,5	44,2	28,8	0,6
Transitions: employment → training more than 2	43,3	13,6	16,4	23,9	12,5	0,6

In the 6th cluster (6), "family formation and parenthood with little and intermittent employment“, which is the smallest cluster and mainly female, the young adults live with children during the largest part of the time (62.4%). 94.5% of the young women have at least one child up to their age of 30. They live, in comparison to all clusters, the shortest time in the parental household and the longest time in their own household, where they spend 34.7% of the time with domestic work. In this trajectory type the lowest portion of transitions is from training into gainful employment (27%) and a high percentage (of about 40%) of the young adults do not accomplish any vocational education.

The accumulated doings and beings of an individual at each point in time can be seen as the basis for describing a life span as a whole within a dynamic capability approach. As shown above, different functionings were cumulated for each individual and the individuals' trajectories were finally grouped by similarity. Each of the six types of trajectories into adulthood represents a characteristic set of accumulated functionings that differs from that of the other clusters of individuals for the life span of age 17 to age 30. The consistency of trajectories is partly due to the dependence of every functioning bundle at each point in time on the antecedent functioning bundle, every functioning bundle influencing on its part the subsequent capability set. Furthermore, each functioning bundle at each point in time is the result of choice and, as the case may be, also of institutional intervention.

Trajectory one (1) "long and recurrent education and late household formation" shows, summarized, the result of repeated positive educational choices which lead, in terms of educational career, to a successful educational biography, but in terms of family to a less lucky career of family foundation.

For this quantitative analysis, choice and institutional intervention could not be operationalised. Therefore the results do not show whether for instance young adults of type (1) intended to choose a successful educational trajectory and what kind of impact institutional intervention (would have) had. To address the question of choice as well as of institutional intervention, the trajectories were investigated by a more narrative and therefore more 'qualitative' approach, as proposed by Singer et al. (1998): Out of the cases clustered as trajectory type (1) one person and his biological sibling were singled out. For these persons, narratives of individual life histories were reconstructed, as richly detailed as possible, based on the evidence from the longitudinal dataset.

The siblings Aishe (*1970) and Murat (*1971) are one pair of these chosen siblings. Murats' transition into adulthood was clustered in type (1) and Aishe followed the trajectory type (6). They are of Turkish origin and have four more siblings. Aishe, the girl, achieves only general basic education. She marries with 21, and in 2006, with 29 years, she is not working or attending school or in any way integrated in the labour market. She is still staying at parental home and doing domestic work. The choices she made were probably expected by her family, but this is unknown, because she made no statements about her own aims and attitudes concerning her professional and future private life.

The trajectory of Murat, Aishe's younger brother, belongs to the "long training" type (1): He graduates at middle school and finishes an apprenticeship as a car-mechanist. After finishing school he is working in full time and does some further in-firm education. He becomes a father at the age of 24 and moves out of the parental household within the same year. His attitudes and statements concerning his aims are in accordance with his choices: he wanted a good education and to be responsible for his wife and children.

Both siblings' transitions into adulthood seem to be clearly gender-biased: Aishe is assumedly expected to live a traditional female life-course, centered within the private sphere with commitments to the family. Her choices are according to these expectations, independently of her aims, of which we do not have knowledge. Meanwhile Murat lives a traditional male life course, with the financial responsibility for the family, but in accordance with his expressed aims. We can observe Aishe's decisions leading to a lock-in situation with a very small capability set, whereas Murat's decisions enlarge his capability set. To improve the situation of Aishe at the end of the observed trajectory, institutional intervention could still offer her opportunities to catch up on the training not taken earlier. As well, it could have assisted her in the beginning of the observed period, creating alternatives subjectively acceptable. This could have been done, for example, by offering culture sensitive further education programs or child care facilities.

4. Evaluating institutional intervention from a capability point of view

In this last section, the capability approach shall be presented as a framework for policy evaluation. It has been argued that life courses can be regarded as sequences of beings and doings which have to be observed before the background of a specific biographical opportunity structure. Consequently, for comparing life courses, both the cumulative functionings shown at the surface of a biography and the underlying capabilities present in crucial decision situations have to be taken into account. However, as has been argued, capabilities are not distributed at random. Their configuration is socially structured, and one of the structuring elements is institutional intervention. The impact of policies is reflected in people's capability sets and their realized functionings. Therefore, despite all the unresolved methodological issues, the capability approach is essentially about politics: it is above all a paradigm for assessing outcomes of public action and policy design, proposing as evaluation criterion to what extent they empower individual to act and to choose (Bonvin 2008).

For addressing life course issues in public action (Klammer 2009), Leisering (2004: 217) proposed to distinguish life course sensitive and life course relevant policies. 'Life course sensitivity' refers to the degree to which present entitlements and interventions depend on facts of the past, on the person's biography. The angle is retrospective. Conversely, the 'life course relevance' of policies refers to their prospective qualities, asking about the difference intervention makes for the subsequent life course. While these characteristics are not mutually exclusive, both should be separated analytically.

In the theoretical example and in the empirical cases presented above, it has been obvious that the courses of people's lives are determined by the choices they make among existing options. The capability approach may be construed to make a case for life course sensitive policies that hold individuals responsible for what they choose and how their choices affect their well-being over time. On the other hand, Leßmann (2009: 1) argues that the "ability to choose develops in human beings" by experiences. Also, decisions will be based on an evolving set of values. And even if values were static or "universal", informational problems as raised by Comim (2004: 8) would apply, both in respect to decisions under uncertainty and to a human preference for the present. As Kanbur puts it, cited by Comim (ibid.): "I do not think, in human terms, knowledge can be so perfect that tomorrow's hunger can be felt today". And, most importantly, "the capability approach insist on two necessary preconditions of responsible behaviour: adequate means and power to act and real freedom to choose one's way of living" (Bonvin 2008: 368), thus providing a strong argument for collective supports and against excessive life course sensitivity of policy. While ardently advocating personal responsibility[13], Sen also explains that "[r]esponsibility *requires* freedom. The argument for social support in expanding people's freedom can, therefore, be seen as an argument *for* individual responsibility, not against it" (Sen 1999: 284). As life course sensitive policy tend to make individual lives more path-dependent, they have the adverse effect of exacerbating inequalities, widening the gap between those with an adequate and those with a deficient trajectory.

Therefore, 'capability friendly' life course relevant interventions should promote equality in diversity by substantially extending the freedom of the targeted person. In order to do this, they must make an actual impact on his or her capabilities. For example, policy should not restrict itself to guaranteeing formal rights or to providing resources without verifying that the individual can actually use them (Bonvin & Farvaque 2007: 11). On the other end of the scale, life course relevant policies that exaggerate the 'realness' of the offered new opportunities by imposing them on the target persons (Bonvin & Farvaque, ibid.) are no more 'capability friendly'. In capability terms, they would not provide a better capability set but only prescribe functionings. Rather, interventions should help to create capabilities which are valuable to the targeted person and which she also has reason to value, i.e. which are generally agreed as desirable for the members of their society.

---

13 „Any affirmation of social responsibility that *replaces* individual responsibility cannot but be, to varying extents, counterproductive" (Sen 1999: 283).

However, it is known that different people value options differently, and the value of a capability can not be judged independently from who the person is and has been. Whether someone will perceive a specific new capability bundle as a substantive increase of freedom depends not only on the objective characteristics of these capabilities, but on how they relate to the capabilities which the person had before the intervention. Equally, preferences and goals pursued by the person as an agent have developed along the course of her life. Beyond this, the life course affects the personal conversion factors that are crucial for the *effectiveness* of institutional intervention. They develop continuously, and social support which does not take their current state into account might fall into the trap of not being 'convertible' into capabilities (cp. also Yaqub 2008: 443). In order to reach similar capabilities, people with different histories may need different modifications of resources and/or conversion factors. Also, Yaqub argues that the *efficiency* of institutional help has a lot to do with its *timing* in the life course. He warns that "[m]any interventions to expand adult capabilities might be made when they are least likely to succeed" (Yaqub 2008: 438). He gives two basic reasons for this, one having to do with particularly "sensitive periods" for influence from environmental factors during a human life (ibid.: 444), the other having to do with path-dependence, which can take positive as well as negative routes. Taking the life course into account in policy making would, according to Yaqub, lead to early intervention, as prevention is much more efficient and effective than fixing. All these arguments indeed suggest accounting for the life courses of targeted persons when designing policies, however not in order to constrict the means of support or the array of supported capabilities, but to adjust them where possible to the needs and aspirations of these persons.

Rather than holding individuals responsible for increasingly unequal outcomes and achievements, the normative individualism of the capability approach calls for life course relevant policies that increase the 'fault tolerance' of increasingly diverse individual trajectories, limiting the adverse effects of path-dependency and extending the capabilities of a person over time.

References

Aassve, A., Billari, F. & Piccarreta, R. (2007): Strings of Adulthood: A Sequence Analysis of Young British Women's Work-Family Trajectories. European Journal of Population, 23, 369–388.

Aisenbrey, S. & Fasang, A. (2007): Beyond Optimal Matching: The 'Second Wave' of Sequence Analysis. CIQLE. Yale University. New Haven. (Working Paper, 2007-02).

Bartelheimer, P., Moncel, N., Verd, J.M. & Vero J. (2009): Towards Analysing Individual Working Lives in a Resources/Capabilities Perspective. In: Bartelheimer, P., Büttner, R. & Moncel, N. (Eds.): Sen-sitising life course research? Exploring Amartya Sen's capability concept in comparative research on individual working lives. Marseilles and Göttingen: Céreq and SOFI: 21-51. http://www.sofi-goettingen.de/fileadmin/Peter_Bartelheimer/Literatur/Net-Doc-50.pdf

Bonvin, J.-M. (2008): Activation Policies, New Modes of Governance and The Issue of Responibility. In: Social Policy & Society 7, 3, 367-377.

Bonvin, J.-M. & Farvaque, N. (2007) : L'accès à l'emploi au prisme des capabilités, enjeux théoriques et méthodologiques. Formation emploi, 98, 9-20.

Brückner, H./Mayer, K.U. (2005): De-standardization of the life course: what might it mean? And if it means anything, whether actually took place? In: Macmillan, R. (Ed.): The Structure of the Life-Course: Standardized? Individualized? Differentiated? London, 27-53.

Comim, F. (2004): Time and Adaptation in the Capability Approach (draft paper).

Diewald, M. & Mayer, K.U. (2008): The Sociology of the Life Course and Life Span Psychology. DIW Discussion Paper 772, Berlin.

Elder, G.H., Johnson, M.K. & Crosnoe, R. (2004): The Emergence and Development of Life Course Theory. In: Mortimer, J.T., Shanahan, M.J. (Eds.) (2004): Handbook of the Life Course. New York, 3-19.

Elliott, J. (2005): Using Narrative in Social Research. Qualitative and Quantitative Approaches. London.

Giddens, A. (1988): Die Konstitution der Gesellschaft. Grundzüge einer Theorie der Strukturierung. Frankfurt a.M. & New York.

Heinz W.R. & Marshall V.W. (Eds.) (2003): The Social Dynamics of the Life Course. New York.

Kohli, M. (1992): Lebenslauf und Lebensalter als gesellschaftliche Konstruktionen: Elemente zu einem Vergleich. In: Matthes, J. (Ed.): Zwischen den Kulturen? Die Sozialwissenschaften vor dem Problem des Kulturvergleichs. Soziale Welt, 8, Göttingen, 283-303.

Klammer, U. (2009): The Life Course Research Perspective on Individual Working Lives: Findings From The European Foundation Research. In: Bartelheimer P., Büttner, R. & Moncel, N. (Eds.): Sen-sitising life course research? Exploring Amartya Sen's capability concept in comparative research on individual working lives. Marseilles/Göttingen: Céreq and SOFI, 53-71. http://www.sofi-goettingen.de/fileadmin/Peter_Bartelheimer/Literatur/Net-Doc-50.pdf

Leisering, L. (2004) Government and the Life Course. In: Mortimer, J.T. & Shanahan, M.J. (Eds.): Handbook of the Life Course, New York, 205-229.

Lesnard, L. (2006): Optimal matching and the social sciences. CREST (working paper, 01).

Leßmann, O. (2009): The Capacity to Choose as an Essential Ingredient to Freedom of Choice. Unpublished paper.

Leßmann, O. (2009a): Freedom of Choice and Poverty Alleviation. URL: http://www.capabilityapproach.com/pubs/, accessed 30th January 2010.

Mayer, K.U. (2001): The Paradox of Global Social Change and National Path Dependencies: Life Course patterns in Advanced Societies. In: Woodward A.E.,

& Kohli, M. (Eds.): Inclusions and Exclusions in European Societies. Milton Park, New York, 89-110.

Mayer, K.U. (2004): Whose Lives? How History, Societies and Institutions Define and Shape. Life Courses. In: Research in Human Development 1, 161-187.

Mayer, K.U. (2005): Life Courses and Life Chances in a Comparative Perspective. In: Svallfors, S. (Ed.): Analyzing Inequality: Life Chances and Social Mobility in Comparative Perspective. Palo Alto, 17-55.

Mayer, K.U. (2008): New Directions in Life Course Research. CIQLE Working Paper, New Haven.

Mayer, K.U. (2009): Global Pressures and Transformation Turbulences? Work Biographies and Skill Formation of West and East German Men Born 1971. In: Bartelheimer, P., Büttner, R. & Moncel, N. (Eds.): Sen-sitising life course research? Exploring Amartya Sen's capability concept in comparative research on individual working lives. Marseille/Göttingen: Céreq and SOFI, 225-249. http://www.sofi-goettingen.de/fileadmin/Peter_Bartelheimer/Literatur/Net-Doc-50.pdf

Naegele, G., Barkholdt, C., de Vroom, B., Goul Anderson, J. & Krämer, K. (2003): A new organisation of time over working life. European Foundation, Luxembourg.

Schokkaert, E. (2008): The capabilities approach.

Sen, A. (1999): Development as Freedom. New York.

Sen, A. (2002): Rationality and Freedom. Cambridge, Mass.

Singer, B., Ryff, C., Carr, D. & Magee, W. (1998): Linking Life Histories and Mental Health: A Person-centered Strategy. Sociological Methodology, 28, 1-51.

Streeck, W. (2008): Flexible Markets, Stable Societies? Köln, MPIfG Working Paper 08/6.

Wagner, G.G., Frick J.R. & Schupp, J. (2007): The German Socio-Economic Panel Study (SOEP) - Scope, Evolution and Enhancements. Schmollers Jahrbuch 127, 1, 139-169.

Yaqub, S. (2008): Capabilities over the lifecourse: At what age does poverty damage most? In: Comim, F., Qizilbash, M. & Alkire, S. (2008): The capability approach: concepts, measures and applications. Cambridge.

Jérôme Ballet, Mario Biggeri & Flavio Comim

Children's Autonomy, Education and Capabilities[1]

Introduction

The capability approach constitutes undeniably an important renewal of thought on development and well-being. However, applying this approach to areas such as health and education is somewhat problematical, and works have recently looked into these questions.[2] Concerning education, Sen (1992, 1999 for example) underlines the central role this approach may play in the promotion of capabilities. As for Nussbaum (1997, 2002, 2006), she has tackled this facet of capabilities more thoroughly.

Other works have expanded on this line of thinking (for example Brighouse 2000; Saito 2003; Swift 2003; Unterhalter & Brighouse 2003; and recently a set of contributions edited by Walker & Unterhalter 2007). However, there is a fundamental question which still remains inadequately explored: the possibility of applying the capability approach to children while respecting a basic principle of the liberal theories of justice – of which the capability approach is part – i.e. the principle of autonomy.[3] So, beyond the debate on education, what needs to be broached is the possibility of applying this approach to childhood-related issues.[4] This article specifically touches on the links between *i)* childhood, *ii)* education, and *iii)* the principle of autonomy along the lines of the capability approach, and it evaluates the approach's capacity to apply to this triptych. Consequently, our purpose is not to examine the most appropriate form of education in the sense of an educational curriculum[5], but the possibility of thinking out education within the framework of the

1 Some parts of this paper are based partially on the second chapter of the book *Children and the Capability Approach*, edited by Biggeri, Ballet and Comin (2010).

2 See for example the website of the Human Development and Capability Association.

3 Here we should underline, however, that the contributions of Saito (2003) and Flores-Crespo (2007) tackle this question directly.

4 A number of contributions in the tradition of this approach address childhood issues broadly, not focusing on education specifically. See for example Klasen (2001) and Biggeri (2004) for a discussion on the significance of this approach to understand children's well-being, but also Di Tommaso (2003) for a measurement of well-being, Biggeri (2003), Biggeri et al. (2006), Ballet et al. (2006a, b) for a link with the problem of child labour, Ballet et al. (2004), Horna (2007), Arnich et al. (2007) for an application to street children.

5 See all of the above-quoted contributions on this point.

capability approach, it being considered that the principle of autonomy is central to such an approach.[6]

In a first part, the article addresses the applicability of the capability approach to children with regard to the underlying principle of autonomy. Three points of view are considered, from the most minimalist point of view of the approach to the most maximalist. The first two points of view are compatible with a paternalistic conception of education, whereas the third is more demanding. The first is limited to functionings, the second shifts the emphasis of the problem by bringing up the children's future autonomy in adulthood, and the third takes the children's autonomy seriously. Note that these three points of view are not mutually exclusive in the sense that the most demanding point of view may very well – and must logically – encompass the two others, while the reverse is not true.

In a second part, the article assumes that children's autonomy – at the age they are and not only as future adults – is an issue of some importance. On this basis, it expands on the capability approach by tackling the two notions of redefined functioning and capability to aspire. The capability to aspire constitutes the very core of the development of autonomy, while redefined functioning permits to reduce the question of choice opportunities to achievable choices. In that sense, these two contributions speak in favour of a low, but developing, autonomy.

In a third part, the article, which takes up Sen's distinction (2005) between substantive opportunities and freedom of processes, invites us to go beyond an approach based on substantive opportunities in order to adopt a view of education which is more in conformity with freedom of processes. Doing so leads to children being given a voice in their education.

1. Applying the Capability Approach to Children: The Question of Self-Determination

The application of the capability approach to children is particularly delicate in that it raises the question of their autonomy. In fact, the capability approach

6 It does seem that A. Sen and M. Nussbaum's views of this principle are somewhat different insofar as Sen insists on the impassability of freedom, it being intrinsically important. More particularly, according to Sen, a list of capabilities cannot be defined without public consultation. Nussbaum, in a more Marxian/Aristotelian perspective, is rather inclined to favour a perfectionist conception, and thus formulates a list of basic capabilities. The fact that A. Sen and M. Nussbaum differ on the list of capabilities induces us to think that they do not address the principle of autonomy in quite the same way, even if, on the whole, it appears unquestionable that both authors refer implicitly to such a principle.

obviously implies the individuals' capacity for self-determination.[7] As Kymlicka (1992) underlines full well, the liberal theories of justice all agree on the principle of self-determination. They agree on the idea that the best way to promote the individuals' interests is to let them choose the lifestyle they wish to have. And if they do not agree on the combination of rights and resources with which the individuals should be provided to be in a position to pursue their own conception of good, at least there seems to be a general agreement about the principle of self-determination insofar as its negation would amount to treating individuals not as equals. A. Sen's proposed capability approach encompasses this idea of the importance of self-determination, especially when it makes a distinction between well-being freedom and agency freedom, the latter implying the persons' capacity to exercise their own free will (Sen 1999). After all, opening up the maximum number of choices for individuals is equivalent to supposing that they, alone, can judge what is good for themselves. What would be the use of freedom of choice if the individuals were not in a position to resort to it?

Should we consider that all individuals are concerned, including children? Saito (2003), for example, wonders about the possibility of applying the capability approach to children insofar as they are not mature enough to take decisions for themselves. Most of the time, liberal theories leave out children, as well as mentally ill and temporarily handicapped persons who, unlike other people, are the subject of paternalistic benevolence. This exclusion rests on the inability of the individuals concerned to make choices for themselves, and thus implies their lack of cognitive capacity to decide on what is good for themselves.[8]

Applying the capability approach to children therefore entails taking a stand with regard to their capacity for self-determination. But it seems clear that denying children the capacity for self-determination results in losing the very substance of the capability approach. After all, why talk of capabilities if children do not have freedom of choice? We may certainly consider that freedom of choice does not apply due to the children's lack of cognitive capacity to decide for themselves, but then the capability approach is limited to a set of specific measures which provide children with opportunities without it being really possible for them to choose or not. Three points of view permit to overcome this problem partially.

---

7 Note that the notion of autonomy used here is synonymous with that of self-determination. It does not relate, strictly speaking, to the more complex notion of autonomy as developed in Kant's works.

8 There is an obvious connection here between liberal theories and rationality. In fact, liberal theories are based on the assumption that the agents are rational. If, indeed, the individuals were not in a position to choose for themselves, with a minimum amount of rationality, it would then become legitimate that someone – the State – chooses for them (Unger 1984; Jaggar 1983; Sullivan 1982).

According to the first, the question of the children's mental attitudes is not central to assess their well-being, but functionings are. In that sense, self-determination is not a real problem since it is enough to wonder about what children can actually do. However, such a point of view does not really solve the problem as it leaves two questions entirely open: that of educational choices and who takes the decisions as regards these choices. So, this first point of view is fully compatible with a paternalistic view of education.

According to the second point of view, the question of self-determination should not specifically be addressed at non-mature age but over the whole life cycle, so that what actually needs to be taken into account is the adults' autonomy which they acquire during childhood. Saito (2003: 26) interprets the capability approach along these lines. She thus points out: "In this sense, when dealing with children, it is the freedom they will have in the future rather than the present that should be considered. Therefore, as long as we consider a person's capabilities in terms of their life-span, the capability approach seems to be applicable to children". This second point of view goes beyond the first by providing an answer to the question of educational choices. Educational choices must be made on the basis of a guiding line favourable to the development of the individuals' autonomy in adulthood. Nevertheless, like the first, this second point of view does not seem sufficient to answer seriously the question of the place of autonomy as far as children are concerned. In support of this, we may, for example, introduce the notion of learning effect without which children are not able to choose as they do not know. Note that this effect would also apply perfectly to the first point of view. But the argument could be valid for adults just as well. It could certainly be objected that if the above-mentioned educational guiding line were well-defined so as to favour the adults' autonomy, then the argument would no longer hold for adults and would thus be limited to children. Such an objection is yet compatible with a paternalistic view of education insofar as children are merely regarded as future adults.

The third point of view takes the reasoning further. Note that this point of view is fully compatible with the two others, but is more demanding. It, indeed, encompasses the two others whereas, conversely, it is quite possible to subscribe to one and/or the other first two points of view without subscribing to the third. This point of view sets out to acknowledge a minimal self-determination principle for children. As a matter of fact, the exclusion of children from the principle of self-determination is fundamentally based on a view of individuals as having moral capacity to determine their conception of good. Rawls (1980: 40) expresses this point of view full well when he asserts that "as free individuals, the citizens mutually recognise each other as being endowed with the moral capacity to have a conception of good. This means that they do not perceive themselves as being inevitably linked to the specific conception of good and its objectives which they espouse at some or other moment of their life. On the contrary, as citizens, they are regarded as being generally capable of revising and changing their conception on reasonable and rational grounds. The citizens can thus distance themselves from the different conceptions of good and endeavour to examine and evaluate their various ultimate objectives". This passage underlines two key aspects of liberal theories. On the one hand, the individuals are rational and reasonable; on the other, these faculties enable them to reappraise their judgment. So, the exclusion of children, as well as of mentally handicapped persons, implies that they are neither rational nor reasonable, and are therefore not in a position to revise their judgment. In other words, the problem is not about making a bad choice but being in a position to revise this choice. After all, we are all confronted with bad choices, but the capacity to evaluate and revise choices is essential even more so when these affect our life and our conception of good. Nussbaum (2000: 78) expresses the same opinion when she asserts that the human capability of practical reason consists in "being able to form a conception of the good and to engage in critical reflection about the planning of one's life". The distinction between capacity to make choices and capacity to evaluate and revise choices is of some importance. The problem is not so much that children are unable to make choices – they are –, but that they are unable to evaluate and revise the choices they make. In many cases, however, this distinction is not really taken seriously. Children have long traditionally been regarded as totally vulnerable and dependent upon their parents. Such a view is based on a sentimentalist and maternalistic cult (Boulding 1979) which does not correspond to the situation of a great deal of children in the world. For this reason, they are considered incapable of making choices, and paternalism implies that choices are made by parents. But if the problem is not so much one of choice as one of choice evaluation and possible revision, then it is necessary to provide children with a choice space, instead of making choices for them, in such a manner that rational and reasonable decision-making is favoured. The question is not to defend a strong self-determination principle for children but to acknowledge a weak self-determination principle. On the one hand, a strong self-determination principle would imply that the individual is the best judge of what is good for himself insofar as he, more than anyone else, is in a position to evaluate and revise his judgment. On the other hand, a weak self-determination principle only implies that the individual is in a position to make choices but that the framework within which he makes these choices must be defined so that his capacity for evaluation may develop and that certain particularly harmful choices may thus be eliminated. Brighouse (2000) goes along these lines when he makes a distinction between autonomy-facilitating education and autonomy-promoting education. Autonomy-facilitating education, contrary to autonomy-promoting education, is not aimed at passing on instrumental knowledge with a view to developing choice autonomy in adulthood (in terms of employment choices for example), but attempts to develop freedom of choice in the sense of a capacity to evaluate and revise choices. Now the question is can individuals learn to be autonomous if they are not given any autonomy space? Or in other words, can we really think out the autonomy of adults without thinking out, at the same time, the autonomy – at least weak – of children? The following sections develop a point of view in favour of children's minimal autonomy.

2. Liberal Education, Capacity to Aspire and Redefined Functionings

Ryan (1999) defines liberal education as an education which prepares children for autonomy, that is to say an education which moulds the children's critical mind so as to enable them to assess and revise the choices they make, but also those which society makes. Such an education is largely incompatible with paternalism. Indeed, the internalisation constraint defended by the liberals (for example Dworkin 1989; Raz 1986) stipulates that the individuals cannot really attain a better and autonomous life if their existence is directed from the outside in accordance with values they have not internalised. Such a constraint would doom to failure any paternalism attempt which would be aimed at compelling the individuals to seek the ways of life that are most worthy of interest only to avoid penalties or to react to incitements (Waldron 1989; Lomasky 1987).

Now, the internalisation constraint obviously is central to the development of autonomy in childhood. It is through the internalisation process that children conceive an idea of the good life which is worth living. This process may of course take place in a paternalistic perspective, but such a perspective is not in line with the capability approach. As Nussbaum (2003: 42) underlines, in a society of democracy and tolerance, children should "not be held hostage to a single conception (of the good life)". In other words, following J. S. Mill, liberal theories, including the capability approach, are not ready to admit that society is structurally coercive even if such a structure ensures everyone's autonomy. Society must structurally respect the autonomy of its members even if this results in depriving some individuals of autonomy. Nussbaum (2000) clearly endorses this point of view. So ideally, in the perspective of liberal education, it is necessary to implement an educational structure which guarantees a minimum amount of autonomy and whose result is the production of autonomy in adulthood.[9]

9 Yet, as underlined by White (1973), adopting an extreme liberal position with regard to children is irrational in the sense that this may result in low autonomy in adulthood.

In order to address children's autonomy in line with the third above-discussed point of view, we propose to go beyond the capability approach by introducing two recent developments: redefined functioning and capacity to aspire.

The notion of redefined functioning consists in associating functioning with capability into a single indicator, in such a way that choosing to do A is associated with doing A. More fundamentally, a redefined functioning associates the desire to do A with the fact of managing to do A (Vero 2000). Freedom of choice is therefore associated with choice achievement. This entails limiting choices to the really competing alternatives. So, a redefined functioning is *i)* a *narrow-based functioning* since it must not take into account the alternatives which are not really ones or which are not really possible, and *ii)* a *wide-based functioning* since it integrates desire or freedom of choice. This notion of redefined functioning is closely linked to that of autonomy insofar as it incorporates a freedom of choice principle, together with the concept of achievable choice. This induces us to think out the question of choice in relation to a given context and its revision in relation to contextual changes.[10] This notion is also compatible with a conception of the capability approach in which choices are not individual choices isolated from external influences. Indeed, Sen (1993: 44) underlines that viewing an individual's choices without considering the choices of others would be an excessive position: "Being free to live the way one would like may be enormously helped by the choices of others, and it would be a mistake to think of achievements only in terms of active choice by oneself".

As for the capacity to aspire, it relates to the dynamic and situated nature of aspirations. Appadurai (2004) has recently put forward the notion of capacity to aspire. According to that author, the capacity to aspire provides capabilities with an ethical horizon by giving them a meaning. Conversely, exercising these capabilities reinforces the capacity to aspire and thus contributes to turning wishful thinking into thoughtful thinking. This capacity to aspire is situated in that it takes into account the social embeddedness of aspirations. It is dynamic in that aspirations, even if they may arise statically at a given point in time, refer to a process of projection into the future.

These two developments permit to formulate a view of autonomy in the case of children. On the one hand, autonomy cannot be regarded as complete. It is acquired in time, in a given social context which delimits aspirations. On the other hand, the real alternatives children have at their disposal must not be limited to choices but, in accordance with the notion of redefined functioning, must closely associate choice with freedom of choice. The question of children's autonomy is therefore conceivable in the form of a weak autonomy

---

10 Note that Lallau (2007) has given a very pertinent illustration of this notion of redefined functioning in his essay on the market gardeners' strategies in Kinshasa (Democratic Republic of the Congo).

defined on the basis of a set of limited and achievable choices for children, whose basic purpose is to teach them choice capacity and revision as their capacity to aspire develops. In that sense, liberal education would be based on *i)* a minimal amount of freedom of choice (as learning freedom of choice and its consequences is not possible without freedom of choice) and *ii)* the development of aspirations to be and to do which, in time, will ensure the desire to reappraise and revise choices. These two developments are thus closely akin to the notion of autonomy as proposed by Elster (1983) under the name of *freedom to do otherwise*. Such a conception goes beyond the usual framework of the capability approach (Teschl & Comin 2004) since it focuses on the conditions in which the decision is taken.

3. Capability to Aspire: Substantive Opportunities vs. Freedom of Processes

If, fundamentally, the capacity to evaluate and revise one's choices constitutes the core of autonomy, beyond freedom of choice itself, the capacity to aspire plays an essential part too. Indeed, how can a capacity to revise one's choices be conceived of if the aspirations do not change? The only possibility would be to consider that the previous choices were erroneous choices which it is necessary to put right in time. Another avenue which the capacity to aspire opens up consists in thinking that the previous choices were good choices after all in view of the aspirations of the moment, but that these choices are no longer in keeping with the new aspirations. Enabling the new aspirations to take shape is then at the heart of autonomy. Here we can suggest extending the *capacity to aspire* to the *capability to aspire*. While the capacity to aspire relates to the aspirations as such, the capability to aspire is connected with freedom to aspire, which entails examining the processes behind aspiration.

Sen (2004, 2005) has clearly opposed two views of justice which, when confronting them with the issue of autonomy, permit to integrate, to various degrees, the aspirations: *i)* an approach to justice in terms of substantive opportunities and *ii)* an approach in terms of freedom of processes. He illustrates this distinction through the example of a young woman called Natacha. If we suppose that Natacha is compelled, by an authority, to go out in the evening, then she is not free to choose whether she wants to or not. Even if she wants to go out in the evening – in which case the constraint tallies with her own choice – she is not free to choose. This situation presents two characteristics. On the one hand, there is a violation of the freedom of choice principle; on the other, there is a lack of opportunities as there precisely is no choice. The capability approach focuses mainly on the second aspect, *i.e.* the fact that there is no real alternative opportunity. So, first, the approach in terms of freedom of processes deals with the question of the limits of the freedom of choice process, even if the choice is made by an authority. Second, the approach in terms of substantive opportunities is concerned with the fact that the choice has been made by another and would not have been made had the authority been absent and freedom present. The capability approach therefore concentrates on the alternative choice possibilities, whereas the freedom of processes principle focuses on the choice-making procedure, including if there is no alternative to choice. Thus, as Sen (2005) points out, the capability approach is in a position to provide an argument in favour of freedom of opportunities, but cannot deal adequately with the choice process itself. In other words, the capability approach is concerned with the alternative choice possibilities, but not with the process leading to choice achievement. Thus, for example, the capability approach permits to emphasise the importance of electoral choices, but does not specifically treat the democratic choice process in itself.[11] Furthermore, Ballet et al. (2006b, 2007b) consider that, when applied to children, the capability approach limited to substantive opportunities is insufficient, especially because child-related choices are generally made by their parents or guardians. More particularly, addressing freedom of choice if this freedom concerns only choices, and not the process by which these are made, constitutes a restrictive view of the problem, which is certainly applicable if we confine ourselves to a static analysis at a certain point in time, but is problematical when the analysis turns on a dynamic question, as is precisely the case with children. Moreover, it seems inadequate to defend the application of the capability approach to children by referring only to their future – when they are adult and autonomous – while overlooking the choice-making process in childhood.

Can the process of learning autonomy really be conceived of on the basis of a wider range of choices offered to children only? The answer is clearly no

11 Walker & Unterhalter (2007: 12) give us to understand, however, that Sen defends as much the decision-making process as substantive opportunities. "*Freedom, for Sen (following educators such as John Dewey and Paolo Freire), is concerned as much with the processes of decision making as with the opportunities to achieve valued outcomes*". In support of this reading, they quote Sen's following sentence (1999: 22): "*In making us free to choose something we may or may not actually choose*". There is absolutely no doubt that Sen is as much concerned about the decision-making process as about the ensuing decisions themselves, but the interpretation of Walker & Unterhalter seems excessive insofar as what Sen only appears to say here is that freedom of choice is as important as choice itself, which is not equivalent to saying that the choice process is as important as choice itself since freedom of choice does not constitute the choice process, but is simply a conditionality for the expression of a possible process. I shall therefore consider here that substantive opportunities reflect merely freedom of choice, while the process tells us more about the way this freedom of choice is built. The various opportunities are but means to express a choice process.

since such a perspective could just as well lead to the opposite of autonomy, like for example behaviours of passive consumers who are accustomed to having a set of choices at their disposal but who do not lend real importance to their choices. As far as the question of autonomy is concerned, the process by which choices are made is even more important than choices themselves. Autonomy takes on a meaning only through the choice-guiding process, *and not* through choice. If autonomy does correspond to the capacity to evaluate choices and revise them, the opening up of choice opportunities becomes a means to express this autonomy, and not the condition of this autonomy, which, for its part, requires learning the choice procedure. As White (1973) has underlined, giving a child temporary freedom of choice does not mean he will have such freedom in the future. More precisely, opening up choice opportunities for children does not mean they will be in a position to exercise their freedom of choice in the future. From this point of view, learning decision-making takes precedence over the decision itself. This obviously does not mean that choices should not be opened up, but simply that opening up choices without learning the choice procedure first will probably prove counter-productive in the acquisition of autonomy. If the internalisation constraint has a meaning, then it is necessary to internalise freedom of choice through the choice process, and not through choices themselves.

Taking the internalisation constraint seriously entails considering that autonomy cannot be achieved by defining externally the rules to be respected under pain of penalty. This does not mean that certain rules are not desirable, or even necessary, but these turn more on the way of defining rules than on the rules themselves. Giving children a voice in their choices is not equivalent to opening up choice opportunities. Choice opportunities constitute means of expression, whereas the choice procedure and rules constitute the condition of choice. And giving children a voice so that they may develop their autonomy to the full presupposes an internalisation of rules even before choices can be expressed.

Accepting the rules and wanting to change them if they are not consistent with one's conception of the good life then entails learning the definition of rules (or else wanting to change rules is very likely to turn into 'changing rules by fair means or foul, including violence'). Developing autonomy to the full therefore requires being involved in the definition of choice rules. So, favouring children's autonomy requires that we agree to their being a party to the rules on which choices are based.

4. Concluding Remarks

The capability approach is in line with the liberal theories of justice and, as such, is confronted with the issue of respect for the principle of autonomy – a founding and unifying principle of that trend of theories. The article suggests considering, from this point of view, a minimal self-determination principle for children. Here, minimal self-determination does not relate so much to a set of opportunities which children could be offered as to the process by which choices are made. In particular, the voice of children should be given a significant place in the choices concerning them. But this voice does not turn so much on a set of opportunities as on the way of choosing amongst opportunities. In other words, even in the event of a limited set of opportunities, an important place should be given to the process which leads children to choose amongst opportunities. It is therefore necessary to provide children with learning, as well as with a voice in the learning process, in terms of choice-guiding rules. If we take the internalisation principle seriously, rules cannot be imposed from the outside or they are likely to be perceived as non-valid; they must be the subject of an argued discussion with children, who will thus come to participate in the elaboration of decision rules concerning them. In such a perspective, it is obvious that *i)* a more democratic school is essential and *ii)* the role of families is also to provide a learning framework to the democratic decision rules in connection with the choices affecting children. Again, it is not a question of opening up multiple opportunities – even if this may sometimes be desirable – but seeing to it that, amongst a set of limited and achievable choices, children may develop a capability to aspire through their involvement in the choice-making process.

References

Arnich, R., Biggeri, M., Libanora, R. & Mariani, S. (2006): Street Children in Kampala: Understanding Capabilities Deprivation through a Participatory Approach. Paper presented at the Workshop on Children Capabilities, March, Florence, Italy.

Appadurai, A. (2004): The Capability to Aspire: Culture and the Terms of Recognition. In: Rao, V. & Walton, M. (Eds.): Culture and Public Action. Standford, 59-84.

Ballet, J., Bhukuth, A. & Radja, K. (2004): Emotional Capability as Basic Capability. Application to Street Child in Mauritania. Paper presented at the 4th Conference on the Capability Approach: Enhancing Human Security, 5-7 September, University of Pavia, Italy.

Ballet, J., Bhukuth, A. & Radja K. (2006a): Travail des enfants, enfants des rues et capabilities: enjeux et questions méthodologiques. Ethique économique/Ethics and Economics, 4(1), http://ethique-economique.net.
Ballet, J., Bhukuth, A. & Radja, K. (2006b): Child labour, Human Rights and the Capabilities Approach. Paper presented at the 6th Conference on the Capability Approach, Groningen, Netherlands.
Ballet, J., Bhukuth, A. & Radja, K. (2007a): Child Labour, Street Children and the Capability Approach. Paper presented at the Workshop on Children Capabilities, March, Florence, Italia.
Ballet, J., Bhukuth, A. & Radja, K. (2007b): Fighting against Child Labour: The Capability Approach Considered. In: Rajasekhar (Ed.): Child Labour – Global perspectives. Hyderabad, India, 93-110.
Boulding, E. (1979): Children's Rights and the Wheel of Life. New Brunswick.
Biggeri, M. (2003): Children, Child Labour and the Human Capability Approach. Paper presented at the 3rd Conference on the Capability Approach: From Sustainable Development to Sustainable Freedom, Pavia, 7-9 September.
Biggeri, M. (2004): Capability Approach and Child Well-Being. Studi e discussioni, 141, Dipartimento di Scienze Economiche, Università degli Studi di Firenzi.
Biggeri, M., Libanora, R., Mariani, S. & Menchini, L. (2006): Children Conceptualizing their Capabilities: Results of a Survey Conducted during the First Children's World Congress on Child Labour. Journal of Human Development, 7(1), 59-83.
Biggeri, M., Ballet, J. & Comim, F. (Eds.) (2010, forthcoming): Children and the capability approach. Basingstoke, UK.
Brighouse, H. (2000): School Choice and Social Justice. Oxford.
Brighouse, H. (2002): What Rights (If Any) do Children Have? In: Archard, A. & Macleod, C. (Eds): The Moral and Political Status of Children. Oxford.
Di Tommasio, M.L. (2003): How to Measure Children's Well-Being Using Capability Approach? An application to Indian Data through a Multiple Indicators Multiple Causes Model. Paper presented at the 3rd Conference on the Capability Approach: From Sustainable Development to Sustainable Freedom, University of Pavia, 7-9 September.
Dworkin, R. (1989): Liberal Community. California Law Review, 77, 3, 479-504.
Flores-Crespo, P. (2007): Situating Education in the Human Capabilities Approach. In: Walker, M. & Unterhalter, E. (Eds.): 45-65.
Horna, M. (2007): Development of Emotional Capabilities as a Strategy for Human Development among Marginalized Children. Paper presented at the Workshop on Children Capabilities, March, Florence, Italy.
Jaggar, A. (1983): Feminist Political and Human Nature. Totowa, NJ.
Klasen, S. (2001): Social Exclusion, Children and Education: Implications of a Rights-Based Approach. European Societies, 3, 4, 413-445.
Kymlicka, W. (1992): Contemporary Political Philosophy: An Introduction. Oxford.
Lallau, B. (2007) : Capacités et gestion de l'incertitude: essai sur les stratégies des maraîchers de Kinshasa, RDC. Journal of Human Development, 8, 1, 153-173.
Lomasky, L. (1987): Persons, Rights and the Moral Community. Oxford.
Nussbaum, M.C. (1997): Cultivating Humanity. A Classical Defence of Reform in Liberal Education. Cambridge, MA.
Nussbaum, M.C. (2000): Women and Human Development. The Capabilities Approach. Cambridge.

Nussbaum, M.C. (2002): Education for Citizenship in an Era of Global Connection. Studies in Philosophy and Education, 21, 289-303.

Nussbaum, M.C. (2003): Political Liberalism and Respect: A Response to Linda Barclay. Nordic Journal of Philosophy, 4, 25-44.

Nussbaum, M.C. (2006): Education and Democratic Citizenship: Capabilities and Quality Education. Journal of Human Development, 7, 3, 385-398.

Rawls, J. (1980): Kantian Constructivism in Moral Theory. Journal of Philosophy, 77, 9, 515-572.

Raz J. (1986): The Morality of Freedom. Oxford.

Ryan, A. (1999): Liberal Anxieties and Liberal Education. What Education Is Really For and Why It Matters. UK.

Saito, M. (2003): Amartya Sen's Capability Approach to Education: A Critical Exploration. Journal of Philosophy of Education, 37, 1, 17-33.

Sen, A.K. (1983): Poor, Relatively Speaking. Oxford Economic Papers, 35.

Sen, A.K. (1992): Inequality Reexamined. Oxford.

Sen, A.K. (1993): Capability and Well-Being. In: Nussbaum, M.C & Sen, A.K. (Eds.): The Quality of Life: Studies in Development Economics. Oxford.

Sen, A.K. (1999): Development as Freedom. Oxford.

Sen, A.K. (2004): Elements of A Theory of Human Rights. Philosophy and Public Affairs, 32, 4, 315-356.

Sen, A.K. (2005): Human Rights and Capabilities. Journal of Human Development, 6, 2, 151-166.

Sullivan, W. (1982): Reconstructing Public Philosophy. Berkeley, California.

Swift A. (2003): How Not to Be A Hypocrite: School Choice for the Morally Perplexed. London.

Unger, R. (1984): Knowledge and Politics. New York.

Unterhalter, E. & Brighouse, H. (2003): Distribution of What? How Will We Know If We Have Achieved Education for All by 2015? Paper presented at the Third Conference on the Capability Approach: From Sustainable Development to Sustainable Freedom, September, Pavia, Italy.

Vero, J. (2002) : Mesurer la pauvreté à partir des concepts de biens premiers, de réalisations primaires et de capabilities de base. Paris, PhD dissertation, EHESS.

Waldron, J. (1989): Autonomy and Perfectionism in Raz's Morality of Freedom. Southern California Law Review, 62, 3-4, 1097-1152.

Walker, M. & Unterhalter, E. (2007): Amartya Sen's Capability Approach and Social Justice in Education. New York.

White, J. (1973): Towards a Compulsory Curriculum. London.

Jürgen Volkert & Kirsten Wüst

Early Childhood, Agency and Capability Deprivation – A Quantitative Analysis Using German Socio-Economic Panel Data

Child Poverty and the Capability Approach (CA) in Germany

The challenge of child poverty has been discussed with increasing intensity in Germany since the publication of the third official Poverty and Wealth Report by the German government in the second half of 2008, which – inter alia – focused on the state of children and families (Bundesregierung 2008). In 2007, some 2.4 million children and adolescents under the age of 18 had lived in low-income households with a disposable income of less than 60 % of the median equivalent income. This "at-risk-of-poverty rate", predefined by the European Union, reached 17.7 % in 2007 for children and adolescents in Germany.[1]

However, child poverty is not caused and reflected by low household incomes alone. The Capability Approach (CA) takes account of this multidimensionality of well-being and poverty of children. The CA conceptualizes human well-being as not only depending on financial means but gives at least the same importance to personal and social conversion factors which determine how (far) financial means can be converted into personal well-being.

Until 2008, the CA had been applied only to the well-being of adults in Germany (Arndt & Volkert 2007; Strotmann & Volkert 2008) and not specifically to the well-being of children. Meanwhile, non-representative studies have been published that explore the state of children from a CA perspective. Andresen & Fegter (2009) assess the well-being of socially disadvantaged children aged six to thirteen in Berlin and Hamburg with a reference to Martha Nussbaum's CA. Another study of Schäfer-Walkmann et al. (2009) explores the well-being of children aged nine to ten years in Baden-Wuerttemberg.

These are remarkable steps, although neither the results of these studies nor those of the former analyses for adults can in general be applied to child

1 Bundesregierung (2009: 63). As in Germany, also in the EU Member States the at-risk-of-poverty rate of children and adolescents (19 %) is higher than the respective rate for the whole population (16 %).

poverty in Germany. Firstly, because the new child studies are not representative of Germany and focus explicitly on socially disadvantaged children. Secondly, Biggeri et al. (2006) have shown that the capabilities which children will conceptualize and find to be most valuable depend on the age of the children. Therefore, representative data for specific age groups of children in Germany are necessary to assess child poverty.

Against this background the main goals of our paper are as follows: For the first time, we present a representative analysis of capability deprivation in early childhood in Germany. We focus on children three years of age and younger. We use a new database based on German Socio Economic Panel (SOEP) data that allows assessing characteristics and interdependencies of major determinants of capabilities in early childhood. Our main interest is in determinants of well-being in early childhood such as social opportunities like early childhood stimulation and social participation.

To achieve this, we will first of all sketch major CA positions in Section 2 as far as they are relevant for assessing major determinants of capabilities in early childhood. In Section 3, we introduce the database and our indicators before analyzing socio-demographic differences in the determinants of early childhood well-being in Germany. We end with a discussion of our findings and further conclusions in the last chapter.

Capabilities in early childhood: a CA-perspective

Capabilities, functionings and real freedoms are core concepts in the CA. A 'functioning' is an achievement, i.e. what a person manages to do or be. These 'beings and doings' can vary from being adequately nourished, living a long and healthy life and being well educated to rather complex achievements such as social participation, having self-respect and the ability to appear in public without , etc. The various combinations of functionings (beings and doings) that a person *can* achieve are called 'capabilities'. The *freedom* that is needed to achieve functionings is central for the CA (Sen 1992: 39-40). Poverty is defined as capability (or functioning) deprivation (Sen 1999a,b; Volkert 2006).

We concentrate on (major determinants of) capabilities to assess the well-being of children, including means to achieve like income. Although the CA vehemently argues that income is not sufficient to assess a person's well-being, an income analysis is necessary in order to take the importance of this means for a variety of important ends into account; and to reflect on deprivation of capabilities or very extensive capability sets for which adequate indicators are not available (Anand & Sen 2000; Sen 1992: 111).

Nevertheless, the same financial means (including wealth and debts) are not always associated with the same opportunities to transform financial means into commodities. Reasons for this are an unequal income and wealth distribution within a household, complementary public in-kind transfers (instead of cash transfers), assistance and transfers by family or neighborhood networks, inability to efficiently dispose of income.[2]

The CA is specifically interested in "conversion factors" that are major causes of why people succeed to differing extents in converting their means (financial means and commodities) into personal well-being. In this respect, we can distinguish "personal conversion factors" and "social conversion factors". Personal conversion factors include issues like age, sex, health, disability, education, and nationality. For instance, children of different ages have different financial and material needs in order to achieve the same degree of well-being (Robeyns 2005: 99). Whether a sufficient level of well-being can be reached also depends on the social context, which the CA terms "social conversion factors". Major social conversion factors of children consist of social opportunities; notably access to family and social networks, social participation, access to health care as well as protection from violence (domestic and other).

Although adult-specific determinants of capabilities (access to gainful employment, capital and land), elements of social protection such as access to social security, political freedoms and guarantees of transparency (absence of corruption and limited bureaucracy)[3], may not be directly relevant for children; they indirectly affect well-being in early childhood in a manifold of ways.[4] For instance, parental unemployment affects the whole family as a result of scarce material means, but can also have non-material consequences, as income poverty has been shown to be associated with the way parents educate their children and with the parent-child relationship as a whole (UNICEF 2008).

Contrary to other welfare theories, the CA has developed a concept of "agency" that allows the taking account of interdependencies that characterize the capabilities of parents and children. Agency is an assessment of "what a

---

2 Sen (1987a, 2003: 7).

3 Determinants of capabilities for adults in Germany are discussed in Arndt & Volkert (2007).

4 Biggeri et al. (2006) have presented their findings of interviews at international congresses against child labor. They let children conceptualize the kind and importance of their capabilities (valuable beings and doings). They find that children (who are older than three years) state that, for themselves, the most important capabilities are education, love and care. Andresen & Fegter (2009) also report, in their study of disadvantaged children in Berlin and Hamburg aged six to thirteen years, that love, care and education are among those things that are decisive for a good life. They also report that personal relationships, friends, the ability to express one's opinion, being taken seriously and access to a doctor are important dimensions of a good life for more than 90 % of the responding children.

person can do in line with his or her conception of the good" (Sen 1985: 206). Agency implies that people engage in action congruent with their values and goals; accepting, for instance, sacrificing personal well-being in order to foster the well-being of a child. *"Well-being"* consists of goals with respect to one's own life and of goals that are driven by sympathy or antipathy (Sen 1987: 28). Agency goes even further than this kind of well-being because it represents the realization of all goals and values a person has reasons to pursue. Agency may, in addition to its coverage of well-being achievement, also relate to "other-regarding goals" (Alkire 2009: 458) that are not driven by sympathy and antipathy alone, but also by commitments. Therefore, a child's well-being can increase his or her parents' well-being as long as common activities are motivated by the parents' sympathy. However, obligations that exceed sympathy (e.g. attending medical checks) may be among a mother's or father's agency goals even if they are not well-being goals of the mother. The opposite of agency would be to be *coerced* to follow less desirable life plans, remain passive, submissive and desirous of pleasing or alienated from one's own behavior (Alkire 2008; Sen 1985; Peter 2006).[5] This is of particular importance for early childhood development since during this period the child is more profoundly affected by the agency of his or her guardians than at any other stage in life: for example, when parents devote time, personal care and support to the well-being of their children by playing, singing or reading with them;[6] they perform activities that have been shown to be decisive for development of cognitive, language and social skills in early childhood (UNICEF 2008). Even social participation and contact for small children, that are decisive for their social competence in the long run, are normally organized by the parents.

Time, personal care and support devoted to children are not only depending on the life plans, goals, preferences and willingness of the parents and other caretakers. As the above explanation of the agency concept expresses, agency requires not only the willingness, but also the ability and opportunity to engage in action (on behalf of the children). This ability is called "agency freedom". Agency freedom may be impaired due to parents' restricted personal or social conversion factors.

Therefore, an analysis of capabilities (and capability deprivation) in early childhood has to extend to parental agency and include the ability of parents and other caretakers to engage in (sufficient) action on behalf of a child.

5 In short, we can move from agency to well-being by ignoring commitments and move further back to the standard of living (which is restricted in the CA to the personal well-being only as it is related to one's own life) by excluding other-regarding goals motivated by sympathies and antipathies. See (Sen 1987: 29); Robeyns (2005: 102).

6 This is the reason for a specific challenge regarding capability analyses in early childhood; in this age group, it is difficult to determine whether a decision in favor of certain functionings is a personal decision by the child or whether it is driven primarily by parental education and influence; Addabbo et al. (2004: 4).

Parental agency freedom can be reduced by a lack of major determinants of parental capabilities; for example, income poverty and insufficient material standards of living. Impaired personal conversion factors (e.g. resulting from disease or poor education) can also affect the inability of parents to engage in action. Moreover, a lack of parental social conversion factors, following difficulties in access to health care systems, social and family networks and/or good quality child care can make it difficult to act on behalf of one's child in an optimal way.

Further impediments of parental agency may indirectly result from restrictions of other social conversion factors, e.g. limited economic facilities because of unemployment, lack of social protection due to insufficient social security or lack of political freedoms and participation.[7]

All this indicates that well-being in early childhood directly depends on a child's capabilities and functionings that are heavily influenced by the agency and capabilities of his or her care givers. The well-being of a child will depend on capabilities such as the capability to play to have social contacts etc, However, functionings play a more important role for children as a child's functioning may be necessary for the future capability of the adult (including the role of education for later choices in an adult life) (Nussbaum 2000: 90). This calls for (also) analyzing the agency freedom of parents and other caretakers to assess the determinants of capabilities and functionings in early childhood.

In our study, we perceive three steps in the interaction between parents and children to be constitutive for early childhood development and future capabilities of small children (Figure 1).

The first step includes the conversion of parents' and care people's personal and social conversion factors into their agency freedom; the agency freedom may be restricted as a result of lack of conversion factors such as education, knowledge, information, time and/or qualified childcare.

The second step recognizes that parents' or third persons' agency freedom has to be transformed into personal and social conversion factors of the child. For our paper, we have selected early childhood stimulation and social participation as examples of a child's conversion factors. For instance, a small child benefits from early childhood stimulation by singing, reading and/or playing with the child and the child's "social participation" (visiting other families, using public playgrounds, etc.).

The last step of this interaction captures the conversion of a small child's means into his or her own capabilities and functionings via personal and social conversion factors. For Germany, the literature[8] has shown that early

7 Lack of political participation of families with children can indirectly reduce the capabilities of children if it results in a neglect of the needs of families and especially (e.g. insufficient investment in) child care etc.

8 Among others, we refer to Biedinger (2009), Klein & Biedinger (2009) and the studies that

childhood stimulation and social participation of children enhance children's development of emotional, cognitive, social and physical skills in important ways.

In our paper, we focus on the first two steps and ask how financial means and personal and social conversion factors (education, nationality, time, occupation, access to childcare etc.) of the parents will – via the parental agency freedom – affect the selected conversion factors of their children.

Figure 1: Conversion processes: from parental means to children's capabilities

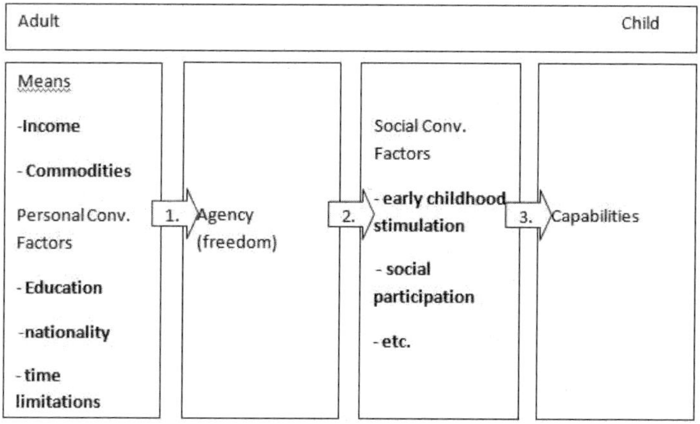

For the present study, data from the German socioeconomic panel (SOEP) was used. The SOEP is a representative panel survey of private German households that is carried out annually since 1984 with the same persons in Germany. Currently, there are 24 waves (1984-2007) of data based on single persons and whole households. Until 2003, no interviews for adolescents under 17 years of age had been carried out. There were only a few questions pertaining to children living in the households. Since 2003, mothers whose children were one year old or younger at the time of the survey, have been surveyed using a new baby questionnaire. The infant questionnaire that was filled out in 2005 and 2006 by mothers of children who were two or three years old at the time of the survey again contains questions about the health and care situation of the child as well as about activities that were carried out together with the child (e.g. reading to the child, going to the playground, etc.) as well as to the child's competences.

are mentioned there.

Our study includes all children whose mothers filled out the infant questionnaire, i.e. 479 children. Only mothers were asked to answer the questionnaires for their children. Therefore, children of single fathers were not included in the study. If the father of the child still lived in the same household he could be identified as the father. Otherwise a link to the father was missing in the data. The study used the current partner of the mother as the male guardian. All in all, the focus of the study lies on mother-child relationships.

Definition of indicators

The capability approach emphasizes that two people who have the same income at their disposal may, due to differing individual potentials and social situations, have very different capabilities. Nevertheless, income is an important factor in the determination of a child's opportunities. Financial means help to fulfill numerous wants and allow participation in cultural, social and sporting events. A household's per-capita income also influences non-quantitative factors. It has been shown that, in Germany, families' lack of material possessions is associated with family members' health and the upbringing of children, as well as with the development of intelligence, social attitudes and problem solving abilities of children living in those families (Biedinger 2009: 199). To what extent early childhood stimulation and the social participation of children aged three years and younger are influenced by income poverty shall be discussed together with other determinants of capabilities.

In 2007, the median monthly net equivalent income[9] in Germany amounted to 1,348 €.[10] Children living in households with a per-capita net equivalent income below 60 % of the median monthly net income, i.e. those who had less than 808.80 € of disposable income per month and person, were classified as income poor. Although the threshold of 60 % of the median income is methodically highly disputable[11], it is widely used by the European Union and we therefore apply it in this study.

Personal care and support foster the intellectual and emotional development of small children and significantly contribute to the child's growing

9 Including "Imputed Rent", i.e. the advantage resulting from the use of proprietary. The monthly net income in households cannot be compared with each other without further ado. To analyze a per-capita income we calculated an equivalent income using the modified OECD scale. The first adult in a household gets a weight of 1, further adults and adolescents above 14 years old a weight of 0.5 and children under 14 years a weight of 0.3. The net income of the household is divided by the sum of the weights of all persons living in the household.

10 See SOEP-Monitor 1984-2007.

11 See e.g. Volkert (2005, 2006).

sense of agency. Along with adequate nutrition, intimate loving one-to-one interaction has been shown to be crucial for the development of the child's emotional, physical and cognitive skills. Such "serve and return" interactions are best integrated in an ongoing relationship between a child and an adult who individually responds to the child's personal needs. Interactions of this kind are prerequisites for the child's mastery of increasingly complex skills. Moreover, it is the adult response, i.e. the encouragement in these intimate relations that have been shown to foster confidence and competence and result in the child's sense of "agency" (UNICEF 2008: 5-7). Income-poor parents read, talk and play less with their children. According to international and recent German studies, these differences in home activities have a significant effect on the developmental differences among children (Bradley et al. 2001; Klein & Biedinger 2009). We try to capture at least a part of these decisive interactions between children and parents with the information in our data set. The mothers of two- to three year-old children were asked how often they or other care givers had done activities like reading to the child, singing, etc. in the last 14 days before the interview. The result was ranked from "1: daily", "2: several times a week", "3: at least once a week" up to "4: not at all". To generate the indicator "early childhood stimulation", the scores of all four variables "reading to children", "singing", "looking at picture books" and "drawing" were added. A value of 11 points was defined as the cut-off point between "a lot of time is spent on an early childhood stimulation" and "not much time is spent on early childhood stimulation".[12]

Neuroscience has begun to confirm that stable, secure and stimulating relationships with family members and caregivers are important not only for the development of a child's stress management system, but also for almost all other aspects of a child's development (UNICEF 2008: 5-6). In support of these findings, Huster (2003) has shown that regular family activities stimulate a child's well-being. The database that we use also allows the assessment of the issue of "social contact" by including family and group activities like "going for a walk", "going to the playground" and "visits at other families' houses". Responses were based on activities performed during the last 14 days prior to the interview. They could also take on the above-mentioned scores from one to four and were added to give a variable "sum of social participation". A value of nine points was defined as the cut-off value between "a lot of time is spent on social participation" and "not much time is spent on social participation".[13] If not much time is spent on social participation the child is assumed to be deprived with respect to social participation.

12 Choosing this cut-off point, the answers must at least contain the value "4 - not at all" for one activity if for another activity the answer is "1 - daily".

13 For this cut-off point, the answers to both other activities must be "4 - not at all" if for another activity the answer had been "1 - daily".

It is of particular interest which parental conversion factors lead to deprivation in the child's social conversion factors. For this aim, several group variables were formed. The variable "region" designates in its values "East" (new German federal states) and "West" (old German federal states) for the regions in which a child can live. The distinction between East and West Germany in analyzing the state of small children and their caregivers in Germany is relevant due to differences that remain evident after German re-unification: On the one hand, East Germany remains characterized by lower levels of economic activity and standard of living, notably by lower per capita income, and much higher unemployment. On the other hand, dating from its socialist era, East Germany has had and continues to have a remarkably better child care infrastructure than does West Germany.[14] Furthermore, we distinguish between household types in which a child lives, i.e. with a single mother[15] with one child, a single mother with two or with three or more children, a couple with one child, a couple with two or with three or more children or a multi-generational household. The mother and her partner who might live in the same household are classified according to their educational degrees (without degree, lowest school track (nine years of school (German Hauptschule)), middle school track (ten years of school (German Mittlere Reife)) university track (at least twelve years of school), as well as foreign degree). Also, the mother and her partner were classified according to their respective vocations (self-employed, public officer, employee, blue-collar worker, in vocational training, unemployed and (perhaps voluntarily) not working). Additionally, the nationality of the mother and the partner ("German" or "non-German") was used in the analysis. Also, the child care situation, i.e. the number of hours per week that a child was not cared for by his or her mother, can have an influence on parental agency and the determinants of children's capabilities.[16]

14 In almost every fourth district in West Germany child care coverage is even lower than 5 %. In Denmark child care coverage of the same age group reaches 60 %, together with a much higher employment rate of mothers; UNICEF (2008: 5).

15 Only mothers answered the questionnaires for their children.

16 Because of the random effect groups with a size below 10 are omitted from the report. An exception is made for single households with 3 or more children (8 households) to be able to compare this group to the couples with three or more children.

Table 1: Overview of the used determinants and indicators

Determinants	
Region	East (new German federal states), west (old German federal states)
Household type	Single (with one child , with two children, with three or more children), couple (with one child , with two children, with three or more children)
Vocational position of the mother, vocational position of the mother's partner	Self-employed, public officer, employee, blue-collar worker, unemployed, in vocational training, (voluntarily) not working
Educational degree of the mother, educational degree of the mother's partner	Low (Hauptschule), medium (Mittlere Reife), high (Abitur), other degree, without degree
Nationality of the mother, nationality of the mother's partner	German, non-German
Non-parental child care	In hours
Indicators	
Income poverty	Equivalence-weighted per-capita income in the household figures below 60% of the median of the per-capita net income (incl. imputed rent) of the population.
Deprivation in early childhood encouragement	The sum of the activities "singing", „reading to children", „looking at picture-books together" and „drawing" in the last 14 days before the interview had a value of 11 or more (per activity: "1 – every day" up to "4 – not at all")
Deprivation in social participation	The sum of the activities "going for a walk", "going to the playground" and "visiting other families in the last 14 days before the interview had a value of 9 or more (per activity: "1 - every day" up to "4 - not at all")

Statistical methods

We initially report descriptive statistics including rates, means and medians. For the inductive test on differences between the considered groups, chi-square tests were carried out. We chose a type one error rate $\alpha=0.05$. A p-value $p<0.05$ is regarded as significant. In the reported tables we also distinguish whether a result is significant at a significance level of 0.05 (*) or would be significant at a level of 0.01 (**). We report two-tailed p-values throughout the paper. As we carry out an exploratory analysis, no adjustment for the multiple test situation is made.

We start with a univariate analysis of the non-financial poverty indicators dependent on the groups defined by educational achievement, occupation and nationality of the mother and her partner, as well as household type and region in which the household members live. Additionally, a multivariate analysis clarifies the question to what extent the non-financial indicators of deprivation in early childhood are induced by income poverty and to what extent they result from different factors. We calculate logistic regressions. For this purpose the categorical group variables are split up into dummy variables. As reference values we chose "couple with 1 child" for the household type, "Mittlere Reife" for the educational degree, "West-Germany" for the region and "German" for the nationality.

Due to the fact that, for single households, data for the partner is missing (missing values), a regression analysis that takes the household type as well as the partner variables into account cannot be carried out. Thus, we primarily carry out a logistic regression containing household type and the mother's attributes as independent variables. Additionally, we report the variables that were included in a regression model on the mother's and her partner's attributes excluding the household type.

The column exp(B) in Table 3 shows the change of the odds $P(Y=1)/(P(Y=0)$, i.e. the risk that a child belonging to the reported group is experiencing a deprivation with respect to the analyzed indicator which is measured as an elevation or reduction, in comparison to the reference value of the group. Values of the odds below one indicate a lower risk of being deprived and values above one raise an elevated risk.[17] For the number of hours that a child was not cared for by the mother, we calculate a linear regression.

17 To give an example: the value of 17.7 for mothers without an exam (school degree) indicates that the risk of their children to suffer from deprivation in early childhood stimulation is 17.7 times higher than for children of mothers with "Mittlere Reife" as highest school degree.

Results

Early childhood stimulation

Table 2 compares the groups with respect to the indicators for "early childhood stimulation" and "social participation".

In total, 8.7 % of the children were deprived with respect to early childhood stimulation. The univariate analysis indicates that the parents' nationalities play a remarkable role in this respect. For children of non-German women deprivations were found in 19.1 % of cases compared to 7.3 % for German women. Similarly, deprivations were found in 20.5 % of cases in which the children's mothers had non-German partners vs. 6.5 % for those whose mothers had German partners. It is interesting that the rate of children for whom a deprivation in "early childhood stimulation" can be found is significantly higher in relatively rich Western Germany (10.4 %) compared to poorer East Germany (2.8 %). This may be a sign of the positive impacts of the above-mentioned better East German child care infrastructure in comparison with the low West German child care coverage. Differentiating with respect to the mother's level of education, we find that the following percentages of children experience deprivation of early childhood simulation: 20.8 % of mothers with the lowest school track, 20.7 % of those whose mothers attended school in a country other than Germany and 42.9 % of those whose mothers did not complete school are deprived with respect to early childhood stimulation.

*Table 2: Percentages of children that had a score of 11 or more points for early childhood stimulation and respectively a score of 9 or more points for social participation during the last 14 days prior to the interrogation (** significant at a level of 0.01, * significant at a level of 0.05) – in parentheses: median of the score*

	Early childhood stimulation		Social participation	
Population groups				
Total	8.7%		16.5%	
Region	(p=0.014)*		(p=0.477)	
East	2.8%	(6)	15.8%	(7)
West	10.4%	(7)	18.7%	(7)
Household type	(p=0.319)		(p=0.171)	
Single with one child	17.6%	(8)	11.8%	(5)
Single with two or more	9.7%	(7)	3.3%	(6.5)

children				(6)
hereof: with 2 children	11.5%	(7)	3.8%	(7)
with 3 or more children	0%	(6)	0%	
Couple with one child	4.9%	(6)	14.9%	(7)
Couple with two or more	8.9%	(7)	19.1%	(7)
children			16.8%	(7)
Thereof: with 2 children	7.7%	(6)	23.7%	(7)
with 3 or more children	11.5%	(7)	14.3%	(6)
Multi-generational household	25%	(8.5)		
Vocational position of the mother	(p=0.011)*		(p=0.644)	
Selfemployed	9.1%	(6)	22.7%	(7)
Public officer	4.8%	(6)	23.8%	(6)
Employee	2.3%	(6)	14.6%	(7)
Blue-collar worker	22.6%	(8)	25.8%	(7)
Unemployed	15.2%	(7.5)	17.8%	(7)
In vocational training	11.1%	(5)	11.1%	(7)
(Voluntarily) not working	9.0%	(7)	15.6%	(7)
Vocational position of the mother's partner	(p<0.001)		(p=0.751)	
Selfemployed	7.0	(6)	25.6%	(7)
Public officer	0%	(5.5)	17.4%	(6)
Employee	2.8%	(6)	15.5%	(7)
Blue-collar worker	13.4%	(7)	17.5%	(7)
Unemployed	14.7%	(7.5)	20.6%	(6)
Educational degree of the mother	(p<0.001)**		(p=0.754)	
Low (Hauptschule)	20.8%	(8)	22.2%	(7)
Medium (Mittlere Reife)	4.6%	(6)	15.0%	(7)
High (Abitur)	3.4%	(6)	17.1%	(7)
Other degree	20.7%	(7)	17.9%	(7)
Without degree	42.9%	(10)	14.3%	(6)
Educational degree of the mother's partner	(p=0.016)*		(p=0.796)	
Low (Hauptschule)	14.3%	(7)	17.9%	(7)
Medium (Mittlere Reife)	3.8%	(6)	15.0%	(7)
High (Abitur)	5.5%	(6)	18.8%	(7)
Other degree	17.9%	(8)	25.0%	(7)
Without degree	-	-	-	-

Nationality of the mother	(p=0.006)**		(p=0.725)	
German	7.3%	(6)	16.9%	(7)
Non-German	19.1%	(8)	14.9%	(6)
Nationality of the mother's partner	(p=0.002)**		(p=0.949)	
German	6.5%	(6)	17.5%	(7)
Non-German	20.5%	(8)	17.9%	(6)
Equivalent income <60% of the median	(p=0.049)*		(p=0.941)	
yes	14.7%	(8)	15.7%	(6)
No	7.4%	(6)	16.1%	(7)
Non-parental child care	(p=0.169)		(p=0.580)	
0-20h	12.0%	(7)	19.1%	(7)
20-40h	6.2%	(7)	12.6%	(7)
40-60h	5.9%	(6)	15.3%	(7)
60-100h	5.4%	(6)	16.2%	(7)
>100h	0%	(7)	9.1%	(7)

The logistic regression of the early childhood stimulation (Table 3) on the attributes of the mother shows significant effects of the degree of education and the professional occupation of the mother. For children of mothers without a degree (factor 17.7), with a foreign degree (factor 4.4) or with the lowest school degree (factor 4.6) the risk of deprivation in early childhood encouragement is drastically higher.[18] For children of blue-collar working mothers the child's risk of deprivation in singing, reading etc. is seven times higher than for children whose mothers are employees. The analyzed conversion factors of the mother's education and employment affect her agency and with it the "early childhood stimulation" of her children. In the additional regression including the partners' variables the risk of deprivation in early childhood stimulation was five times higher for children of mothers with non-German partners. Furthermore, the risk is even higher for self-employed and unemployed mothers. According to the SOEP monitor the median of the monthly equivalent income (including imputed rent) amounted to be 1348 €. In total, 16.2 %[19] of the children included in our study are income poor. How-

18 This is in line with other empirical findings for the age group of three to four-year old children in Germany. Biedinger (2009) has shown that income poverty only has a considerable impact on a child's cognitive and language skills as long as this is not controlled for education and parental activities with the child at home (playing, reading books etc.). Well-educated parents tend to activate their children more than less educated parents.

19 According to the third official German Poverty and Wealth report (Bundesregierung 2008)

ever, the equivalent income does not have a significant effect on deprivation in early childhood stimulation and is therefore not included as an explanatory variable in the model. Hence, the difference between income-poor and non-income poor households is explained by other conversion factors.

Table 3: Logistic regression: Significant explanatory variables for a deprivation in early childhood stimulation

Regression on:	Variables included in the model	p-value	Exp(B)
Educational degree of the mother, vocation of the mother, household type, region, nationality of the mother, OECD2-weighted net income, external child care in h	Mother without exam Mother has lowest secondary school track Mother has a foreign degree Mother is blue-collar worker	0.001 <0.001 0.027 0.027	17.7 6.0 4.4 7.1
Above Without: Vocation of the mother Additionally: Educational degree of the partner, vocational position of the partner, nationality of the partner	Nationality of the partner Mother has lowest secondary school track Mother is self-employed Mother is blue-collar worker Mother is unemployed	0.037 0.016 0.014 0.004 0.030	5.0 4.4 15.9 17.5 10.3

Social participation

Table 2 shows that 16.5 % of the children are deprived with respect to social participation. In the univariate analysis it can be observed that the percentage of children lacking social participation is higher in the old federal states (18.7 %) than in the new ones (15.8 %). There was nearly no difference between poor households (15.7 %) and non -poor households (16.1 %). It is remarkable that children of single mothers have a higher social participation with respect to the chosen indicators than children of couples. For single

18 % of the total population are – on the basis of SOEP data – income poor, i.e. the net income at their disposal lies below 60 % of the median of the net equivalent income. According to a study by UNICEF (UNICEF Report No. 6, 2005: 5) who use 50 % of the median of the equivalent income to define income poverty, 10.2 % of the German children are income poor. This rate has increased by 2.7 % in the 1990s.

mothers with one child, the percentage of deprived children amounted to 11.8 %; for single mothers with two or more children only 3.3 % in comparison to 14.9 % for couples with one child and 19.1 % for couples with two or more children. However, no significant differences were found between any of the groups. Furthermore, in a logistic regression on the indicator "social participation" (nine or more points) no significant explanatory variables were found.

Discussion and conclusions

Children perceive their parents' love, personal care and support as major capabilities. This has been shown in international studies (e.g. Biggeri 2006) as well as in a regional, non-representative German study on socially disadvantaged children by Andresen and Fegter (2009: 23-24). Parental time as a major pre-condition and driver of early childhood development becomes manifest in several dimensions. It is also a main component of the analyzed determinants of children's capabilities such as early childhood stimulation and social participation.

Looking at the univariate results, the risk of a child being deprived in early childhood stimulation is twice as high for children of single mothers. Single mothers might not have the time to do activities such as reading and drawing with their children. This brings up the relevance of time for capability and poverty analyses of early childhood. Both should take into account that households and parents have not only an income budget constraint, but also a time budget constraint.

Income poverty is often associated with deprivation in early childhood. It has been shown that single parent households and households with three or more children have the lowest income position with 77 % and 87 % of the mean net equivalent income.[20]

Our analyses show, however, that the mother's educational level and vocation, rather than household income, is the primary factor in inducing deprivation in early childhood stimulation. The risk that a child will be deprived with respect to early childhood stimulation is higher if his or her mother is poorly educated. This confirms the CA thesis that focusing on household income may often not be adequate to assess the well-being of family members. Further political implications include that, instead of relying on ineffective income redistribution, society and state may have to assist low educated mothers (and fathers) in ensuring sufficient early childhood stimulation by providing highly competent and stimulating childcare infrastructures.

20 18. Cp. Bundesregierung (2008: 90) based on the harmonized EC survey EU-SILC.

Our study shows also no difference in social contact for children under three who live in income poor households in comparison to children from non-poor households. This may be explained by the creation of social nets that seem to be especially advanced by people with a lower income.

However, our results are at odds with the findings of Holz et al. (2005) and it is worthwhile to discuss the possible reasons for these differences in more detail. Holz et al. found that children in income poor households in Germany invite friends over and celebrate birthdays less frequently while we find no difference in social contact of children living in poor households.

A reason for the differences could be that Holz et al. (2005) focus on older children than we do. Social contacts of children under the age of three are often free of charge (visiting and playing on playgrounds, in the yard and with other families). In contrast, social contact for older children (birthday parties, going to the movies and other forms of entertainment) are time consuming *and* costly. One reason for the differences of both studies could be a trade-off between income and time budget constraints, which may change with the age of the children and deserves more attention.

Another reason could be that the capability to invite friends without being ashamed may vary not only with living conditions but also with age. This could mean that small children under three years of age in poor households may not comprehend the social differences between themselves and their friends and are thus not ashamed to play with wealthier friends at home. The older the children get, the more sensitive they may become to these social differences, which might explain why, contrary to small children, older children do not invite friends into their poor households. This would be in line with the findings of Andresen and Fegter (2009: 58), who conclude that socially disadvantaged children aged six to thirteen are easily ashamed – also by the stigmatization that society attaches to families of their social background which is often at odds with how they view their parents. This implies that a capability analysis of child poverty would have to assess the causes as well as a potential age dependency of children's capabilities to appear in public without shame.

For the selected factors we do find that, in multivariate analysis, the effects of income are insignificant and differences in parental agency are explained by parental conversion factors other than income.

Although income has no significant impact on the results of our study, it cannot be concluded that income is unimportant for the well-being of children in general. This is the case because other factors for early childhood development that we have not yet analyzed may depend on household income. Moreover, the effects of income may be more important when children grow older.

As in the SOEP data set only mothers were asked to answer the questionnaires for their children, our analysis focuses on the mother-child relationship.

The father or partner of the mother was addressed and analyzed in the study if he lived in the same household. Children of single fathers could not be reached by the study. Here, there is room for further research. However, as the percentage of single fathers is with 12.3 % small[21] and our study includes 78 single mothers the estimated number of fathers missing in the study is with 11 fathers relatively small.

Our paper has focused on the transformation of parents' conversion factors and agency freedom – into their children's conversion factors. However, we did not explicitly assess parental agency as the link between parents' and children's conversion factors. Further research might additionally focus on parental agency and its transformation into a child's personal conversion factors, capabilities, and functionings. This step may be substantially affected by the quality of the relationship between parent and child and by the amount of time that they (can) spend together. The third step, i.e. the conversion of a child's means into capabilities and functionings (via conversion factors) may also deserve additional attention. A number of social science studies may provide a basis for specific capability analyses and could be helpful in an analysis from a capability perspective in Germany.

To sum up: this first capability approach assessment of early childhood, based on representative data, has re-emphasized the importance of education for parental agency and children's capabilities. This is in line with a large number of existing studies that were not carried out from a capability perspective. However, the factors that did not show significant impacts on early childhood capabilities in our study are perhaps even more remarkable; the skepticism of the capability approach with respect to the (exclusive) role of income as a means to freedom has been confirmed by the finding that income affected neither early childhood stimulation (where other variables were significant) nor social contact. For social contact, no significant variables could be identified, which calls for further capability analyses to assess the major determinants of this important field.

References

Addabbo, T., di Tomaso, M.L. & Facchinetti, G. (2004): To what extent fuzzy set theory and structural equation modeling can measure functionings? An application to child well-being. In: University of Centre for Household, Income, Labour and Demographic Economics, 30.

21 According to Statistisches Bundesamt (2010) the percentage of single fathers in 2004 with children under 18 years is 12.3 %. For fathers with children under 3 years old it may even be smaller.

Alkire, S. (2008): Concepts and Measures of Agency. OPHI Oxford Poverty and Human Development Institute Working Paper 9.

Alkire, S. (2009): Concepts and Measures of Agency. In: Basu, K.. & Kanbur, R. (2009): Arguments for a better World. Essays in Honor of Amartya Sen. Vol. I: Ethics, Welfare, and Measurement, Oxford, 455-474.

Anand, S. & Sen, A. (2000): The Income Component of the Human Development Index. Journal of Human Development. 1, 1, 83-106.

Andresen, S. & Fegter, S. (2009): Spielräume sozial benachteiligter Kinder. Bepanthen-Kinderarmutsstudie: eine ethnographische Studie zur Kinderarmut in Hamburg und Berlin – vorläufiger Bericht, Bielefeld.

Arndt, C. & Volkert, J. (2007): A Capability Approach for German Poverty and Wealth Reports: Conceptual issues and first empirical results. IAW-Discussion Paper, 27, Institute for Applied Economic Research, Tübingen.

Biedinger, N. (2009): Kinderarmut in Deutschland: der Einfluss von relativer Einkommensarmut auf die kognitive, sprachliche und behavioristische Entwicklung von 3-4jährigen Kindern. Zeitschrift für Soziologie der Erziehung und Sozialisation, 29, 2, 197-214.

Biggeri, M., Libanora, R., Mariani, S. & Menchini, L. (2006): Children Conceptualizing Their Capabilities: Results of the Survey During the First Children's World Congress on Labour. Journal of Human Development, 7, 1, 59-83.

Bradley, R.H., Corwyn, R.F., McAdoo, H.P. & García Coll, C. (2001): The home environments of children in the United States. Part I: variations by age, ethnicity, and poverty status. In: child development, 72, 6, 1844-1867.

Bundesregierung (2008): 3. Armuts- und Reichtumsbericht der Bundesregierung, Bonn.

Bundesregierung (2009): Familienreport 2009. Leistungen, Wirkungen. Trends. Hrsg. vom Bundesministerium für Familien, Senioren, Frauen und Jugend, Berlin.

Holz, G., Richter, A., Wüstendörfer, W. & Giering, D. (2005): Zukunftschancen für Kinder. Wirkungen von Armut bis zum Ende der Grundschulzeit, Zusammenfassung des 3. Endberichts der AWO-ISS-Studie, Frankfurt a.M.

Huster, E.-U. (2003): Kinderarmut in Deutschland. Zentrale Ergebnisse der AWO/ISS-Studie "Gute Kindheit – schlechte Kindheit?". Sozialer Fortschritt, 1, 10-17.

Klein, O. & Biedinger, N. (2009): Determinanten elterlicher Aktivitäten mit Vorschulkindern. Der Einfluss von Bildungsaspirationen und kulturellem Kapital. Mannheimer Zentrum für Europäische Sozialforschung, Working Paper 121, Mannheim.

Nussbaum, M.C. (2000): Women and Human Development. The Capability Approach, Cambridge.

Peter, F. (2006): Gender and the Foundations of Social Choice. In: Agarwal, B., Humphries, J., & Robeyns, I. (Eds.): Capabilities, Freedom, and Equality. Amartya Sens Work from a Gender Perspective. Oxford, 17-38.

Robeyns, I. (2005): The Capability Approach: A Theoretical Survey. Journal of Human Development 6, 1, 93-114.

Schäfer-Walkmann, S., Störk-Biber, C., Rieger, G. & Ross, P.-S. (2009): Arme Kinder und ihre Familien in Baden-Württemberg. Eine sozialarbeitswissenschaftliche Studie. Hrsg. vom Caritasverband der Diözese Rottenburg-Stuttgart e.V., Stuttgart u.a.

Sen, A. (1985): Well-Being, Agency, and Freedom. Journal of Philosophy 82, 169-221.

Sen, A. (1987): The Standard of Living. Cambridge.

Sen, A. (1992): Inequality Reexamined. Oxford, New York.

Sen, A. (1999a): Development as Freedom. Oxford.

Sen, A. (1999b): Commodities and Capabilities. New Delhi, Oxford.

SOEP-Monitor (1984-2007): Zeitreihen zur Entwicklung ausgewählter Indikatoren.

Statistisches Bundesamt (2010): Leben und Arbeiten in Deutschland. Tabellenband zum Sonderheft 1 - Ergebnisse d. Mikrozensus 1996-2004.

Strotmann, H. & Volkert, J. (2008): Lack of instrumental freedoms: Social exclusion from and unfavourable inclusion into the labour market – an empirical analysis for Germany. Paper presented at the 8th Human Development and Capability Association Conference, New Delhi.

UNICEF (2005): Child poverty in rich countries. Unicef Innocenti Research Center, Report Card 6, Florence, Italy.

UNICEF (2008): The child care transition. A league table of early childhood education and care in economically advanced countries. UNICEF Innocenti Research Center, Report card 8, Florence, Italy.

Volkert, J. (2005): Armut als Mangel an Verwirklichungschancen: ein „Adäquater Methoden-Ansatz“ (AM-Ansatz). In: Volkert, J.: Armut und Reichtum an Verwirklichungschancen. Amartya Sens Capability-Konzept als Basis der deutschen Armuts- und Reichtumsberichterstattung, Wiesbaden, 73-94.

Volkert, J. (2006): E.U. Poverty Assessment – a Capability Perspective. Journal of Human Development, 7, 3, Special Issue: Selected Papers from the 5th International Conference on the Capability Approach: 'Knowledge and Public Action' at UNESCO, Paris, September 2005, Fall 2006, 359-383.

Michael Watts

Symbolic Capital and the Capability Gap

Introduction

The notion of a capability gap – the focus of this edited volume – implies that some individuals have more freedoms to choose and lead lives they value and have reason to value than others. Whilst this is inevitably the case, care must be taken to avoid looking for gaps that do not necessarily exist from a capability perspective. This chapter sets out to address two particular and interrelated matters concerning the analysis of human well-being: the risk of confusing freedoms and resources; and, following on from this, the danger of dogmatically attributing adaptive preferences to those who possess fewer resources. Adaptive preferences typically operate as subtle and insidious limitations on the individual's freedom to choose and lead what Nussbaum describes as a truly human life (Nussbaum 2000): they are generated by the internalisation of external constraints and so signal the individual's resignation to reduced circumstances. They can, therefore, significantly widen the capability gap. However, as argued in this chapter, it is important to distinguish between choices that are restricted by the adaptation of preferences and those that enhance capability.

The foregrounding of human diversity in the capability approach requires the capability analyst to account for different interpretations of the good life whilst taking care to avoid valorising adaptive preferences. The capability approach de-emphasises the importance of goods in well-being assessments but their possession can significantly influence the individual's freedom to achieve and aspire to particular signifiers of capability. This problem is addressed here through the example of higher education in the UK. Higher education can enhance individual well-being but opportunities to benefit from it are unequally distributed across social strata. It can, therefore, be argued that the lack of freedom to participate in higher education diminish individual capabilities. However, reduced opportunities to participate in higher education do not equate with reduced opportunities to achieve different functionings referencing the same capability.

Adaptive preferences are a central justification and ongoing problem for capability assessments of well-being. Education has a special place in the capability approach not only for its potential to enhance other capabilities but also because it can enable the individual to challenge her non-reflective acquiescence in the unjust circumstances of her life. Governmental policies seeking to address social inequalities typically aim to increase participation in education but education and educational contexts can generate adaptations. Moreover, there is often a tendency to prioritise participation in certain forms of education as the end of well-being rather than as a means to that end. This failure to acknowledge the significance of what Nussbaum refers to as multiple realizability risks overwriting the human diversity that is central to the ethic of the capability approach; and the subsequent attribution of adaptations to young people's lives can widen rather than close the capability gap. This is not to devalue the importance of education but to suggest that great care needs to be taken when conducting capability assessments of education and educational opportunities.

The measurement of freedoms must be sensitive to these different specifications of capabilities as the wrong metric can distort the capability gap. Pierre Bourdieu's sociology of education is used here to address this concern and the potential for his work to enhance capability analyses is considered. Bourdieu's work is typically used to highlight the reproduction of social inequalities in and through education. He argues that educational resources have a socially constructed value so that qualifications, for example, are worth what the individual is worth. His work also offers an insight into the relationship between goods and preference formation and deformation. Holding structure and agency in tension, his concept of the habitus incorporates the internalisation of external circumstances and the externalisation of the internal world to account for the delimitation of choices that tend to make the individual complicit in the reproduction of social injustices that may inhibit her well-being. These policies and processes can be seen in the attempts to widen participation in higher education in the UK which serve to illustrate the arguments here. However, research on higher education is often used to show how opportunities for capability expansion are constrained and therefore illustrate the widening of the capability gap. Here, Bourdieu's sociology is used to close that gap through his concept of symbolic capital – that is, the social sanction of particular goods and resources. Little attention has been paid to symbolic capital in educational research but it can be deployed to challenge the hierarchical frameworks that valorise the acquisition of the cultural capital which is the main currency in educational fields. As such, it enables a focus on what the individual values and has reason to value (that is, her functionings). This offers a means of closing the capability gap by providing a framework that sees education as a means to an end rather than the end itself whilst still taking into account the social structures that shape identities, values and adaptations.

This chapter offers an overview of higher education in the UK and then summarises the problem of adaptive preferences and multiple realizability before considering Bourdieu's notion of habituation and the potential for his concept of symbolic capital to inform capability analyses.

Higher education and capability

Education can significantly enhance well-being by opening up opportunities to choose and lead the good life (Saito 2003; Walker & Unterhalter 2007). It can also enable people to reflect upon the unjust circumstances of their lives and thereby avoid the adaptive preference problem: they may not be able to close the capability gap, but they need not accept it. Nussbaum explains how education can empower people to form a conception of the good life and to engage in critical reflection about the planning of their lives (Nussbaum 2000: 97). It is, therefore, hardly surprising that an 'adequate education, including, but by no means limited to, literacy and basic mathematical and scientific training' is found on her list of central human functional capabilities (*inter alia*, Nussbaum 2000: 78-79). As 'capabilities do not develop in isolation but relationally' (Walker 2006: 37) education can also enhance the other capabilities she argues are needed to enable the truly human life. Sen too, constantly references education as a fundamental capability that can enhance individual freedoms.

Within the broader capability frameworks proposed by Sen and Nussbaum, the particular forms of education to be advanced in order to increase well-being should be determined within local contexts; and it could therefore be argued that widening participation policies in the UK frame the need to consider higher education as the baseline against which freedoms and adaptations should be assessed. Moreover, Nussbaum has proposed that higher education is necessary to human flourishing (Nussbaum 2002) and even Sen, who is typically more concerned with basic capabilities, has highlighted its contribution to the development of intellectual thought in India (Sen 2005). Sen tends to view education as instrumental – it is a means to other, usually economic, ends (Sen 1999) – and several authors have addressed the potential for higher education to tackle economic impoverishment (Tilak 2002; Comin 2007; Deprez & Butler 2007; Flores-Crespo 2007) and so also lead to the development of other capabilities such as community participation. Others are less concerned with these economic benefits and focus on the role of higher education in promoting other capabilities: Walker, for example, addresses its potential to enhance Nussbaum's central human functional capabilities of practical reason and affiliation (Walker 2006, 2007).

The UK's higher education sector has undergone considerable expansion in the last two decades and many of the formal barriers to participation have been dismantled. The sector remains socially stratified and students from middle class backgrounds and those attending socially and academically selective schools are far more likely to obtain the high academic qualifications that are still required for entry to the most academically elite institutions (Ball 2003; Power et al. 2003; Reay et al. 2005). However, a diverse society requires a diverse higher education sector and a wider range of entry level qualifications are now accepted across the sector as a whole and there is APEL (the accreditation of prior and experiential learning) for those with no or few formal qualifications. Although higher education is no longer free, it remains heavily subsidised and funds are available to those in most need of them. Furthermore, full time study is no longer the norm and there are opportunities (albeit opportunities that are often subject to other limitations) for part time study and distance learning for those unable or unwilling to follow traditional full time residential programmes. In short, there are now significantly greater formal opportunities for more people from more diverse backgrounds to obtain a university degree; and these contexts of policy and practice should serve to reduce the capability gap.

Given the benefits associated with higher education, reduced opportunities for participation can contribute to the widening of the capability gap; and even though the widening participation agenda in the UK means that there are more opportunities for more people with more diverse learning experiences to engage with it, individual freedoms to progress to and through higher education remain unequal. The educational capabilities of the adult are constrained by those of the child (Biggeri 2007) and early learning experiences – both formal and informal – delimit future learning opportunities. Educational resources remain unequally distributed and despite the often valiant efforts of teachers, many schools and colleges remain under-resourced to meet the learning needs of their pupils and students (and beyond the UK, particularly in the Global South, the lack of resources places far more severe constraints upon learning opportunities).

The capability approach de-emphasises the significance of resources in well-being assessments but they nonetheless remain important, particularly inasmuch as they shape perceptions of the good life. Educational opportunities are framed by more than just the availability of educational resources: the UK government has pumped significant financial resources into the education sectors (and, in the context of the current economic crisis, has promised to safeguard spending on primary and secondary schooling whilst threatening severe cuts to other public sector services) but many young people, particularly those from lower socio-economic backgrounds, continue to show no interest in higher education. For many, it is still seen as a typically middle class activity that is not part of their lives – of their identities, if you like – and that holds no benefit for them (Archer et al. 2003). For some, their earlier experiences may have ground down and limited such educational aspirations (Nussbaum 2002; Walker 2006, 2007) but others may not have aspired that far in the first place (Watts 2006, 2009a; Watts & Bridges 2006; Hart 2007; Burchardt 2009). This presents considerable analytic problems when determining the extent to which their freedoms and adaptations contribute to the widening of the capability gap.

Adaptive preferences

The drive to widen participation in the UK means that there are now significantly greater opportunities for individuals to obtain a higher education but the sector remains split along class-based fault lines and the government argues that low aspirations continue to prevent more young people from social groups previously under-represented in higher education from enjoying its benefits (DfES 2003, 2006). Such adaptations can make individuals 'implicit accomplices to injustices that are reified through traditions, norms and social rules' (Watts 2007: 25) and so leave the capability gap wide open. It cannot be assumed that education automatically promotes valued doings and beings (Flores-Crespo 2007: 50) as individuals may learn to accept and value certain doings and beings (which cannot properly be termed functionings as they are not constitutive of their good living) even though they have a negative impact upon their well-being (Nussbaum 2000; Deneulin 2006; Galeotti 2007; Unterhalter & Walker 2007). Nussbaum explains that

> "just as people can be taught not to want or miss the things their culture has taught them they should not or could not have, so too they can be taught not to value certain functionings as constituents of their good living" (Nussbaum 1988: 175).

The capability approach is concerned with adaptation as self-abnegation – that is, the individual's failure to recognise a better life for herself – arising from habituation to impoverishment. It seeks to address the adaptive preference problem by regarding well-being as the freedom to choose and lead the good life; and this focus on freedom requires consideration of the counterfactual nature of capabilities. Counterfactuality allows the capability analyst to take into account what the case might have been if the circumstances had been different. In this context of higher education, for example, it offers the analyst the opportunity to consider what a working class individual might value and what she might do if she were not subject to class-bound social disciplines or if she had access to greater educational resources (Watts 2009a). Although central to the notion of capability, counterfactuals are all too often overlooked (Comim 2008; Watts 2009a) but their complexity is neatly untangled by Sen when he suggests asking what people would do if they controlled the levers of power (Sen 1992: 64-69). Some counterfactuals can be easily identified – for example, if they have the real opportunity to acquire basic educational skills, people will not choose to be illiterate or innumerate – but 'social discipline' (Sen 1992: 149) may lead to the internalisation of sub-optimal choices. Women in oppressive societies, for example, "will often tend to form a negative value regarding education because they have internalized the belief that women should not receive an education" (Deneulin 2006: 5). Capability analyses, whether drawing on Sen's *de facto* list of basic capabilities or Nussbaum's *de jure* list of central human functioning capabilities, should be sensitive to such self-abnegation and should therefore recognise the adaptive preference.

However, the adaptive preference problem becomes more complex when considering more complex capabilities. Walker, for instance, highlights the problem of adaptive preferences in higher education (Walker 2006, 2007) but whilst the non-reflective rejection of higher education may indicate the adaptation of preferences in Elster's sense of the sour grapes phenomenon (Elster 1983) it does not necessarily constitute an adaptive preference within the capability approach as higher education is but one means to the end of well--being (Watts & Bridges 2006; Watts 2009a). Identifying adaptive preferences in education requires an understanding of what people would choose if they were not constrained by their adaptation but the respect for human diversity that is central to the capability approach means that counterfactuality (what would be the case if the circumstances were different) should not be confused with counteridenticality (what would be the case if the person were different). Nonetheless, interpersonal comparisons (particularly from a Senian interpretation of the capability approach) may be a useful means of identifying adaptations and the capability gap. Yet they also present the analytic problem that different people have different levels of access to different resources. These varying circumstances inevitably inform different interpretations of the good life but they also limit opportunities:

> "We get used to having the bodies we do have, and even if, as children, we wanted to fly like birds, we simply drop that after a while, and are the better for it. Again, someone as a child may want to be the best opera singer in the world (as I did), or the best basketball player – and most people adjust their aspirations to what they can actually achieve… I am not free to be a leading opera singer, nor is the short adult free to be a leading basketball player. We have failed to reach the grapes and we have shifted our preferences in keeping with that failure, judging that such lives are not for us. But clearly this is often a good thing, and we probably should not encourage people to persist in unrealistic aspirations" (Nussbaum 2000: 137-38).

Nussbaum does not consider adaptive preferences to be uniformly negative and suggests that adaptations to less important capabilities – such as the specific capabilities to sing opera or play basketball rather than the more fundamental capability of 'Being able to laugh, to play, to enjoy recreational activities' (*inter alia*, Nussbaum 2000: 80) – may even be beneficial. So, whilst she recognises such adaptations, unlike Elster, she downplays their significance. Drawing on Nussbaum's interpretations of capability and adaptation, then, and with the caveat that what may seem impossible is merely improbable, it is not necessarily a bad thing if those for whom higher education is out of reach (perhaps because they cannot achieve the formal entry level requirements) come to terms with their adaptation. The allegorical grapes, as

Nussbaum suggests, may really be out of reach for some people and it is difficult to comprehend the morality of encouraging people to aspire to that which is beyond them (Watts 2006).

Adaptation and multiple realizability

So, for all the advantages that higher education can confer, unless the specific focus of capability analyses is on higher education, it must be remembered that it is one of many means to the end of well-being: the specific functioning of higher education can enable the realisation of other functionings (Walker 2006) but the fundamental capabilities they reference can be achieved through other specified means. Moreover, some young people 'simply do not want to enter HE because it will not enable them to achieve valued aspirations' (Watts & Bridges 2006: 284). Higher education does not allow all individuals to flourish (or, perhaps less controversially, it is not the best means of allowing all individuals to flourish) and to unquestioningly assert its primacy over other means of achieving well-being is to deny the acknowledgement of and respect for human diversity that is central to the capability approach.

Although all functionings are, by their very definition, valuable they are not equally valuable to all people. To presume adaptations where they do not exist or to over-emphasising their relative weighting is to privilege certain means to the same end and to therefore 'consciously or subconsciously... justify and privilege elitist conceptions of well-being' (Clark 2009: 35). The problem with Clark's argument is that it is founded on the somewhat mischievous claim that adaptive preferences are overstated in the capability approach but he nonetheless points to the potential dangers of overstating them in capability analyses. Underlying his argument is the concern that heterodox interpretations of the good life can be seen as the product of 'mental conditioning' (Sen 1985: 188) and 'social discipline (Sen 1992: 149) with the adaptive preference argument being marshalled to explain how the 'poor and deprived lack the necessary education, knowledge and experience to harbor grand desires or make rational choices' (Clark 2009: 24-25). This apprehends the general understanding of the deprivation that may generate adaptive preferences but, as Clark goes on to suggest, the poor and deprived are 'arguably just as capable as anyone else [of] imagining, articulating and demanding a substantially better or "good" form of life' (Clark 2009:25-26).

The capability analyst must remain aware of the adaptive preference problem, but she must also be prepared to acknowledge the manifestations of the good life as it is envisioned by others. As Sen explains, capability assessments must take note of '*all* the barriers – including those from 'social discipline'' in determining the real freedoms people have (Sen 1992: 149, original emphasis) they must also 'be sensitive to the person's preferences and reasons for them' (Sen 2002: 14). Too great an emphasis on adaptations to particular means to the end of well-being 'may lead to the derogation of people's chosen and valued ways of living' (Watts 2009a: 427) and risk imposing the sort of colonialist judgements that Nussbaum argues are antithetical to the capability approach (Nussbaum 2000: 149).

Nussbaum acknowledges the importance of recognising human diversity through the notion of 'multiple realizability' (Nussbaum 2000: 77) which gives evaluative space for the specific interpretation of general functional capabilities. Although she criticises Sen for the deliberate incompleteness of his approach, his refusal to specify a *de jure* list of basic capabilities gives similar room for diverse manifestations of the generalised doings and beings individuals value and have reason to value. Capability analysts may make use of a list of capabilities 'without consideration of the *multiple realisability* of its elements' (Comim 2008: 167, original emphasis) and in doing so, and in this context, widen the capability gap instead of closing it. Human diversity means that there are many different ways of living the good life and this, in turn, means that

> "there may be more agreement on the need to be entertained, or to have the capability to take part in the life of the community, than on the form that entertainment must take, or on the particular way the life of the community may be shared" (Sen 1992: 109).

This respect for human diversity, though, must not valorise the self-reported satisfaction of those who have 'come to terms with their deprivation because of the sheer necessity of survival' (Sen 1999: 62-63). Well-being assessments that fail to take account of adaptations not only fail to represent the true circumstances of individual deprivation but sanction it with the argument that it frames the individual's well-being. Elsewhere, Sen argues that

> "people living under tyranny may lack the courage to desire freedom, and may come to terms with the deprivations of liberty, taking whatever pleasure they can in small reliefs, so that in the scale of utility (measured either in terms of mental satisfaction, or in terms of intensities of desire), the deprivations may be muffled and muted... Tyrannies operate not just by violating freedoms, but often by making collaborators out of victims" (Sen 2002: 634).

Sen's description of tyrannies may seem a little strong with reference to higher education but his argument that people can become willing accomplices to their own deprivation is at the heart of Bourdieu's concern that individuals accommodate the perpetuation of educational inequalities that disadvantage them; and Bourdieu's sociology enables a means of treading the line between multiple realizability and adaptation.

Bourdieusian habituation

Adaptive preferences – the tendency of people to content themselves with their deprivation – frame what Sen describes as the 'illusion of cultural destiny' which is 'not only misleading [but] can also be significantly debilitating, since it can generate a sense of fatalism and resignation among people who are unfavorably placed' (Sen 2006: 111-12). Much of Bourdieu's work (*inter alia*, Bourdieu & Passeron 1990; Bourdieu & Wacquant 1992; Bourdieu 1996) is concerned with the role of education in producing and reproducing such illusions of destiny and it therefore has the potential to offer insights into the adaptive preference problem. For Bourdieu, the resignation of those in socially subordinate positions (that is, those Sen describes as being 'unfavorably placed') typically means that having 'adapted to the demands of the world which has made them what they are, they take for granted the greater part of their existence' (Bourdieu 2000: 231). His concepts of field, capital and habitus link macro-level structures to micro-level processes and enable the interrogation of Nussbaum's assertion that most of the 'interesting' instances of adaptation 'involve lifelong socialization' (Nussbaum 2000: 139).

These concepts shed light on the self-held truths of social phenomena that lead individuals to exclude themselves from the communities from which they are excluded (Bourdieu 1984: 471) and so illuminate the processes whereby '[we] adjust our hopes to our probabilities, even if these are not in our best interests' (Walker 2006: 58). They link the possession of resources, particularly those inherited and acquired by the individual in her youth, to the mental dispositions that generate her understanding of what it is reasonable to expect (Bourdieu & Passeron 1990: 226) and therefore legitimate the perpetuation of relative advantage and disadvantage that can keep the capability gap wide open. The individual is located in a social field by the capital she initially possesses – and which signifies her identity – and that position influences her perception of the world and of her place in it. The routine experiences of her lifeworld, marked out by her capital, leads to the limits she encounters being internalised and sets the boundaries of what is likely to be possible.

The habitus, as the nexus of the externalised internal and the internalised external, generates 'a practical anticipation of objective limits acquired by experience of objective limits' (Bourdieu 1984: 471). Bourdieu argues that it is shaped by hegemonic elites and that although 'individuals have agency… the kind of agency they have is partially prescribed by the culture of which they are members' (Cleaver 2007: 226). By filtering the individual's perception of her lifeworld, the habitus mediates her sense of what her resources are worth and the probability of their deployment in social fields. Drawing on Bourdieu's work, and in the context of the widening participation debate,

Walker observes that this may lead to people failing to see 'particular practices and obstacles to their developing capabilities as problematic' with the result that 'they may not even identify certain capabilities as of value to themselves' (Walker 2006: 59). That is, the experiential delimitations of the habitus can inhibit individual capabilities by putting identity before reason. Given its potential to enhance well-being, the non-reflective rejection of higher education should not be dismissed lightly. Yet the disadvantaged are unlikely to be too concerned about this capability gap because, having internalised their external circumstances, they do not recognise it: 'the work of legitimation of the established order is extraordinarily facilitated by the fact that it goes on almost automatically in the reality of the social world' (Bourdieu 2000: 181).

The problem with a Bourdieusian analysis of adaptation, though, is that it privileges the manifestations of cultural capital – such as higher education – sanctioned by social elites. It can, therefore, erase the notion of multiple realizability. However, there is a moral dimension to the classed habituses which reproduce the taxonomies within which individuals are defined and define themselves. The habitus frames principles which provide members of the taxonomic groups with

> "a sense of their own value… Each principle tells its own story and provides a particular virtue that places its adherents above others. On this basis, people may aspire to stay as they are, to affirm their membership and its virtues, and to resist the call of education to 'improve' themselves by acquiring the distinctions of cultivation" (Moore 2004: 81).

The habitus, particularly in its non-reflective state, can delimit opportunities but it can also signal those doings and beings the individual values and has reason to value because she is a member of a community which values them (Watts & Bridges 2006; Watts 2009a). The issue, then, is not whether the individual is able to identify certain capabilities as being of value to her but how and why she identifies particular means of achieving that which she values. The task of the capability analyst is to balance these multiple realisations of general capabilities with the concern for adaptive preferences. Focusing on the Bourdieusian notion of cultural capital alone may lead to the identification of adaptations to privileged realisations of capabilities and may therefore distort the capability gap. This is not to argue that cultural capital should be made redundant in capability analyses but to suggest that it requires greater contextualisation. Bourdieu's notion of symbolic capital offers one way of closing the capability gap by acknowledging the moral dimensions of diversity produced and reproduced through the filter of the habitus.

Symbolic capital

Symbolic capital is typically seen as pernicious as it enhances the relative value of capital – or, rather, the goods and attributes that assume the form of capital – recognised as dominant in social fields. As such, it acts as an index to the cultural domination of social elites by assigning its value to their lives and lifestyles (Bourdieu 1984, 2000). Bourdieu describes it as '*worldmaking* power… that is, essentially, power over *words* used to describe groups' as it legitimises the visions and divisions of the social world (Bourdieu 1987: 13-14, original emphasis). Symbolic capital therefore apprehends the acceptance of social order and those possessing it are admired and visible. It gives them 'a kind of continuous justification for existing' (Bourdieu 2000: 240) whereas those who lack personal or institutional authorisation are 'all the more powerless to gain recognition, and thus to exert a truly symbolic effect' (Bourdieu 1991: 239). Whilst symbolic capital renders its possessors visible, its close articulation with cultural capital tends to render it invisible in educational analyses. Moreover, its assignation to heterodox valuations (that is, those that challenge the orthodoxy of the dominant form of capital at stake) in other fields is usually prefixed by negativity (Bourdieu et al. 1999) thereby adding analytic sanction to the social derogation of that capital. The orthodox interpretation and analytic use of symbolic capital as the legitimation of power relations 'whereby dominant groups secure esteem in public opinion for their activities' (Swartz 1997: 92) would therefore seem to only keep the capability gap wide open.

However, social fields are in a constant state of flux, even if it is muted by the effect of the habitus operating to limit individual preferences, as orthodox manifestations of capital struggle to maintain dominance over heterodox challenges for recognition. Thus, symbolic capital can be used in Bourdieusian analyses to account for the successful progression of students from working class backgrounds (that is, from backgrounds defined by relatively low levels of cultural capital) to elite universities (Watts 2007, 2009b). Such analyses, though, take place in social fields built around orthodox hierarchies of education privileging not only higher education but also certain higher education institutions (Bourdieu 1996; Reay et al. 2005) and these working class successes, often requiring significant capital investment, do little more than throw a few bridges across a wide capability gap. Yet, unless widening participation is the specific focus of the analysis, there is a danger of conflating capital and capability. Again, the potential benefits of higher education mean that these social structures should not be discounted in capability analyses but the respect for human diversity that is at the heart of the capability approach demands that the means to the end of well-being must be teased out from the end itself. Even if it initially appears somewhat paradoxical given the role that it plays in Bourdieusian analyses, symbolic capital can help untangle the means from the end of well-being.

Symbolic capital 'is one of the mechanisms which (no doubt universally) make capital go to capital' by raising the group's 'standing in the eyes of other groups' and inspiring 'actions which are very directly material' (Bourdieu 1977: 181). Although Bourdieu typically sees it lodged in the capital of social elites (the capital that allows them to maintain their dominant positions in the relevant fields) others argue that symbolic value is distributed throughout social hierarchies where it enhances that which is valued within subordinate classes (Skeggs 1997, 2004, 2008; Moore 2004; Järvinen & Gundelach 2007; Watts 2007, 2009b; Lin 2008). The sort of sub-cultural capital that it marks may not 'have much value outside of the field of the sub-culture and is unlikely to improve chances of social movement' (Skeggs 2004: 149) but such interpretations of symbolic capital nevertheless articulate with the recognition of diversity in the capability approach.

Sen observes that the reality of people's concerns means that their 'priorities and actions are influenced by all of their affiliations and associations' (Sen 2006: 162). This can lead to the adaptation of preferences: in order to maintain their position in society, for example, women may accept and even learn to value subordinate positions that preclude the freedom to choose and lead a different and better life (Nussbaum 2000; Deneulin 2006; Walker 2007). However – and this is where great analytic care is needed to distinguish between heterodox specifications of functionings and adaptations to orthodox capabilities – those affiliations and associations also influence the social determination of the doings and beings individuals have reason to value. In delimiting what is probable and improbable, the Bourdieusian habitus frames the valuation of class-based forms of cultural capital which typically reaffirm the individual's place in educational fields and that reaffirmed placement tends to generate adaptations which lead to the non-reflective rejection of other forms of cultural capital (specifically here, the working class rejection of higher education).

Following Bourdieu's usual insistence on the symbolic sanctification of dominant aspects of capital may therefore lead to the conclusion that adaptations to higher education widen the capability gap. However, symbolic capital is recognised as legitimate (both by those possessing it and by those accepting the orthodoxy of the field) because of its

> "relationship with a habitus predisposed to perceive it as a sign, and as a sign of importance, that is, to know and recognize it on the basis of cognitive structures able and inclined to grant it recognition because they are attuned to what it is. Produced by the transfiguration of a power relation into a sense relation, symbolic capital rescues agents from insignificance, the absence of importance and meaning" (Bourdieu 2000: 242).

Conclusion

The capability approach is concerned with the substantive freedoms people have to choose and lead lives they value and have reason to value. Adaptive preferences address the individual's attempts to resolve the psychological conflict between what she really prefers and what her circumstances make her prefer (Teschl & Comim 2005: 236). Individual desires are highly malleable and people 'adjust their preferences to what they think they can achieve, and also to what their society tells them a suitable achievement is for someone like them' so that they 'often learn not to want things that convention and political reality have placed out of their reach' (Nussbaum 2006: 73, 283). However, social conventions and political realities also frame individual specifications of capabilities.

The fundamental principle of the capability approach – that individuals should have the freedom to choose and lead lives they value and have reason to value – therefore presents significant analytic problems. The notion of freedom as the index to well-being rather than the acquisition of goods and resources is difficult enough but the deliberate incompleteness of Sen's interpretation of capability and the multiple realizability that Nussbaum advocates add further layers of complexity. In foregrounding respect for human diversity, capability analyses must be open and responsive to many different understandings of the good life. In the context of this chapter, well-being may be apprehended through successful engagement with higher education or by its rejection. So, despite the advantages that it may confer upon the individual, the opportunity to make use of a higher education should not be automatically privileged over other means of achieving well-being.

Assessing individual freedoms to choose that which is of value requires the interrogation of the social structures that shape and distort individual constructions of the value attached to doings and beings. The Bourdieusian concepts of capital and habitus offer considerable insight into the 'social discipline' framing individual capabilities. However, they are located in social fields that typically privilege orthodox interpretations of what is considered to be of value and they may therefore disregard what individuals actually value as a means of attaining well-being. That is, whilst Bourdieu's conceptual toolkit may illuminate the adaptive preference problem, it may also cast a shadow of the fundamental notion of multiple realizability. Cultural capital, for example, which is the main currency in educational fields, typically reifies educational hierarchies that place certain types of education, such as higher education, over others. Whilst indicating that which may be worth striving for, and so signposting educational adaptations, it can also stifle the voices of those whose identities are shaped around and by other forms of education.

If it is to be used in capability analyses, cultural capital therefore needs to be supplemented by other metrics that can capture the relative value of what individuals value. Although it typically works to maintain the doxa (that is, the self-evident nature of social arrangements) symbolic capital can also be appropriated in order to subvert it by recognising what is known and recognised as legitimate, and therefore valued, by subordinate groups in Bourdieusian fields. The analytic recognition of symbolic capital enhances the value of the capital already possessed by individuals and adds to it (Watts 2007, 2009b) and invests them with 'a power which is proportional to their symbolic capital, that is, to the recognition they receive from a group' (Bourdieu 1991: 238). It can, therefore, be used to challenge orthodox presumptions of the relative valuations given to specific realisations of capabilities. As such, it offers a means of accounting for both the multiple realizability of the capability approach and the adaptive preference problem and so can be used to reassess – and perhaps even reduce – the capability gap.

References

Archer, L., Hutchings, M. & Ross, A. (2003): Higher Education and Social Class: issues of exclusion and inclusion. London.

Ball, S. (2003): Class Strategies and the Education Market: the middle classes and social disadvantage. London.

Biggeri, M. (2007): Children's valued capabilities. In: Walker, M. & Unterhalter, E. (Eds.): Amartya Sen's Capability Approach and Social Justice in Education. Basingstoke.

Bourdieu, P. (1977): Outline of a Theory of Practice. Cambridge.

Bourdieu, P. (1984): Distinction: a social critique of the judgement of taste. London.

Bourdieu, P. (1987): What makes a social class? On the theoretical and practical existence of groups. Berkeley Journal of Sociology, 32, 1-17.

Bourdieu, P. (1991): Language & Symbolic Power. Cambridge.

Bourdieu, P. (1996): The State Nobility. Cambridge.

Bourdieu, P. (2000): Pascalian Meditations. Cambridge.

Bourdieu, P., Accardo, A., Balazs, G., Beaud, S., Bonvin, F., Bourdieu, E., Bourgois, P., Broccolichi, S., Champagne, P., Christin, R., Faguer, J-P., Garcia, S., Lenoir, R., Œuvrard, F., Pialoux, M., Pinto, L., Podalydès, D., Sayad, A., Soulié, C. & Wacquant, L. (1999): The Weight of the World: social suffering in contemporary society. Stanford.

Bourdieu, P. & Passeron, J.-C. (1990): Reproduction in Education, Society and Culture. 2nd edition, London.

Bourdieu, P. & Wacquant, L. (1992): An Invitation to Reflexive Sociology. Cambridge.

Burchardt, T. (2009): Agency goals, adaptation and capability sets. Journal of Human Development and Capabilities, 10, 1, 3-19.

Clark, D. (2009): Adaptation, poverty and well-being: some issues and observations with special reference to the capability approach and development studies. Journal of Human Development and Capabilities, 10, 1, 21-42.

Cleaver, F. (2007): Understanding agency in collective action. Journal of Human Development, 8, 2, 223-244.

Comin, F. (2007): Concepts of development: the role of education. In: Bridges, D., Jucevičienė, P., Jucevičius, R., McLaughlin, T. & Stankevičiūtė, J. (Eds.): Higher Education and National Development. London.

Comim, F. (2008): Measuring capabilities. In: Comim, F., Qizilbash, M. & Alkire, S. (Eds.): The Capability Approach: concepts, measures and applications. Cambridge.

Deneulin, S. (2006): The Capability Approach and the Praxis of Development. Basingstoke.

Deprez, L. & Butler, S. (2007): The capability approach and women's economic security: access to higher education under welfare reform. In: Walker, M. & Unterhalter, E. (Eds.): Amartya Sen's Capability Approach and Social Justice in Education. New York.

DfES, Department of Education and Skills (2003): The Future of Higher Education, cm 5735. Norwich.

DfES, Department of Education and Skills (2006): Widening Participation in Higher Education. Annesley, DfES.

Elster, J. (1983): Sour Grapes: studies in the subversion of rationality. Cambridge.

Flores-Crespo, P. (2007): Situating education in the human capability approach. In: Walker, M. & Unterhalter, E. (Eds.): Amartya Sen's Capability Approach and Social Justice in Education. New York.

Galeotti, A. (2007): Relativism, universalism, and applied ethics: the case of female circumcision. Constellations, 14, 1, 91-111.

Hart, C. (2007): The capability approach as an evaluative and developmental framework for education policy: the example of widening participation in higher education in England. Prospero, 13, 3, 34-50.

Järvinen, M. & Gundelach, P. (2007): Teenage drinking, symbolic capital and distinction. Journal of Youth Studies, 10, 1, 55-71.

Lin, A. (2008): Modernity, postmodernity, and the future of 'identity': implications for educators. In: Lin, A. (Ed.): Problematizing Identity: everyday struggles in language, culture, and education. New York.

Moore, R. (2004): Education and Society: issues and explanations in the sociology of education. Cambridge.

Nussbaum, M. (1988): Nature, function and capability: Aristotle on political distribution. Oxford Studies in Ancient Philosophy, 6, Supplement, 145-184.

Nussbaum, M. (2000): Women and Human Development: the capabilities approach. Cambridge.

Nussbaum, M. (2002): Education for citizenship in an era of global connection. In: Studies in Philosophy and Education, 21, 4, 289-303.

Nussbaum, M. (2006): Frontiers of Justice: disability, nationality, species membership. Cambridge, MA.

Power, S., Edwards, T., Whitty, G. & Wigfall, V. (2003): Education and the Middle Class. Buckingham.

Reay, D., David, M. & Ball, S. (2005): Degrees of Choice: social class, race and gender in higher education. Stoke-on-Trent.

Saito, M. (2003): Amartya Sen's capability approach to education: a critical exploration. Journal of Philosophy of Education, 37, 1, 17-34.

Sen, A. (1985): Well-being, agency and freedom: the Dewey Lectures. Journal of Philosophy, 82, 4, 169-221.

Sen, A. (1992): Inequality Reexamined. Oxford.

Sen, A. (1999): Development as Freedom. Oxford.

Sen, A. (2002): Rationality and Freedom. Cambridge, MA.

Sen, A. (2005): The Argumentative Indian: writings on Indian culture, history and identity. London.

Sen, A. (2006): Identity and Violence: the illusion of destiny. London.

Skeggs, B. (1997): Formations of Class & Gender: becoming respectable. London.

Skeggs, B. (2004): Class, Self, Culture. London.

Skeggs, B. (2008): Making class through fragmenting culture. In: Lin, A. (Ed.): Problematizing Identity: everyday struggles in language, culture, and education. New York.

Swartz, D. (1997): Culture & Power: the sociology of Pierre Bourdieu. Chicago.

Teschl, M. & Comim, F. (2005): Adaptive preferences and capabilities: some preliminary conceptual explorations. Review of Social Economy, 63, 2, 229-247.

Tilak, J. (2002): Education and poverty. Journal of Human Development, 3, 2, 191-207.

Unterhalter, E. & Walker, M. (2007): Conclusion: capabilities, social justice, and education. In: Walker, M. & Unterhalter, E. (Eds.): Amartya Sen's Capability Approach and Social Justice in Education. London.

Walker, M. (2006): Higher Education Pedagogies. Maidenhead.

Walker, M. (2007): Selecting capabilities for gender equality. In: Walker, M. & Unterhalter, E. (Eds.): Amartya Sen's Capability Approach and Social Justice in Education. New York.

Walker, M. & Unterhalter, E. (Eds.) (2007): Amartya Sen's Capability Approach and Social Justice in Education. New York.

Watts, M. (2006): Disproportionate sacrifices: Ricoeur's theories of justice and the widening participation agenda for higher education in the UK. Journal of Philosophy of Education, 40, 3, 301-312.

Watts, M. (2007): Capability, identity and access to elite universities. Prospero, 13, 3, 22-33.

Watts, M. (2009a): Sen and the art of motorcycle maintenance: adaptive preferences and higher education in England. Studies in Philosophy and Education.

Watts, M. (2009b): Widening participation in higher education in the UK: the significance of educational leadership. International Journal of Urban Educational Leadership.

Watts, M. & Bridges, D. (2006): The value of non-participation in higher education. Journal of Education Policy, 21, 3, 267-290.

Iris Sadlowski

A Capability Approach Fit for Children

When I started to develop a framework for the evaluation of child poverty in Germany in the context of the capability approach, I found that there is some very basic work missing. I did not find an overview concerning the key terms of the CA and their relation to *child well-being*. This paper tries to fill the gap. The Capability approach focusses on human development. But does the CA's understanding of development embrace *child*-development as well? The child-development process should be evaluated based on the background of development psychology and educational sciences. Does this psychological-educational "upgrade" will be compatible with the comprehension of development and well-being provided by the CA?

The relation in fact will be revealed as very close: Child *development* is the foundational *childhood* capability. Child development means the process to acquire progressively human abilities and capabilities. It means to be able to reach other and more valuable doings and beings every day. And it means to become more and more a "doer": playing an active role in the own live as well as in family and the nearer and farer environment.[1] The normative aim of the capability approach is to enlarge the individual substantive freedoms of every person and thus the understanding of the CA development means the same as the approach by developmental psychology: the expansion of capabilities.

A paradigmatic shift has taken place in developmental psychology: children are now recognized as plain "conductors" of their developmental process. The emphasis shifted from "someone secures me to get educated" to "my development is driven by me". In developmental psychology, *agency* has become a central term has become *agency*.[2] Similar, the core concept of

---

1 E.g. Bandura (2001: 2); Bandura (2008); Brandtstädter (2007).

2 In social developmental psychology and cognitive theory 'agency' means: "To be an agent is to intentionally make things happen by one's actions. Agency embodies the endowments, belief systems, self-regulatory capabilities and distributed structures and functions through which personal influence is exercised, ..." Bandura (2001: 2). Agency (cognitive theory) embraces conversion and choice abilities.
Whereas agency – as understood in the CA – means the valuable freedom to act, but possesses additionally a circular character and embraces then a similar meaning as in developmental psychology and cognitive theory. Agency (CA) is often reduced to "acting for others" or "blaming the own well-being because of actions based on values" as a contrast to the pursuit of well-being which is more oriented on the person herself. This polarity well-being vs. agency is owed to the departure point 'economics' of the CA. See e.g. Crocker (2008).

human being in the capability approach knows the person as an *agent* who shapes not only her own live but also the social and physical environment.[3] "Agency" means – as Sen expresses – that persons value achievements and opportunities "possibly going well beyond the pursuit of one's own well-being." "The 'agency-aspect' takes a wider view [than the well-being aspect, I.S.] of the person, including valuing the various things he or she would want to see happen, and the ability to form such objectives and to have them realized."[4]

If we were working on a report on well-being of adults, we would ask: "Which are the valued doings and beings adults have reason to value?" In this case as a first step we could start to choose *capabilities* – for example by a democratic process as proposed by Sen (Sen 2000: 100). Considering children, we have to ask must ask as a first, which *position* the elements of the CA model will get now.

In order to reach our objective to "readjust" the model and the relations between the individual CA elements, we will discuss their implications and special meaning regarding child well-being: resources, conversion factors, capabilities, the choice process and functionings. My proposal is to identify the main changes compared to the standard 'adult' model and clarify the points to revise.[5] The result of our discussion should be a capabilities-based understanding of the 'process of growing-up' and an enhanced picture of *child well-being*. This discussion will not be concluded by this paper, but I think the paper identifies the key aspects we will have to work on.

The child capability approach "readjustment" discussion relies on the model shown here:

3 Sen (2000: 22); Sen (1985); lecture II.

4 Sen (1987: 59) Due to the different foci of the points of departure – economics and psychology – the capability approach emphasizes the difference between the motivation through a narrow self-interest versus the motivation through values. Developmental psychology emphasises the view on the process of development: is the child an "input-receiver" and development thus unilateral or is development self-conducted and transactional? Bandura (2001: 4).

5 This does not mean that a scientifically acknowledged *Capability Standard Model* exists. But the approach in general was developed for adults. Sen 19.12.2006; Robeyns (2005).

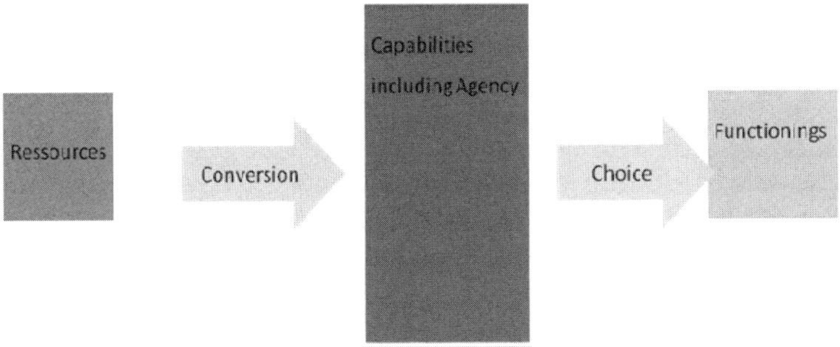

Adapted from Robeyns (2005).

Child well being: will capabilities still play the central role?

What is the main message from developmental psychology for our departure from the capability approach? Developmental psychology emphasizes, that an environment and personal capacities, that permit to pursue and reach personal goals motivates and strengthens persons. In contrary conditions, when people "believe they are being exploited, coerced, disrespected, or manipulated, they respond apathetically, oppositionally, or hostilely" (Bandura 2001: 5). This statement points out that the normative aim in the CA – to judge a life as valuable, if there exists *real* freedom to choose valuable doings and beings – is a condition for human development also from a positivist scientific view. Beside the normative foundation to value freedom and development, in the *child's capability approach* we get a clear vote through integrating developmental psychology in our line of reasoning: *capabilities first*! The motivation for children to shape their own development evolves based on the experience of own capabilities and growing abilities. To come up with these conditions is an aim on behalf of their own families – and "a matter of public policy and social programmes" (Unterhalter 2003: 5).

Is our approach – based on capabilities – adequate to think about child well-being? Capabilities as *freedoms* require the act of *choice* to convert them in real-live functionings. "But can children take their own decisions?"[6] Sen argues that this is not the right question because the promotion of capabilities is often enough – also for adults lives – in the hands of others. "While exerci-

6 Sen (2006: 9); else Sen (1993: 43,44).

sing your own choices may be important enough for some types of freedoms, there are a great many other freedoms that depend on the assistance and actions of others and the nature of social arrangements“.[7] In our interdependent world “the demands of liberty are more complex than the simple rule of leaving everyone to make their own little choices” (Sen 2006: 10).

We may argue analogously with respect to the aspect of *conversion* that it is not crucial who – the child *or* care persons – converts resources into capabilities. Evidently conversion is a capacity that is built up during childhood. Children themselves may not execute conversion to reach certain capabilities. It depends on age and on the specific capability concerned, whether children or someone else converts (or not) the resources into substantive freedoms to choose on what to do, to be or to become.[8]

Does that mean that we should evaluate only on the household level because children's capabilities and functionings depend so much on the actions (and non-actions) of their families? No. First, the mentioned processes though executed by a collective lead to individual results – individual child capabilities or individual child functionings. Second, because the *development* of child's conversion and choice abilities is a crucial *process*: it matters, *who* becomes “capable” inside the family.

Does a capability approach for children should care about resources?

Even if have asserted that resources are not our core criteria, we won‘t deny their crucial importance.[9] An adult with more resources than another person is able to reach a wider range of capabilities of what to do or to bc. But this is true only if these two persons live under the same circumstances and if they have got the same personal characteristics. Otherwise these persons will differ in their capability sets – and we must know a lot about their circumstances of live as well as about their personal characteristics to predict who has at her command a “richer” capability set with the given amount of resources (Robeyns 2005: 99). A resource may only be converted into a valuable doing or being if it is possible to set up a relation between the resource characteristic and the person via conversion. The empiric correlation between resources

7 Sen (2006: 10); similar: Sen (1993: 44).

8 And the relation between resources and capabilities is often co-produced by children and their key care-givers.

9 Sen (1999: 87). “In fact, we generally have excellent reasons for wanting more income or wealth. This is not because income and wealth are desirable for their own sake, but because, typically, they are admirable general-purpose means for having more freedom to lead the kind of lives we have reason to value” Sen (1999: 14).

and capabilities varies and can be very loose.[10] For children the relation is even much more indirect than in the case for adults, because they don't dispose directly over resources and the transition from resources to capabilities by conversion is often co-produced by children and adults. Children don't acquire resources by themselves – and it's usually not seen as their responsibility to contribute resources to the household.[11] Children participate in resources that are mostly owned by all or someone else in the family. Additionally we will recognize that important capabilities rely for the most part on non-market resources: save neighbourhoods, schools, and health care as some examples.

The level of their available individual *resources* does not only depend on the general economic situation of their family but depends deeply on distributional routines *inside* the household.[12] We don't know up to which amount the household resources will be used in favour of the child or the children living in a family. There is no fix distributional routine, the resources are allocated by a household mediation process and the resulting decisions upon the use of resources will differ from household to household and by situation.[13]

But how will *capabilities* be assigned and distributed? The range of child capabilities reached with certain resources is influenced by the child's age-corresponding conversion ability and by the quality and the amount of co-conversion and proxy-conversion executed through agency by adults, mainly by their key-caregivers.[14] The child's conversion ability is restricted and will broaden according to age by learning shaped through the input and opportunities endowed by their families, care-givers and the society as a whole. We face a dynamic conversion relation between resources and capabilities (and functionings) which changes and evolves during growing-up and development. A view which relies on resources would imply a static relation between resources and the capabilities well-being status achieved. This means, we can handle much better child *development* within the perspective that capabilities matter.

10 E.g; Holz, Puhlmann (2005: 67); Volkert, Wüst (this volume); Klasen (2005: 211).

11 The contribution of resources to the household by children would be the case of child labour, in Germany we will find few cases of child labour and will neglect here in this article the case of child-labour.

12 Vgl. Sen (1999: 91); Kanbur (1991).

13 The outcome for the child depends on the intrahousehold power relation. See Jeanette Findlay, Robert E. Wright (1996).

14 See FN 18.

The processes of conversion and choice

We focus in our context on the process of *acquiring* and using conversion and choice abilities. Education and social politics have a great bearing on the *execution* of conversion and choice processes as well as they do have a great influence on the *development* of conversion and choice abilities. Education intends to support their acquisition and development – while social policies (and other policies) shape the conditions for conversion and choice.

Conversion abilities determine the availability of capabilities. They are built up during childhood through self-driven development and through learning by experience and education. Educating conversion abilities is the main target of formal and informal education.[15] For example, someone who knows how to prepare potatoes can convert this resource into the capability "to have the opportunity to be adequately nourished". These abilities expand during development and lead – given the same amount of resources to a larger capabilities range. Choice abilities evolve by the development of values and the representation of a live plan. These latter abilities are influenced by 'Bildung' as broad human education.[16] Both, conversion and choice process are presented in the context of the capability approach to have a twofold character dispaying personal and social conditions.[17] Considering the arguments above about the execution of conversion and choice whether by children or by care persons, we will introduce a view which is threefold: first there is *personal conversion* and *choice*. Secondly, *proxy conversion* and *choice,* which in the terms of the CA is *agency*, being executed by someone else for a child.[18] Thirdly, conversion and choice processes are shaped by *societal* and *political* conditions. Conversion and choice rely on individual characteristics and abilities, on agency of others for children and they are based on societal settings.

---

15 Volkert, Wüst (this volume); Vaughan (2007: 115).

16 The notion of 'Bildung' refers to an understanding that goes beyond formal and informal education in that it includes the evolution of values and cultural habits.

17 E.g. Robeyns (2003); Scholtes (2007); In terms of developmental psychology this reflects the actual position inside the discipline concluding the debates about "nature and nurture" (e.g.: Shonkoff (2000: 3; 39ff.) and the transactional character of the development process (Bandura 2001: 4).

18 This term is borrowed from „proxy agency" Bandura is referring to: Bandura (2001: 13). The case, where adults *assist* and *back* conversion and choice executed by the child should additionally be mentioned here.

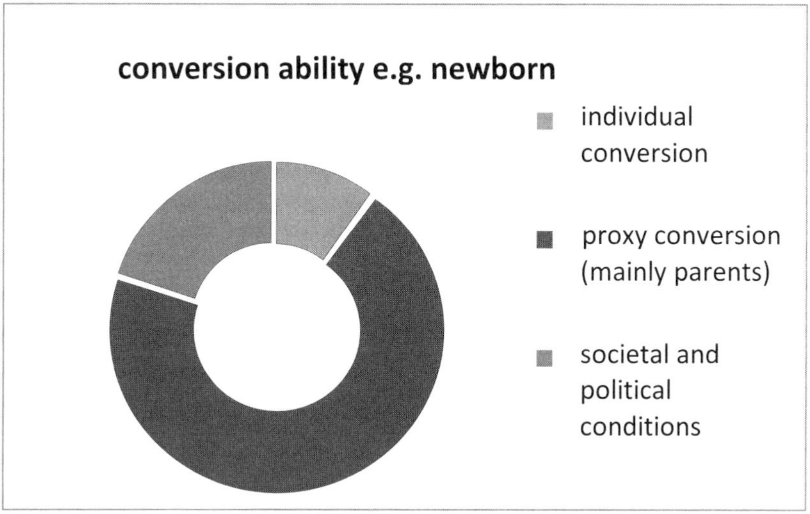

Any individual choice as well as any public debate and reasoning will be shaped by social norms and cultural values.[19] But we must distinguish between "what people really prefer and what they are made to prefer".[20] *Adaptive* preferences are preferences adapted to the persons live context but *additionally* they do not reflect her real needs (Steckmann 2008: 102). The problematic issue on adaptive preferences is not, that preferences are not built completely independent from others or that they are not context independent. Child live is much more interwoven with its environment than adult live and is especially interwoven with the child's caregivers by attachment[21]. Due to this narrow interdependency children adapt their wishes and preferences more than adults, but in a changing scale.

19 The adaption of preferences to the social and material circumstances is the product of socialisation and part of the human condition as a social being.

20 Teschl & Comim (2005: 236). See the discussion on the rising risk of paternalism in this context: e.g.: Steckmann (2008).

21 'Attachment' is a close emotional relationship with at least one primary caregiver every child needs to develop for social, emotional and physical development to occur normally. The attachment system is very robust and young humans form attachments easily, even in far less than ideal circumstances. Mooney (2010).

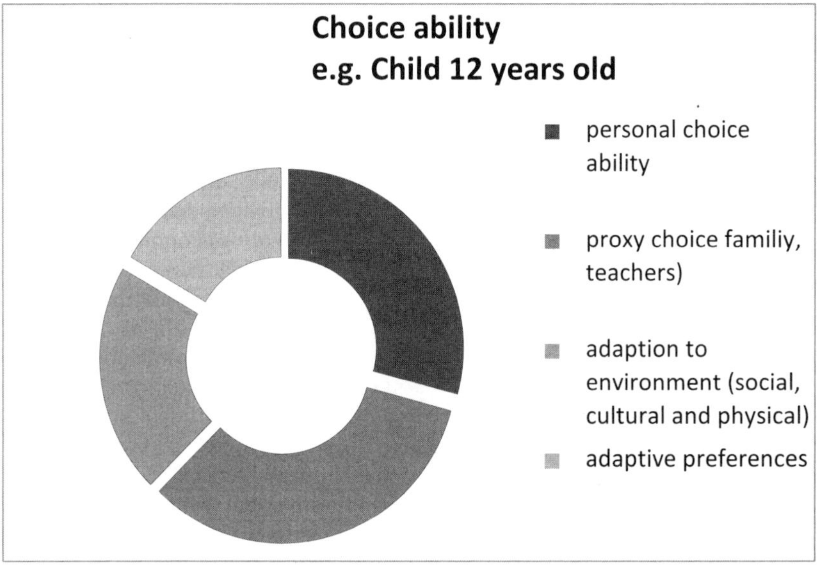

Another reason for limited choice ability is owed to the fact, that one of the intrinsic developmental aims of childhood is the construction and evolvement of a life plan. Children in every age do have explicit and implicit life-plans but the complexity of a fully human life plan will not be reached in childhood and will increase together with the growing self-determination ability.[22] In general, children tend to orientate themselves to the visions and the possibilities of live expressed by parents and other key-persons.[23] This means for example in the developmental stages of around 6 to 9 years old children that values and preferences are mainly adopted from their key care-persons. Later in the developmental stage of 10 to 12 years old children values and preferences notably are shared with peers.[24] In addition they switch between different values dependent to the situation and the persons in the actual context.[25] The narrow relation of child preferences with the presented opportunities and values by adults opens both a sphere of power over child development as well

22 See e.g. the arguments of Steckmann (2008: 111) concerning reduced self-determination abilites and the consequences for education to promote these abilites.

23 See e.g. the results on educational goals of children in Hurrelmann (2007:111).

24 Phasen und Stufen in der kindlichen Entwicklung, 31.08.2009.

25 Lansdown (2005); Woodhead, Faulkner (2004). This fact is owed beside the developmental stage to child socialisation in family and school environments, which do not promote virtues for civil courage.

as a cope for learning by adult model. If, so – who knows and how could someone know the 'real' valued capabilities and functionings of children?

The dynamic perspective of development

Childhood can be characterised by 'change'. Considering child development implies 'naturally' a dynamic perspective. Child *development* is the core *childhood* capability, and therefore for children more than for adults we emphasize that "valued states are those that expand capabilities".[26] There are a lot of childhood specific capabilities we will have to identify (for example to be able to play, to have a closely related caregiver ...) – and they will all be interrelated with *development*.

Regarding the more general human capabilities, there is some scope to discuss whether an adult's life may still be judged as a good live if there is no development.[27] In the case of child well-being it is more than clear that this must be denied. The neglect of development would violate the main characteristic of this period of live. For children development is vital and childhood without development is not possible.[28]

Therefore the conceptualisation and measurement of capabilities must be advanced into a dynamic model if we want to assess child well-being. The *process* of growing up and being educated is not restricted to be regarded as *capability* extension – to broaden the approach for this aim, it is crucial to shed more light on the building-up of the individual *conversion* and *choice* abilities. Compared to capabilities they rely on different mechanisms, but have not been focused and evaluated sufficiently yet. Ortrud Leßmann shows that developing conversion and choice abilities might be explained by the experiences made based on former capabilities and their realization as functionings.[29]

When we want to identify the "doings and beings children have reason to value" it is important to note that child psychological development is at the same time continuous *and* discontinuous: the differences between a baby, a

26 Unterhalter (2003: 3). For developmental psychology see Oerter et al. (2008) – at least in this period of live the role of development is considerably larger than in other periods of live. Recently, the topics "development" and "change" are not any more "reserved" to evaluate children's live. Adult live is nowadays perceived as dynamic and changing during the whole live-time.

27 This can only be discussed on the functionings level – on the capability level – inside CA thoughts – there can't be good live without an expansion of the freedoms to choose valuable doings and beings.

28 Shonkoff (2000: 3); "Core Concepts of Development".

29 See e.g Leßmann, September 2009.

five-years old child and the same 30-years old adult person will be so big that – based on the description of certain characteristics: e.g. their interests and their physical abilities – it will not be possible to identify them as identical persons. Anyway, simultaneously continuous development takes place. For example, normally the vocabulary of children will grow *continuously* when they get older. But a 1 ½ years old, a 4 years old and a 10 years old child will use it in very different patterns (Oerter et al. 2008: 40, 534). The changes during this development process in the quality of characteristics and abilities in certain categories are so big, that a quantitative adaption of the measure ('more'/'less') would fail. We cannot apply the same evaluation scheme for the same person over time. When we come up with indicators for childhood well-being, we must identify different sets of doings, beings and becomings[30] for each 'step' of child development.[31]

Instrumental impact of capabilities

Childhood itself is a critical period that offers opportunities for disrupting the intergenerational transmission of poverty (Francesconi Marco et al. 2005; Boyden 2007; Shonkoff 2000: 283ff.; Grundmann et al. 2006: 149). Children's actual doings and beings have a great bearing on their own live in future and will influence the development of the society as a whole. It's been a merit of the CA *not* to pose the instrumental impact of capabilities or functionings as a central evaluation criterion such as, for example, the individual future benefits or the sum of gains for the society as a sum. Capabilities are valued on their own: there is no need of justification, e.g. to prove that literacy or being well-nourished may lead to more individual income later, to increase the wealth of the society or to enhance happiness. Capabilities and functionings are valuable intrinsically.

Here we focus on child well-being and we will state, that *with respect to children* there *is* a broader concernment for instrumental impacts because we have to assess the dynamic aspect of "becoming" (Walker, Unterhalter 2007: 6) in childhood. Capabilities and functionings are instrumental for *development* and *learning*.[32] From birth to the age of 5 and further up to adolescence

30 The term becomings has been added to the discussion by Elaine Unterhalter and Flavio Comim (2007/2003).

31 Oerter et al. (2008: 18). Developmental psychology discusses if development is conducted in steps or is continuous – but there is a consensus about critical periods which we interpret here as steps in development.

32 E.g. development: Sen (2000: 51); learning: Leßmann September 2009. For the aims of this article we define: development is the expansion of the set of real freedoms and capabilities; learning is the expansion of conversion and choice abilities (which leads to capability set

"in addition to their remarkable linguistic and cognitive gains, they (the children, I.S.) exhibit dramatic progress in their emotional, social, regulatory, and moral capacities. All of these critical dimensions of early development are intertwined, ..." (Shonkoff 2000: 5). Developmental psychology provides more arguments to focus on the instrumental role of capabilities: In a row of changes, we have to secure that the latter steps have been concluded because they establish the bases of the subsequent developmental step (James et al. 2008: 18; Shonkoff 2000: 5). A "fundamental paradox" in the early years is, that development "is both highly robust and highly vulnerable.... What happens during the first months and years of live matters a lot, not because this period of development provides an indelible blueprint for adult well-being, but because it sets either a sturdy or fragile stage for what follows" (Shonkoff 2000: 5). Children "need to function in order to develop the mature capability" (Walker & Unterhalter 2007: 15; Nussbaum 2000: 89). Learning in the context of this article is regarded as successive building up of conversion and choice abilities. This learning has been modelled by Leßmann by integrating ideas of John (Dewey 1938) as an outcome of experience won in a sequence of situations or capabilities sets, where the capability set of a person today is linked to the experience in former capability sets.[33]

A new role for functionings?

Because of the conclusive instrumental impact for development and future live, there is some evidence to claim that adults do have not only to provide *capabilities* but they will have to *guarantee* basic *functionings* to children. For example, children need to be healthy to be able to make progress in school, babies need to be attached to someone before they may start to explore and learn, development of motor skills is the condition to come up with language competencies. Care persons like parents, teachers and politicians thus "need to know, if and how capability is being developed, by whom and under what conditions" (Walker & Unterhalter 2007: 15) in order to choose and guarantee in a first step the functionings upon that basic capabilities are conditional which should become feasible in a second step. Since adults are responsible – legally codified e.g. by the 'Convention of the Rights of the Child'– to guarantee "special safeguards and care" [34] due to the

extension).

33 Leßmann, September (2009: 459). I extend her argument here without former discussion to conversion ability building beyond her mentioned choice ability building.

34 United Nations (1990): Preamble.

physical and mental immaturity of the child, certain functionings must be identified and completed.

If we judge the role of functionings this way, should functionings during childhood be valued stronger than capabilities? The conclusion that functionings must attain a *stronger role* than capabilities is not at all inescapable. We already discussed the paradigm shift in development psychology and other disclipines concerning child development: today children are regarded as active participants in their own development. *They* decide about the use of their capabilities.[35] In consequence, education – as intentional input by adults for influencing or supporting child development – produces contingent results from the perspective of the educator. The results will differ from the outcomes that were initially intended by parents, teachers and other care persons. The knowledge which functionings will be the foundation for later valued capabilities is as fortuitous as the educational knowledge how to give "from outside" through care persons or through the social environment direction to behaviours or characteristics (Oerter et al. 2008: 118). Thus owed to the perceived contingency of child development, a broad range of capabilities is even more important to children than to adults to assure their ability to live a full and creative life in both life periods: childhood and adulthood. A set of guaranteed *basic* functionings for children must be complemented by a broad *variety* of capabilities. In case we have to choose among priorities either on 'freedom to choose on capabilities' or on 'guaranteeing basic functionings' – we need to develop criteria that should balance the capabilities of today, the near future and the far-away future.

Agency for children: to be brought up as basic capability

Capabilities or functionings in general are classified as 'basic', if they protect a person from harm, satisfy basic needs or are fundamental for other basic capabilities.[36] Nussbaum defines basic capabilities in contrast to as the "… innate equipment of individuals that is the necessary basis for developing …" (Nussbaum 2000: 84). Some basic capabilities will be named spontaneously if we ask around: to be well-nourished and well-sheltered, to escape avoidable morbidity and premature mortality, to get taught to be literate, to be able to participate in social interactions without shame. Poverty would be the failure

35 In this context 'to decide' includes beside the conscious also 'implicit' decisions by action, re-action and non-action.

36 For a summary see Robeyns (2003: 20) or the discussion in Alkire (2002: 170). Sen (1980: 218/219); Sen (1997: 44).

to satisfy functionings in these mentioned categories up to a certain minimally adequate level.[37]

Independently from the exact interpretation: one capability is so basic, fundamental and intrinsically valuable to children's life that in consequence it fits in every definition: For children the most basic capability is to live in caring, loving and stable relations. These relations are vital in this period of live, in particular in early childhood. Ever since the elementary work of René Spitz on 'hospitalism', Erik H. Erikson on 'basic trust' and of John Bowlby on the role of 'attachment' we know, that a child who falls short of under a certain level of love and care, will not even be able to stay alive, if all material needs are fulfilled (Spitz 2005, 1993; Erikson 2005; Bowlby 1958; Spitz 2005, 1993; Mooney (2010). We can state that in the case of children, the most vital and basic capability is *based on the human ability for agency*.[38]

The whole *process of being brought up and being educated* is called "socialisation" and may be described as a *basic capability* for children. Socialisation includes the impacts of interactions and the influence of the totality of the child's experiences in its social and physical environment: playgrounds, TV, care-persons, neighbours and peers (e.g. Bundesministerium für Familie 1975). "Human infants start life as remarkably helpless individuals who elicit powerful protective responses from their caregivers" (Shonkoff 2000: 93). So mainly all basic functionings or capabilities must be guaranteed in the early years by care persons or members of the society and thus depend on agency of others. Childhood and adolescence are the periods of human live "during which interaction and receptiveness within the household and social environment reach their highest levels" (Biggeri 2007; Shonkoff 2000: 6). Socialisation includes as a subset education as the intended attempt to influence the development of other persons. Education concentrates on the deliberate interaction of children, parents and professional care persons (e.g. teacher) in family, kindergarten, school and university.[39] In contempt of the aim to focus on children, this intense interdependency of child development and agency of others obliges us to assess adult agency abilities and environmental conditions.

37 Sen (1997: 111). Discussion: Terzi (2007: 25).

38 And consequently the function to live 'in caring, loving and stable relations' must be guaranteed. For agency ability see e.g.: Volkert, Wüst (this volume).

39 Hurrelmann (2008: 25, 118); Walker, Unterhalter (2007). Sen and Nussbaum refer to education as a basic capability. But they relate mainly - due to the understanding of *education* in the anglo-american tradition – to institutional education in kindergarten, school and university. In Germany prevails the broader notion of 'Bildung', which leads to an understanding that embraces more than formal and informal education but else the evolution of values and cultural habits.

Children as agents

Intuitively, *agency* seems to be a crucial aspect if understood – as discussed above – as "agency performed *for* children" by individuals or the society as a whole. But we must take additionally in account the paradigmatic shift in developmental psychology and education, that enhances the active agentic role of children as a 'doer'. Education and child development is no longer seen as unilateral. We state that "to be an agent" during the whole child developmental period is fundamental not only for the evolvement of self-esteem and self-consciousness, and the "training" to be a member of a community and a citizen (Edelstein 2009: 9; Grundmann 2008: 133). Beyond that, an environment, which permits children to execute agency is required for a healthy development in all aspects, e.g. mental and physiological dimensions (Bandura 2008). "Agency" in our notion includes "acting for others" as well as "realization of goals and values the person has reason to value, whether or not they are connected with her own well-being" (Sen 1997: 56).

In early childhood the child starts to develop a sense of the self. Through interaction with their environment they learn that they are "a distinct self capable of making things happen" (Bandura 2008: 19). Children choose and select their developmental aims. Additionally they choose, design or influence their environment. In the same time this social and physical environment where children come upon for choosing, selecting, designing and influencing their life is set by others – other individuals or by the society as a whole. So, the sociallisation process is on the one hand relative to other persons and shaped by the social and physical environment and on the other hand it is significantly configured by the children themselves (Brandtstädter 2007: 37). Their development – and thus every educational effort – counts today as transactional and the child is the agent of its own development as well as an agent in its environment and in the world (Bandura 2008: 19).

A missing self-efficacy belief is – following e.g. the results of empirical qualitative studies about child poverty – both the main *reason* and a *result* of poverty understood as capabilities deprivation. Poor children and their parents do not perceive themselves as "doers" in their own life nor in their environment. They don't belief that their actions will be effective.[40] This perspective is caused by their experience of a reduced scope of action due to the low level of resources available in poor households. This leads to a circular process: low resources cause a low activity level in the reduced scope of action which leads in turn to few experiences. These few experiences bring about a low ability to convert accessible resources into capabilities and functionings. The experience of self-efficacy and of being an agent in the own life can only be made if adequate conditions are in reach. Children need resources

40 Schäfer-Walkmann et al. (2009: 138); e.g. 33, 112.

together with the corresponding conversion and choice abilities made available by agency of care-persons. This presupposes the agency ability of the latter and requires apt social environments.[41]

Children and "future adults" who haven't made the experience of being effective are restricted in their active strategies to overcome challenges. But this is not the central point. They are deprived in their *whole* development because – as already explained earlier – we know that personal, psychological learning is tied to an active role in shaping and developing one's life (Ziegenhain 2005; Bandura 2008; Shonkoff 2000).

In Sum

Capabilities do not only play an outstanding role when we want to assess child well-being, because of

- the ethic and normative value of capabilities which emphasizes the human freedom to choose valuable doings, beings or becomings,
- the fact, that an assessment based on capabilities lead to less subjective indicators than happiness or satisfaction or
- that the focus on capabilities helps us to conquer a lot of restrictions that come about if we relied exclusively on resources for well-being assessment.

Considering developmental psychology we have shown that capabilities – the fundamental freedoms to make relevant choices – and agency – the ability to act as a *doer* – are fundamental requirements that matter not only for a full human life from a normative perspective but also from a positivist scientific view that documents why age-increasing capability sets are *the* basic requirements for child health, development and learning.

Child well-being assessment must identify broad age specific capabilities. Further a balance must be found between freedoms and guaranteeing fundamental functionings. Additionally, work on child well-being measurement has to focus on the development of conversion and choice abilities. These latter abilities rely on the agency of others, their interaction with the child, their educational inputs and the social and physical environment shaped by them.

41 On the role of parents agency ability: Volkert, Wüst (this colume: end); Andresen et al. (2007: 361ff.) The authors point to the societal conditions necessary and do draw their discussion on the proverb: "It takes a whole village to raise a child."

References

Alkire, S. (2002): Dimensions of Human Development. In: World Development, 30, 2, 181-205.

Andresen, S., Hurrelmann, K. & TNS Infratest (Eds.) (2007): Kinder in Deutschland 2007: 1. World Vision Kinderstudie. Frankfurt a.M.

Bandura, A. (2001): Social Cognitive Theory: an agentic perspective. In: Annual Review of Psychology, 52, 1-26.

Bandura, A. (2008): Towards an agentic Theory of the Self. In: Lopez, S.J. (Ed.): Positive psychology. Exploring the best in people. Westport, Conn., 15-50.

Biggeri, M. (2007): Children's valued capabilities. In: Walker, M., Unterhalter, E. (Eds.): Amartya Sen's capability approach and social justice in education. New York, 197-214.

Bowlby, J. (1958): The nature of the child's tie to his mother. In: International Journal of Psycho-Analysis, 39, 350-373.

Boyden, J. & Cooper, E. (2007): Questioning the power of resilience: Are children up to the task of disrupting the transmission of poverty? , Oxford, CPRC Working Paper, 73.

Brandtstädter, J. (2007): Entwicklungspsychologie der Lebensspanne. Ein Lehrbuch. Stuttgart.

Bundesministerium für Familie, Senioren Frauen und Jugend (1975): Familie und Sozialisation – Leistungen und Leistungsgrenzen der Familie hinsichtlich des Erziehungs- und Bildungsprozesses der jungen Generation. Zweiter Familienbericht. Bonn.

Crocker, D.A. (2008): Sen's Concept of Agency. Paper prepared for the 2008 HDCA Conference. New Dehli.

Dewey, J. (1938): Experience & education. 1st. ed. New York.

Edelstein, W. (2009): Demokratie als Praxis und Demokratie als Wert. In: Bundeszentrale für politische Bildung (Ed.): Praxisbuch Demokratiepädagogik. Sechs Bausteine. Weinheim und Basel, 7-19.

Erikson, E.H. (1971): Kindheit und Gesellschaft. 14. ed. Stuttgart (2005).

Francesconi M., Jenkins S. & Siedler T. (2005): Childhood Familiy Structure and Schooling Outcomes: Evidence from Germany. University of Essex. (ISER working papers, 22). Available at http://www.iser.essex.ac.uk/pubs/workpaps/pdf/2005-22.pdf (18.01.2010).

Grundmann, M. (2008): Handlungsbefähigung – eine Sozialisationstheoretische Perspektive. In: Otto, H.-U. & Ziegler, H. (Eds.): Capabilities – Handlungsbefähigung und Verwirklichungschancen in der Erziehungswissenschaft. Wiesbaden, 131-142.

Grundmann, M., Dravenau, D., Bittlingmayer, U.H & Edelstein, W. (2006): Handlungsbefähigung und Milieu. Zur Analyse milieuspezifischer Alltagspraktiken und ihrer Ungleichheitsrelevanz. Münster.

Holz, G. & Puhlmann, A. (2005): Alles schon entschieden? Wege und Lebenssituation armer und nicht-armer Kinder zwischen Kindergarten und weiterführender Schule; Zwischenbericht zur AWO-ISS-Längsschnittstudie. Orig.-Ausg. Frankfurt a.M.

Hurrelmann, K. (Ed.) (2007): Kinder in Deutschland 2007. 1. World Vision Kinderstudie. Frankfurt am Main.

Hurrelmann, K. (Ed.) (2008): Handbuch Sozialisationsforschung. 7. revised ed. Weinheim.

James, A. & Christensen, P. (Eds.) (2008): Research with Children. London.

Jeanette F. & Wright, R.E. (1996): Gender, poverty and the intra-household distribution of resources. In: Review of Income and Wealth, 42, 3, 335-351.

Kanbur, R. (1991): Children and intra-household inequality: a theoretical analysis. The World Bank. (Policy Research Working Paper Series). Available at http://ideas.repec.org/p/wbk/wbrwps/685.html.

Klasen, S. (2005): Messung von Armut und Deprivation in Südafrika. In: Volkert, J. (Ed.): Armut und Reichtum an Verwirklichungschancen. Amartya Sens Capability-Konzept als Grundlage der Armuts- und Reichtumsberichterstattung. Wiesbaden, 207-255.

Lansdown, G. (2005): The evolving capacities of the child. UNICEF: Florence (Innocenti insight).

Leßmann, O. (2009): Capability and Learning to Choose. In: Studies in Philosophy and Education, 28, 5, 449-460. Mooney, C.G. (2010): Theories of attachment. An introduction to Bowlby, Ainsworth, Gerber, Brazelton, Kennell, and Klaus. 1st ed. St. Paul, MN.

Nussbaum, M.C. (2000): Women and Human Development: The Capabilities Approach. Cambridge.

Oerter, R. & Montada, L. (Eds.) (2008): Entwicklungspsychologie. 6.revised ed., Weinheim.

Phasen und Stufen in der kindlichen Entwicklung (2009). Available at http://www.familienhandbuch.de/cmain/f_Aktuelles/a_Kindliche_Entwicklung/s_910.html#grundschulkind (12.04.2010).

Robeyns, I. (2003): The Capability Approach: An Interdisciplinary Introduction. In: Department of Political Science and Amsterdam School of Social Sciences.

Robeyns, I. (2005): The Capability Approach: a theoretical survey. In: Journal of Human Development and Capabilities, 6, 1, 93-117.

Schäfer-Walkmann, S., Störk-Biber, C., Rieger, G. & Ross, P.-S. (2009): Arme Kinder und ihre Familien in Baden-Württemberg. Eine sozialarbeitswissenschaftliche Studie. Herausgegeben von Caritasverband der Diözese Rottenburg-Stuttgart e.V., Stuttgart.

Scholtes, F. (2007): Explaining interpersonal differences of power in a capability perspective. Paper prepared for the 2007 HDCA Conference. New York City.

Sen, A. (1980): Equality of What? In: McMurrin, S. (Ed.): Tanner Lectures on Human Values. Cambridge, Massachusetts, London, 353-369.

Sen, A. (1985): Well-being, Agency and Freedom: The Dewey Lectures 1984. In: Journal of Philosophy, 82, 4, 169-221.

Sen, A. (1987): On ethics and economics. Twelth impression 2008. Oxford.

Sen, A. (1993): Capability and Well-Being. In: Nussbaum, M.C. & Sen, A.K. (Eds.): The Quality of Life (Wider Studies in Development Economics). Oxford, 30-53.

Sen, A. (1997): Inequality reexamined. Reprinted, Oxford, New York.

Sen, A. (1999): Development as Freedom. Oxford.

Sen, A. (2000): Ökonomie für den Menschen. Wege zu Solidarität und Gerechtigkeit in der Marktwirtschaft (Original: Development as Freedom, 1999). München, Wien.

Sen, A. (2006): Children and Human Rights. IHD Foundation Day Lecture delivered on December 19, 2006, Institute for Human Development, New Dehli.

Shonkoff, J.P. (2000): From neurons to neighborhoods. The science of early child development. Washington, D.C.

Spitz, R.A. (2005) (1993): Vom Säugling zum Kleinkind. Naturgeschichte der Mutter-Kind-Beziehungen im ersten Lebensjahr. 12. ed., Stuttgart.

Steckmann, U. (2008): Autonomie, Adpativität und das Paternalismusproblem. Perspektiven des Capability Approach. In: Otto, H.-U. & Ziegler, H. (Eds.): Capabilities - Handlungsbefähigung und Verwirklichungschancen in der Erziehungswissenschaft. Wiesbaden, 90-115.

Terzi, L. (2007): The Capability to be Educated. In: Walker, M. & Unterhalter, E. (Eds.): Amartya Sen's capability approach and social justice in education. New York.

Teschl, M. & Comim, F. (2005): Adaptive Preferences and Capabilities: Some Preliminary Conceptual Explorations. In: Review of Social Economy, 63, 2.

United Nations (1990): Convention on the Right of the Child. Entry into force: 2 September 1990. Available at http://www2.ohchr.org/english/law/pdf/ crc.pdf (01.02.2010).

Unterhalter, E. (2003): Education, capabilities and social justice. In: Education for All Global Monitoring Report 2003/4: Gender and Education for All: The Leap to Equality, 4.

Vaughan, R. (2007): Measuring Capabilities. An Example. In: Walker, M. & Unterhalter, E. (Eds.): Amartya Sen's capability approach and social justice in education. New York, 109-129.

Volkert, J. & Wüst, K. (forthcoming): Early Childhood, Agency, and Capability Deprivation. A quantitative analysis using German socio-economic panel data. In: Leßmann, O., Otto, H.-U. & Ziegler, H. (Eds.): Closing the Capability Gap – Renegotiating social justice for the young. Farmington Hills.

Walker, M. & Unterhalter, E. (2007): The Capability Approach - Its Potential for Work on Education. In: Walker, M. & Unterhalter, E. (Eds.): Amartya Sen's capability approach and social justice in education. New York, 1-18.

Woodhead, M. & Faulkner, D.M. (2004): Subjects, Objects or Participants? Dilemmas of Psychological Research with Children. In: Christensen, P. & James, A. (Eds.): Research with children. Perspectives and practices. Reprint. London.

Ziegenhain, U. (2005): Bindungstheoretisch konzeptualisierte Modelle zur frühen Prävention. In: Kinderärztliche Praxis, 6, 378-383.

Matthias Grundmann, Annekatrin Steinhoff & Wolfgang Edelstein

Social Class, Socialization and Capabilities in a Modern Welfare State: Results from the Iceland Longitudinal Study

Introduction

How capabilities can develop and how they can serve to renegotiate social justice for the young generation is a central issue not merely for developing countries but also for modern welfare states. With a pragmatic understanding of capabilities (Zimmermann 2006) focused on the potentials that persons can effectively realize in their life course, the present chapter will consider the interaction between agency and environment and discuss empirical findings concerning individual development and social structure in a modern welfare state. Reformulating these findings in terms of the capability approach – understood as a broad normative framework for the evaluation and assessment of individual well being and social arrangements (Robeyns 2005: 93) – we attempt a reconstruction of the socialization of personal capabilities and achieved functionings that will simultaneously serve to provide information about the freedom of choice.

Modifying the capability approach, we develop a research program that focuses on the reconstruction of individual courses of development under the constraints of varying social conditions in different social milieus with different family structures and different psychological conditions. The empirical findings are based on a longitudinal study of child development and social structure conducted in Iceland (cf. Edelstein, Keller & Schröder 1990). The data permit to reconstruct developmental processes by which individuals acquire skills and agency, learn to look back and reflect their life experiences, and to understand what they feel they have to do or desire to do in their lives. Therefore, we describe capabilities as a set of personal and social characteristics that correlate with well being and a successful conduct of life. In view of this definition of capabilities, social class and educational institutions are seen as means, and educational outcomes and personal chances ("freedoms") to acquire a social position and achieve well being are understood as ends of the socialization process (Grundmann & Dravenau 2010). In consequence individual development is interpreted as a set of conversion factors: personal competencies, psychosocial dispositions, and value orientations are defined as the person's capacity to orient his or her action pragmatically towards achieving life outcomes. Therefore, the focus of the analysis is on the person's ability to experience, recognize, and make use of his or her resources rather than on the nature and composition of these resources. The question that concerns us is: What is it that enables people to realize and value their personal skills, competencies, and personalities? And what are the opportunities which their life-world provides to put these subjective resources to use?

The research program "Individual Development and Social Structure" and the capability approach

One of the aims of the Iceland Study was to map the structural dynamics of individual development within different social classes and ecologies. With this purpose, Edelstein and his coworkers developed an analytical model to identify the matrix of interacting social forces that influence individual development. The model focuses on the intra- and inter-individual dynamics of cognitive, social cognitive, personal and action competencies of the constructive subject. Edelstein et al distinguish between the universal structures of competence development, the historical dimension of the social structures in the system of social inequality, and the structure of biographical determinants of opportunities. Their goal is to reconstruct the micro-social dynamics of socialization interaction as well as the reflexive ego (Edelstein, Keller & Schröder 1990; Edelstein 1999).

The basic purpose of the research program was the reconstruction of individual courses of development under the constraints of varying social conditions in different social milieux, with different family structures and under different psychological conditions. The study focused on the reconstruction of individual trajectories from the beginning of school at age 7 through the individuals' educational careers and vocational achievements to midlife in their late thirties. To accumulate information about psychological capacities, personality resources and micro-social interaction dynamics the empirical data collected concerned various facets of development: cognitive, socio-moral, affective, and personality related. The data are designed to map the realization of the patterns of opportunities in the realms of occupation, family and peer relations as well as the integration into the societal culture (Schröder & Edelstein 1991; Jacobsen, Edelstein & Hofmann 1994; Keller 1996; Grundmann et al. 2006).

Numerous studies document the impact of the system of social inequality (as transmitted by the system of education) on people's conduct of their lives, on their capability of doing well, and to achieve social recognition of various sorts (Edelstein & Grundmann 2006). In terms of the capability approach, the findings concerning effects of social inequality can be interpreted as aspects of individual functioning in the form of achieved personal outcomes (Sen 1999). The capability approach, then, addresses the scope of potentials and opportunities of individuals to live their lives in a given society. According to the capability approach human resources are interpreted as potential for the realization of individual conduct of life and the construction of life practices as measured by the attainment of desired goals and the achievement of successful living and well being.

In contrast to the intra- and inter-individual models of individual development within social structures adopted in the Iceland study, the capability approach directs the researchers' attention to a perspective of freedom in the conduct of life and the realization of aspired goals. The capability approach focuses on how society moves individuals to perceive themselves as competent social actors who have freedom to achieve desirable functionings and goals and to overcome restrictions prevalent in their living conditions. The capability approach thus is a theoretical concept that raises the question what is possible in a given society.

To answer this question an analytical approach is needed that makes it possible to reconstruct how individuals become able to do well or fail to do so. As pointed out by Zimmermann, this interpretation is consistent with a pragmatic understanding of agency as a socially embedded consequence of employability (Zimmermann 2006: 473f.). Employability implies opportunities and developmental processes that enhance cognitive, social cognitive, personal and socio-political competencies for the realization of desirable aims. For example, political participation as an indicator of the freedom of voice in an egalitarian society requires democratic education that enables people to express their needs and to formulate their aims. The capability approach aims at defining the conditions for a democratic and egalitarian (welfare) society. It calls for a society that provides conditions for the optimal realization of personal needs for all – i.e. equality of freedom defined as autonomy and opportunity to develop. This idealization of society as a community of solidarity is, of course, questionable, as is the individualization of freedom of choice in view of the realities of individual opportunities to realize desirable functionings. The entire approach focuses on values and consumption goods as manifestations of aspired functionings.

In a different vein, the research program embedded in the Iceland Study focuses on individual needs and actual competencies of individuals to articulate their needs and desirable aims. The study insists that valuable functioning must be analyzed as a result of individual development and as manifestations of a socialization process that influences certain choices and interests. As the data from the Iceland study demonstrate, these processes depend on the empowerment of individuals to achieve a score above average defined by the reference group that is relevant for the individual. Normally, this reference group is not society, but the social milieu. This calls for an empirical research design that does not only focus on the distribution of characteristics and variables but on information concerning individual cases and the social constraints of their milieu (Edelstein & Grundmann 2006).

From this perspective, an analysis of capabilities must be sensitive to individual variations in functioning within specific socialization contexts and with reference to individual and personal dispositions. Whenever we approach the question how individuals are able to transform resources into aspired functionings we have to consider the context specific rationalities that guide the individual's aims in life. We have to focus on individuals' ability to transform individual and social dispositions towards realizing their aims. These can be defined as "conversion factors" that permit individuals to develop aspired functionings relative to the personal and social constraints as defined by the social environment in which they grow up, in particular social class. This theoretical amplification makes it plausible that the capability approach is more than a concept of human capital (Robeyns 2006). Freedom of choice is not a purely formal argument. Rather, it is an assumption in need of empirical clarification. The results are indeed open, because the postulated freedom of choice will likely be biased by the paternalism of political or administrative actors (Bonvin 2009). Or they may be limited by taking only consumption or life prospects as defined by the labor market into account. Capabilities, however, depend on social action, such as participation in the process of decision making, or in the choice of values that an individual will engage in.

The need for empirical examination calls for a reformulation of the capability model in view of a person-centered approach as suggested by the Iceland study. In this reformulated model, which conceptualizes individual development as a function of life experiences in social contexts, capabilities may be interpreted as a stage of development at a given age that depends on the relation between the actor's individual attitudes and available social opportunities. The freedoms of achievement and the freedoms of agency, on which the capability approach focuses, are conceptualized as conversion factors defined by personal and social resources. From this point of view the meaning of social life is understood as a result of concrete interactions that are embedded in social structures which either restrict or open up opportunities and freedom of action. In terms of the capability approach we focus on the micro-social construction of social experience and social practice as manifested by a set of capabilities which enable a person to engage in valuable acts or to reach valuable states of being, and to combine actions enabling the person to achieve various functionings that are relevant in his or her environment (Sen 1992, 2004). We can then, for example, interpret capabilities as a result of class specific socialization (Grundmann & Dravenau 2010). However, this implies a detailed analysis of how individuals become able to realize their aims in life. In this respect, capabilities can be translated into a grammar of human development defined as a process of enlarging people's choices or achievable functionings. The capability approach then corresponds to life course research as developed by Glen Elder (1995), which focuses on how social environments and dynamic worlds change people and affect their pathways through their lives. These can be measured either by different aspects of personality development or by measurements of the individual's functionings in different structurally determined contexts. A core premise of the life course paradigm asserts that such pathways and developmental processes and outcomes are shaped by the social trajectory that people follow, and, recalling another principle of the life course paradigm, by human agency and self-regulation. "Within the constraints of their world, people are often planful and make choices among options that become the building blocks of their evolving life course. These choices are influenced by the situation and by the interpretation of it as well as by the individual's life history of experience and dispositions" (Elder 1995: 110).

This analytical view focuses on the actual process of the person's agentic orientation, on the multifarious ways people – especially people with different socio-cultural backgrounds – reflect upon, make sense of, and utilize the human and nonhuman resources and socio-cultural schemas available to them. In view of life course research it is primarily during the transition from the educational to the occupational system, from adolescence to adulthood, that major biographical choices and decisions are made. Here we find a field of special interest for the analysis of the development of people's capabilities and their success or failure in accomplishing the transition into the occupational system and into meaningful adult lives. Relative to the concept of agency, it is at this point that capabilities can be described more concretely as personalized action options in specific life transitions and social contexts. As shown in Figures 1a and 1b, the notion of capabilities and achieved functionings as socialization outcomes can be modelled in form of a class specific socialization process (1a) and reformulated in terms of a socialization model of personal capacities (1b).

Figure 1a: A general model of class-specific socialization

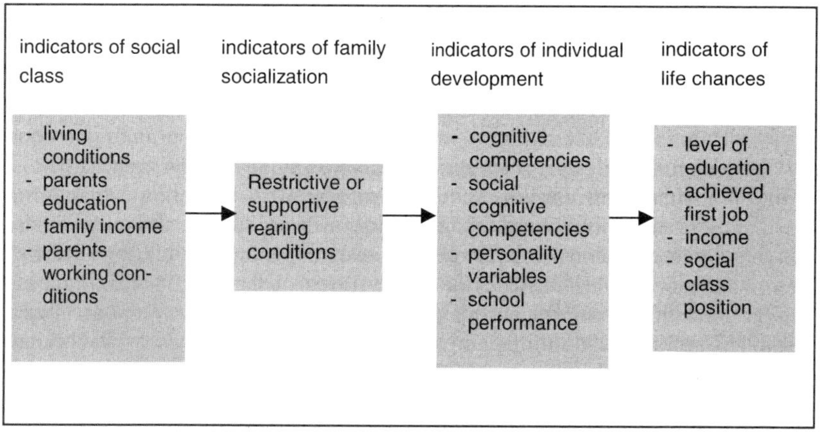

In a general model of class-specific socialization, social class would be measured by living conditions and a set of parental indicators such as educational level, work conditions and income. All these variables are important for defining the restrictiveness or supportiveness of family life in childhood. It is assumed that both social class and family life, either singly or combined, have a strong impact on child development (multifactorially measured) as well as on the life chances of the offspring. Social class, family life and the indicators of individual development can be interpreted as social, economic and cultural resources of the offspring that make life chances more or less probable – or, in the semantics of the capability approach, influence the realization of acquired functionings. Thus, the model can easily be included in a socialization model of a person's capability as shown in Figure 1b. Instead of the simple socialization model, the capability approach takes culturally and politically important conditions into account. Nevertheless, it assumes the same kinds of prediction of life chances, now defined as achieved functionings.

Figure 1b: A socialization model of a person's capability set and achieved functioning

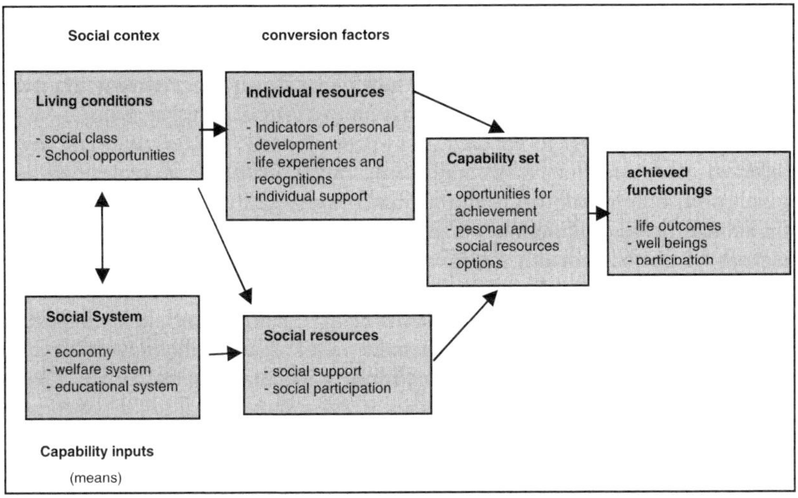

Model 1b permits to describe the unequal opportunities for individual development within class environments in the social system. This is a reason for distinguishing life world aspects and system aspects in the study of human development. In the context of the life world, capabilities represent indicators of individual development, life experiences and recognitions and individual support, whereas, on the system level, social support and participation are defined by institutional arrangements that grant people entitlements or deprive them of opportunities for functionings and well being.

From the perspective of the capability approach, social environments such as social class, the school system, and opportunities provided by the welfare system can be interpreted as means for capabilities. The individual's potentials for the realization of life practices (such as acquired competencies and skills as well as developed personality characteristics, which enable people to enjoy well being and to live an effective life, or social support in family and peer group) can be understood as conversion factors defined as the internal and external conditions that enable the individual to seize an opportunity offered and to effectively take advantage of it. Such a model has been proposed by Robeyns (2005: 98). It can be reformulated in terms of the life course paradigm, or in the perspective of the ecology of human development (Moen, Elder & Lüscher 1995) as shown in figure 1a. The benefit of such a model is its empirical practicability.

Data analysis

To consider this model more closely we return to the Iceland longitudinal study. Our first aim is to use empirical data to demonstrate how the socialization model described earlier can be transformed into an operational empirical model. For practical reasons we restrict the explanation to a limited set of variables: social class as an indicator of social environment restricting the degree of freedom of individual development; parental support as well as a set of personality measures; exemplary life outcomes.

Social class was measured as a multidimensional configuration of socio-economic status including parents' nature of work, parents' educational level, and parents' income. In the analysis we use a dichotomous variable indicating high vs. low SES. Additionally, we refer to the children's individual experiences in the family. Following Grundmann (1998), we computed a variable measuring restrictive versus supportive rearing styles on the basis of information provided by a child's parents.

Furthermore, specific measures inform about personal capacities to regulate relevant dimensions of the conduct of life and learning in adolescence. We focus on recognized important factors in individual and personal development such as ability level at age 7, control beliefs, achievement motivation and social involvement of adolescents at age 15. The child's ability level at age 7 was rated by teachers at the beginning of schooling. The dichotomous variable (high/low) informs about the teachers' expectations for the child's capacities for school performance and his or her personal development. In the perspective of the capability approach, ability level at age 7 could be interpreted as a postulated individual capacity of the child, rated by a teacher at the beginning of school. In order to describe the resulting potentials to effectively take advantage of opportunities offered in adolescence, we first refer to the individual's achievement motivation at age 15. This variable is based on 11 items that represent the individuals' estimate of their own achievement potentials as well as perceived satisfaction at work (cf. Dravenau 2006: 199, 200). Second, we refer to the individuals' perceived self-efficacy at age 15. The variable we use is based on 18 items that were constructed with reference to the Nowicki-Strickland Locus of Control scale for Children (Strickland 1989). On a scale from 0 to 1 values close to 1 symbolize a high rate of internal control belief. Third, we refer to a variable based on 5 items representing teachers' ratings of individuals' observable interest in being socially involved.

We further refer to variables that approximate achieved functionings as described in the capability approach such as education and political participation as well as satisfaction with life as an indicator of well being. The achieved level of education at age 38 is rated on a 6-point scale from 0 = primary school to 1 = university degree. In addition to the achieved level of education we refer to individuals' self-report concerning their interest in political issues as an indicator of political participation. The respondents were asked to rank their personal interest in politics on a 4 point scale from 0 = no interest to 1 = highly interested. Finally, we look at the reported satisfaction with life at age 38 (4 point scale from 0 = very dissatisfied to 1 = very satisfied) as an indicator of individual ability to achieve one's personal aims.

The distribution on the variables used in the analysis is shown in Table 1. 55 cases are complete with all measurements.

Table 1: Measurements of means, conversion factors and achieved functionings

variables	codes	mean	Std.dev.	N
Social and personal resources at age 7 (means)				
social class of origin (SES)	low – high (0,1)	.53	.50	55
ability level	low – high (0,1)	.64	.49	55
parental support	low – high (scale 0 - 1)	.49	.23	55
personal conversion factors at age 15				
achievement motivation	low – high (scale 0 - 1)	.87	.17	55
control belief	external – internal (scale 0 - 1)	.78	.13	55
social involvement	low – high (scale 0 - 1)	.55	.19	55
Achieved functionings at age 38				
achieved level of education	low – high (scale 0 - 1)	.76	.34	55
political participation	low – high (scale 0 - 1)	.73	.23	55
reported satisfaction with life (personal well being)	low – high (scale 0 - 1)	.90	.15	55

The analyses are based on a longitudinal study of urban Icelandic children with the focus on the relationship between social structure and individual development between age 7 and age 38. The sample was stratified according to social class, gender and general ability level at age 7. The sampling design was used in order to maximize the likelihood that the data disclose systematic developmental differences due to important socio-cultural factors and contexts of childhood experience (Edelstein, Keller & Schröder 1990). The project aims at studying the relationship between macro-contexts and micro-processes of individual development, and purports to integrate a sociologically based socialization perspective with a psychological view of developmental dynamics. The richness of the data is due to the amount of data for each case. This allows us to compare the biographical experiences measured in any single case with the mean of all others or rather the means of two selected subsamples.

In the following analysis we ask how social class affects the development of skills and competencies as well as achievable functionings and well being, and we ask how individuals become capable to overcome the restrictions of their social origin. We first show how life outcomes and conversion factors such as personality and social resources depend on social class. Further, we show how personal and social resources (as conversion factors) impact on degree and quality of opportunities for the realization of capabilities from childhood to adulthood. To specify this realization process and to separate it from the restrictions and options generated by social class, we use a case study approach to exemplify how an individual experiences her life world within the socialization process. For this reason we contrast the variable values from two cases from working class families on the one hand, and two cases from upper class families on the other with the mean values of the respective subsample (working class children on the one hand and upper class children on the other). The examples show how the personal conversion factors affect options for the realization of achieved functionings and life outcomes.

Figure 2: Personal characteristics as conversion factors, achieved functioning and well-being by social class (n_{SESlow} = 26, $n_{SEShigh}$ = 29)

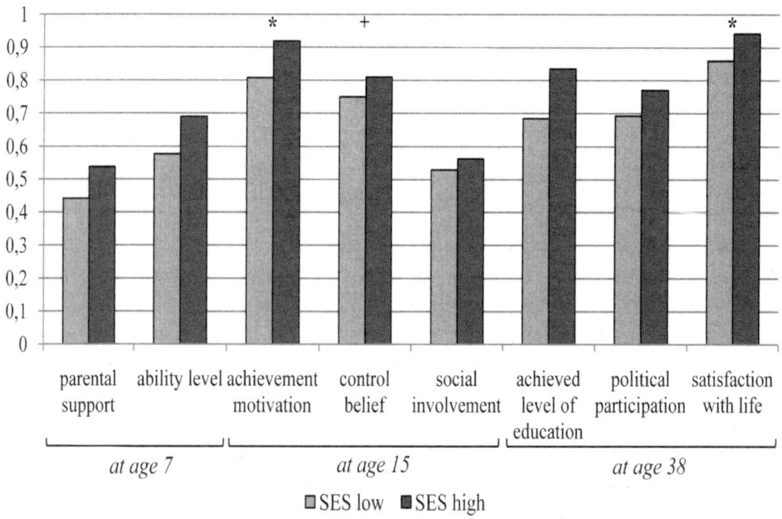

N = 55; level of significance +.10; *.05; **.01; ***.001

Figure 2 shows that the variables used as indicators of the individual's conversion factors vary systematically between social classes of origin. Persons from higher social classes in general possess greater potentials to perform well than their counterparts from the lower social classes. This holds true for outcome variables such as level of education reached, political participation as well as satisfaction with one's life. The surprising result that only achievement motivation and satisfaction with life show significant differences has to do with the sampling design that restricts the original variations in the variables by controlling for social class during the sampling process (Edelstein, Keller & Schröder 1990). In fact, we can assume much greater differences in the natural distribution of class specific characteristics. For our argumentation it is enough to show a systematic difference in the values on all variables.

To demonstrate how life outcomes are influenced by conversion factors as described above, we compute a regression analysis on the achieved level of education as a central concept of the capability approach.

Table 2: Influences of conversion factors on the achieved level of education at age 38 (ordered logit model; estimated coefficients; N = 55)

indicators	achieved level of education
SES – low	- .36
SES – high	*reference group*
ability level at age 7 – low	- 1.80 *
ability level at age 7 – high	*reference group*
parental support at age 7	.38
achievement motivation at age 15	5.60 *
control belief at age 15	- .64
social involvement at age 15	- 1.52
Model Fitting Information	
Chi^2	26.45 ***
df	6
Pseudo R^2 (Nagelkerke)	.42

level of significance +.10; *.05; **.01; ***.001

Table 2 represents the results of the regression analysis. Teacher rated ability level at age 7 as well as achievement motivation exert significant influences on the level of education achieved at midlife. In accordance with the results represented in Figure 2, which were discussed by reference to the sampling design, the analysis shows that in Iceland the opportunity to achieve higher levels of education is statistically independent of social class when controlling for certain personal conversion factors. According to the regression analysis, children's success in the educational system in general depends on their personal resources to perform well at the beginning of schooling and on their motivation to do well. The other variables described do not exert a significant influence on the achieved level of education. While this result holds true when referring to the overall sample, we now try to gain deeper insight into the person specific impacts that personal experiences and developmental characteristics possibly have on people's chances to realize certain achieved functionings – as typical examples or against the odds defined by social class.

For this purpose, we use the strategy of comparing a set of individuals with the mean values of the subsamples described earlier (SES low and SES high). We use a case of a female with low initial social resources (low social class) and low expectable personal capabilities (low teacher rated ability; see Figure 3a) as well as a case of a female from lower social class but with high rated ability at age 7 (Figure 3b).

Figure 3a: Capabilities of an individual from lower class (-) with low ability level (-): a case study (n_{SESlow} = 26, $n_{SEShigh}$ = 29)

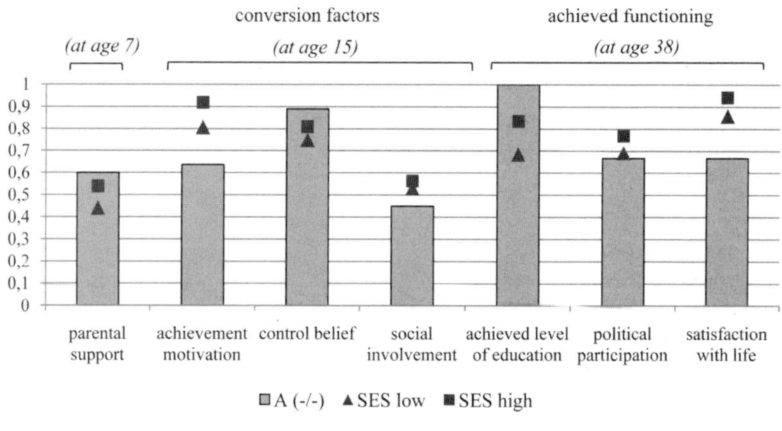

Due to the general class specific distribution in the variables, the individual (case A) exhibited low achievement motivation and little involvement in social activities. In contrast, and possibly due to the high rate of supportive experiences within the family, the female subject achieved a level of control belief in adolescence that even exceeds the upper class sample's average. If we look at achieved functioning at age 38 we also register an above-average value on achieved level of education. To use the semantics of the capability approach, this woman was apparently able to reach unexpectedly high functioning, considering social class of origin and the low ability level at the beginning of schooling. Besides the relatively low selectivity in the Icelandic educational systems (Edelstein 1983), the unexpectedly high level of parental support (which may imply a supportive attitude towards educational efforts) and a high rate of internal control belief may provide possible explanations for the woman's ability to achieve a high above-average educational level, as compared to the subsample of lower class children. In fact, a variety of unconsidered variables such as moral competencies and a supportive peer group may provide further explanations. However, in spite of her educational success, the woman's interest in politics equals the respective subsample's mean value, and she even reports an under-average rate of satisfaction with life. As a relatively low rate of satisfaction with life, according to our analyses, is typical for lower class children, this may be an indication of persisting restrictions due to the individual's social origin. In fact, a closer look reveals the woman's relatively low income. This may imply the personal inability to convert educational achievements into an adequate professional career and therefore provide an explanation for her relatively low satisfaction.

The case illustrated in Figure 3b shows the converse outcome. This female subject reaches a higher level of satisfaction with life than both subsamples' averages. Just as the individual considered above this woman was able to achieve a university degree. As all measured conversion factors at age 15 as well as parental support exhibit low values, typical for children from lower social class, the only explanation for her educational achievements seems to be provided by the woman's high level of general ability, rated by a teacher at the beginning of schooling. This evidence is more or less consistent with the results of the regression analysis described in table 2. With regards to the case study illustrated in figure 3a, we can conclude that this individual (Figure 3b) was, in contrast, able to realize a satisfactory life on the basis of personal achievements in spite of potentially restrictive conditions due to her social origin. The question whether this difference between individuals' satisfaction with their life outcomes can be explained by cognitive abilities in adolescence, unfulfilled expectations concerning one's own capacities or whatever requires a closer look at individuals' development and life outcomes and therefore cannot be conclusively answered at this point.

Last but not least it is noteworthy that in spite of their educational successes both individuals (cases A and B) were apparently not able to overcome class specific restrictions in terms of political participation.

Figure 3b: Capabilities of an individual from lower class (-) with high ability level (+): a case study (n_{SESlow} = 26, $n_{SEShigh}$ = 29)

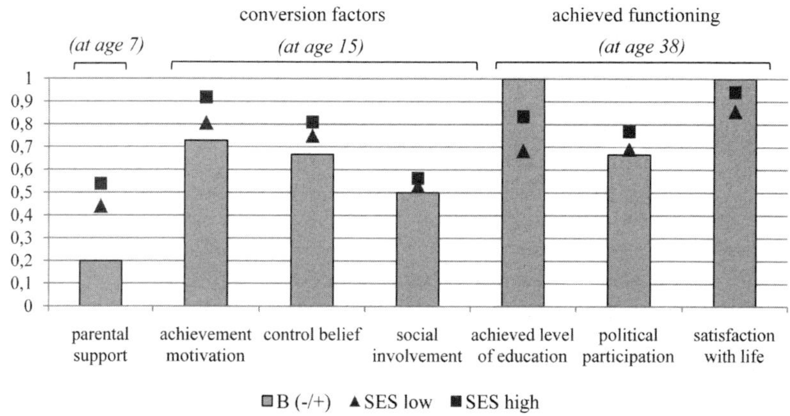

In addition to the case-studies of individuals from lower social class we now turn to two cases from upper social class. In particular, we consider a case of a female subject with high initial social resources (high social class) and low expectable personal capabilities (low teacher rated ability; see Figure 3c) as well as a case of a female subject from higher social class with high rated ability at age 7 (Figure 3d).

Figure 3c: Capabilities of an individual from upper class (+) with low ability level (-): a case study (n_{SESlow} = 26, $n_{SEShigh}$ = 29)

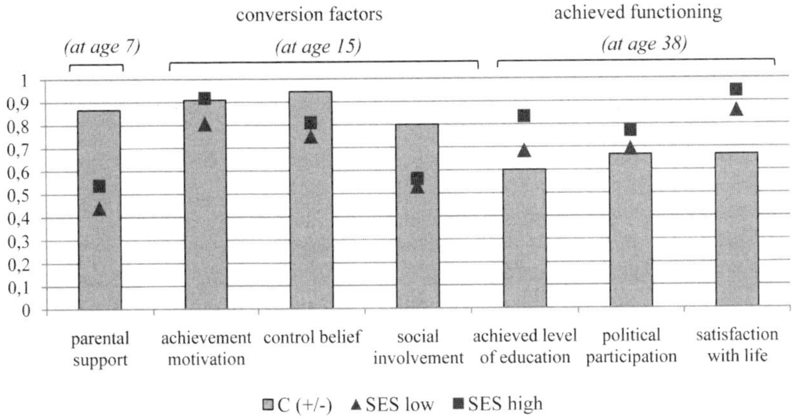

Concerning the conversion factors at age 15 as well as parental support, the individual referred to in Figure 3c appears to be a typical case from the upper class. This female exhibited an average level of achievement motivation compared to other children from the upper social class. Further, she reached above-average rates in control belief as well as social involvement. Similar to our argumentation concerning case A, the highly rated parental support may be a possible reason for the high rated conversion factors in this case as well. Unexpectedly, the woman whose development is illustrated in Figure 3c was not able to finally convert her personal potentials into the socially appreciated goal of higher education. This is probably due to her low rated ability level at the beginning of schooling. As shown in Table 2 as well as in Figure 3b, the ability level at age 7 seems to be an important factor for an individual's chances to realize personal potentials. Accordingly, the rate of political interest reported by the woman at age 38 reaches only the level of the lower class subsample's average. Finally she also reports an under-average rate of satisfaction with life. The latter might be an indicator for personal disappointment as a result of the unexpected inability to achieve certain goals. This assumption arises from the fact that the individuals we have referred to and who exhibited high levels of control belief at age 15, reported relative dissatisfaction with life at age 38 (see Figures 3a and 3c), whereas those whose control belief at age 15 was rated under average reported a high level of personal satisfaction with life later on (see Figures 3b and 3d).

The last case study we describe represents the almost typical development of a child from upper class from adolescence to adulthood. Despite the relatively low rate of control belief, this female, whose general ability level at age 7 was rated high, reaches average or above-average levels in the case of all the conversion factors which we consider. Finally the woman represents the ideal example of a child from the upper class, as she was able to convert social and personal resources into high levels of education, political participation as well as satisfaction with life.

Figure 3d: Capabilities of an individual from upper class (+) with high ability level (+): a case study (n_{SESlow} = 26, $n_{SEShigh}$ = 29)

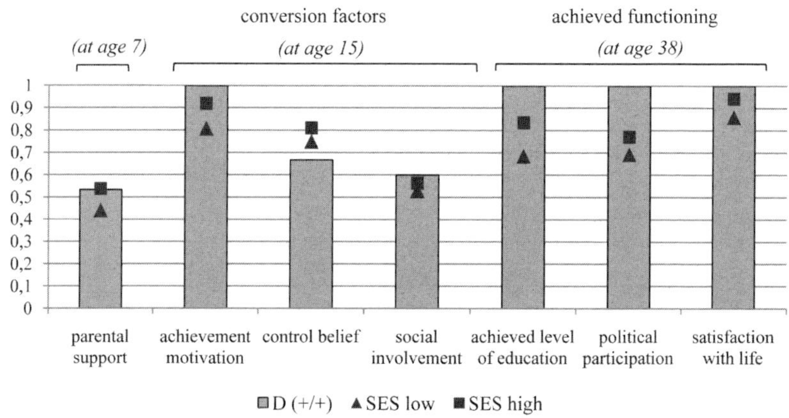

Discussion

The preceding analysis emphasizes the assumption that in welfare states such as Iceland capabilities are to a large extent promoted by the social system, especially education and the labor market. However, the realization of these capabilities does not solely depend on social institutions and political circumstances (such as the educational system and the economy) as our conjectures were in the theoretical considerations at the outset of this paper. More important is the conversion of individual (and social) resources into options for a successful life. According to our analyses, the interplay of general (cognitive) ability of a child, parental support as well as internal control belief has an important impact on his or her life outcomes as well as their meaning for the individual's well being. In order to underpin this argument, we provided four case-studies as examples. The woman we referred to as 'case A', for instance, was able to achieve a university degree against all odds (lower social class and low rated ability level at age 7), possibly due to relatively high rated parental support as well as an above-average level of control belief at age 15. However, and, as pointed out referring to 'case B' (lower social class, high rated ability level at age 7 and low rate of control belief at age 15), possibly due to that specific interplay of personal characteristics as well, she obviously was not able to convert her achieved functionings into a satisfactory way of life. The analysis shows how individual variations in functioning within specific socialization and personality contexts affect success and well-being. The study illustrates how individuals become able to transform personal resources into aspired functionings even in the case of restrictions and low capabilities linked to social origin. Thus, individuals from lower social classes and characterized by low abilities are potentially able to achieve options for a successful life in terms of high educational levels. However, the cases also show that achieved functionings, such as a high level of education, do not automatically affect personal well being – as it is typically assumed in the context of the capability approach. Thus, the process of converting personal resources into achieved functionings and well being is more complex than is often assumed.

Research that relies on the capability approach often tends to focus on capabilities as external resources, measuring people´s employment status, formal education, health, et cetera. In contrast, to assess people´s actual capability to live the lives they desire it appears promising to develop the capability approach further with a perspective on developmental and educational processes that transcend the restrictions of formal education. In fact, other studies show the sustained power of structural constraints on the operation of individual capabilities (Edelstein & Grundmann 2006), which is a much debated problem in view of the selective power of educational systems to determine life courses independent of individual capabilities, especially in educational systems that are more selective than that of Iceland. The case studies we have presented here suggest the general possibility of strengthening one's capabilities and of realizing achieved functionings against the odds defined by restrictive class positions, at least in cases where the social system provides corresponding opportunities. Focusing on individual ways of converting personal resources understood as the possible result of specific social experiences, researchers will be able to enter people´s life-worlds and gain insight into how they make sense of their lives. Major biographical choices and decisions occur in the face of transitions from the educational to the occupational system, from adolescence to adulthood. Here we find a field of special interest for the study of the development of people's capabilities and their success and failure in the process of achieving valuable functionings and living meaningful lives.

The analytical focus on individuals' agency as outlined above grants deeper insight into how resources in the milieux of origin can actually be translated into different pragmatic orientations and thus into different outcomes. Our analyses support the idea that the capability approach can be reformulated in terms of socialization theory and the life course paradigm which permit complex multilevel operationalization and modeling of basic assumptions provided by the capability approach. This permits to reconstruct the processes through which experiences of valuation and recognition in different social environments affect the development of agency as well as an individual's functioning in his or her life course. Moreover, this research perspective entails the option to take social indicators, measures of political and economical change, and parameters of social welfare systematically into account.

The Iceland Study shows how the analysis of capabilities can be put into such contexts. Iceland, even more than other Western societies, has experienced rapid change in the past two decades. Its economy stagnated from 1988, when our respondents were 19 years old, and went into a full-fledged economic recession by 1992, ending in an all time record of Icelandic unemployment of five percent. In 1995 a neoliberally engineered upswing was accompanied by severe cuts in social security spending and liberal tax reforms culminating in rising incomes for those fully employed in the labor market, and leaving behind those who had to rely on the public welfare system.[1] We thus can analyze the interplay of (milieu and person specific) agency and capability in a generation which entered the system of college education and labor markets in a time of rapid change and accelerating competition and complement the micro perspective of milieu specific development of agency and capabilities of individuals by a macro perspective on the educational and occupational outcomes of these micro processes.

The longitudinal data of the Icelandic sample cover the subjects' development from their first school year at age 7 in the late seventies to their adult life at close to 40. Whereas capability research often focuses on capabilities as external resources, we have chosen a more person centered approach. We conceive of milieu specific agency as a person's capacity to pragmatically orient her action, on the one hand towards internal cognitive competencies, psycho-social dispositions such as personal well being and value orientations, and towards external resources such as achievements in terms of education on the other hand. The focus of the analysis therefore is on the person's ability to experience and recognize internal and external resources rather than on capabilities as external resources. The question for which an answer is sought is the following: What kinds of individual resources and experiences enable people to realize and value their personal skills, competencies, personalities and orientations? And what are the opportunities that their life-worlds provide them in order to put these subjective resources to use?

1 The crisis of 2008/2009 remains outside the scope of the present paper.

People do not only differ with regard to their material and sociocultural backgrounds and resources, but also with regard to their milieu specific agency, which allows them to make use of these resources successfully. Since agency is influenced, if not determined, by social structure, we may observe different agentic processes and strategies working on similar resources. We are, therefore, able to evaluate what it is that accounts for the success or the failure of children of the lower social classes in the educational system or the labor market. Focusing on the individual's agency as sketched above grants deeper insight into how different resources in milieus of origin actually translate into different pragmatic orientations and thereby into different outcomes in view of educational and social reproduction.

References

Bonvin, J.-M. (2009): Der Capability Ansatz und sein Beitrag für die Analyse gegenwärtiger Sozialpolitik. In: Soziale Passagen, 1, 8-22.

Dravenau, D. (2006): Die Entwicklung milieuspezifischer Handlungsbefähigung. In: Grundmann, M., Dravenau, D., Bittlingmayer, U.H. & Edelstein, W. (Hrsg.): Handlungsbefähigung und Milieu. Zur Analyse milieuspezifischer Alltagspraktiken und ihrer Ungleichheitsrelevanz. Münster, 191-235.

Edelstein, W. (1983): Cultural constraints on development and the vicissitudes of progress. In: Kessel, F.S. & Siegel, A.W. (Eds.): The child and other cultural inventions. New York, 48-81.

Edelstein, W. (1999): Soziale Selektion, Sozialisation und individuelle Entwicklung. In: Grundmann, M. (Hrsg.): Konstruktivistische Sozialisationsforschung. Frankfurt/M, 35-52.

Edelstein, W. & Grundmann, M. (2006): The persistence of social class: A macro-micro analytical approach to educational performance and attainment in three generations. In: Grundmann, M., Dravenau, D., Bittlingmayer, U.H. & Edelstein, W. (Hrsg.): Handlungsbefähigung und Milieu. Zur Analyse milieuspezifischer Alltagspraktiken und ihrer Ungleichheitsrelevanz. Münster, 96-153.

Edelstein, W., Keller, M. & Schröder E. (1990): Child development and social structure: A longitudinal study of individual differences. In: Baltes, P.B., Featherman, D.L. & Lerner, R.M. (Eds.): Life-span development and behavior. Hillsdale 152-185.

Elder, G.H. Jr. (1995): The Life Course Paradigm: Social Change and Individual Development. In: Moen, Ph., Elder, G.H. Jr. & Lüscher, K. (Eds): Examing Lives in Context. Washington, 101-140.

Grundmann, M. (1998): Norm und Konstruktion. Zur Dialektik von Bildungsvererbung und Bildungsaneignung. Opladen.

Grundmann, M., Dravenau, D., Bittlingmayer, U.H. & Edelstein, W. (2006): Handlungsbefähigung und Milieu. Zur Analyse milieuspezifischer Alltagspraktiken und ihrer Ungleichheitsrelevanz. Münster.

Grundmann, M. & Dravenau, D. (2010): Class, Agency and Capability. In: Otto, H.-U. & Ziegler, H. (Eds.): Education, welfare and the capabilities approach. Opladen & Farmington Hills, 85-102.

Jacobsen, T., Edelstein, W. & Hofmann, V. (1994): A longitudinal study of the relation between representations of attachment in childhood and cognitive functioning in childhood and adolescence. In: Developmental Psychology, 30, 112-124.

Keller, M. (1996): Moralische Sensibilität: Entwicklung in Freundschaft und Familie. Weinheim.

Moen, P., Elder, G.H. & Lüscher, K. (1995): Examining lives in context. Perspectives on the ecology of human development. Washington.

Robeyns, I. (2005): The Capability Approach: a theoretical survey. In: Journal of Human Development, 6, 1, 93-114.

Robeyns, I. (2006): Three models of education. Rights, capabilities and human capital. In: Theory and Research in Education, 4, 1, 69-84.

Schröder, E. & Edelstein, W. (1991): Intrinsic and External Constraints on the Development of Cognitive Competence. In: Chandler, M. & Chapman, M. (Eds.): Criteria for Competence: Controversies in the Conceptualization and Assesment of Children's Abilities. Hillsdale, 131-150.

Sen, A. (1992): Inequality re-examined. New York.

Sen, A. (1999): Development as Freedom. Oxford.

Sen, A. (2004): How does Culture Matter? In: Rao, V. & Walton, M. (Eds.): Culture and Public Action. Stanford, 37-58.

Strickland, B.R. (1989): Internal – external control expectancies. In: American Psychologist, 44, 1-12.

Zimmermann, B. (2006): Pragmatism and the Capability Approach: Challenges in Social Theory and Empirical Research. In: European Journal of Social Theory, 9, 4, 467-484.

Niels Rosendal Jensen

From Inequality to Anomie – And Inequality Revisited by Use of CA

The motto of my intervention at this conference is inspired by Leonard Cohen. He sings a few words which might correspond with our intentions: "First we take Manhattan, then we take Berlin". Amartya Sen did the first; we intend to do the latter.

My presentation is set out in two main parts: some theoretical approaches as the first part and our research in Denmark as the second one.

1. The overall framework – the challenge of the nexus education-work in a broader sense

1.1 Society

Modern societies are framed as knowledge societies. Without further in depth going here the intention is to link an understanding of a knowledge society to the Capability Approach. Here Nico Stehr has presented an outline of much value (Stehr 1994), and to come to the head I quote Nico Stehr who states: "Knowledge may be defined as a *capacity for action*. The use of the term "knowledge" as a capacity for action is derived from Francis Bacon's famous observation that knowledge is power (a somewhat misleading translation of Bacon's Latin phrase: "*scientia est potentia*"). Bacon suggests that knowledge derives its utility from its capacity to set something in motion. The term potentia, that is *capacity*, is employed to describe the power of knowing" (Stehr 1999). In brief: the new societal formation should objectively help us closing the gap and Stehr's point seems supporting our goals.

Important however is to understand: a knowledge based society or a learning society does not operate in a vacuum. It operates – as Castells point at – in a capitalist structure.

1.2 Politics: the Capability Approach and educational discussions

The above mentioned implies a political assessment of our approach:

The first and foremost question is: How can we place the Capabilities Approach within the last 40 years of educational discussion? CA combined with lifelong or even better perhaps life wide education can reopen a chapter of a long struggle for better educational conditions – originally seen as a means of improving enlightenment, equality and social justice. After the Sputnik-chock huge investments were made in order to mobilize the working class kids for education beyond the compulsory 7 years. The barriers were studied, and the main obstacle seemed to be of an economic nature. The slogan in those days was: more equality of education, and the agenda was supported by political parties, popular organizations, trade unions, parents, young people, etc. Lifting the general standards of education had become a national cause.

We might compare the Sputnik-chock then with the globalization chock now. Some new research outcomes have showed up recently pointing to following: Economy still plays a role, but the cultural background of children (e.g. their family) seems to be even more important. Thereby, some researchers almost have forgotten the economic aspect and therefore neglecting what an interpretation of the PISA inquiries may emphasize: at the end school performance has much more in common with objectified cultural capital (access to books, pc, writing desk, etc.) than usually assumed.

At the beginning of the new Millennium the EC became aware that the social critique of growing inequality and marginalization had to be met, and the so called Lisbon Memorandum tried to unite the contradictions between a market economy and social cohesion: "European Union must set an example for the world to show that it is possible both to achieve dynamic economic growth and to strengthen social cohesion. Lifelong learning is an essential policy for the development of citizenship, social cohesion and employment" (EC Memorandum 30.10.2000: 34).

Nevertheless, we must ask whether such contradictions between a life world perspective and an economic perspective simply disappear by proclaiming that we should do a little of both. The discourse of EC seems to be an exponent of a neutralisation of the central dynamic of conflicts in modernity. The guiding principle is likely to understand the needs of the labour market, the democratic civil society, and the individual as one and the same.

We should also bear in mind that the actual crisis – not and primarily not just a financial crisis, but rather a structural crisis – will have a heavy impact on the implementation of our educational work. The crisis has been understood as the personal mistakes or personal greed. In the Hollywood movie from 1987 'Wall Street' Gordon Gekko makes a speech from which at least one sentence has become immortal: "Greed, for lack of a better word, is good". In my opinion greed doesn't only refer to money and markets, but to love, acknowledgement, identity, power, status, etc. as well. Although I dislike greed in Gekko's sense, I find it life-affirming for young people to wish and fight for a better future and to have options. Still greed of brokers or banks just pulled the trigger and does not contain the deeper going reason why the crisis developed that fast.

The young generation among other things shows the optimistic side of greed – which belongs to the kingdom of Bildung, learning, and education. But this greed must be combined with another greed: that of democracy and equality, which to my viewpoint is exactly what the CA is offering..

1.2.1. Equality and social justice

We will now revisit the old discussion of equality and social justice. During more decades the policy of Danish politicians aimed at overcoming poverty and inequality by economic means. This changed in the era of neo-liberalism which now seems to have come to an end. However, the discourse shifted from the 'discourse on inequality' to the 'discourse on anomaly'. In stead of fighting poverty the discourse developed the non mature stile of 'blaming the victims'.

Within the framework of CA some clarification concerning the concept of equality is needed.

The former Norwegian Minister of Education Gudmund Hernes, a well known Norwegian Social Democrat and sociologist, once defined equality in four levels (Hernes 1973):

1. Formal equality	*No formal barriers – 1903*
2. Equality of resources	*In discussion since 1945*
3. Equality of competences	*Performance dependent*
4. Equality of results/outcomes	*Allocation of resources against existing dissemination of resources – "equality through education"*

The year 1903 is mentioned since Danish gymnasiums were opened for working class kids that year. Until then society accepted an education which served to function as a social reproduction of the considerable inequalities in Denmark. Every social class had its "own" school. The working classes had the ordinary Folkeskole, while the middle and upper classes had their private schools and private gymnasiums. Education before 1903 did not signal elevation into another class. 1945 a commission on the future of youth was appointed to document and discuss the problems, because young people had been the most eager participants of the national resistance against German occupation during the Second World War. Equality became top priority, and soon the slogan equality of opportunity opened a new agenda. The new philosophy of equality encompassed an important recruitment perspective, implying that all children and youth, irrespective of social and economic background, should have the opportunity to climb to the top of the educational system. Differences from the past were no longer accepted: social class, gender and geographical origin should be abolished as criteria of selection. This perspective appealed to the sense of justice as well as to the renewed nation-building after the years of occupation. Nation-building was seen as an important task of schooling, because it would develop a sense of belonging, respect, and mutual understanding between pupils from different social classes.

Expanding this perspective meant to understand education as a common good which in turn resulted in comprehensive education and equality of results or outcomes. Intervening for equality of results did not imply that all children should or could reach the same level, but rather aimed at reduction of differences. Hernes stressed that unequal treatment was a necessary tool to overcome differences and create similar chances. During the course of the immediate post-war years equality was developed in three dimensions: the resource dimension – equality of resources invested; the social dimension – the establishing of a public school, common to all children; the cultural dimension – students were to benefit from a joint academic curriculum.

We still need to develop a conceptual framework here in order to combine the CA and equality. An emphasis on equality of outcomes may be our strongest card. Sen may support us in the further struggle for equality (Sen 1979). One of the main problems seems to be a shift from education as a common good to education understood as a private good. The idea of education as a common good is based on the Keynesian concept of a welfare state. Equal distribution of income and opportunity would stimulate economic growth. This argument was completed by the idea of human capital, meaning that education was seen as an investment. Eventually this argumentation was used to enhance comprehensive school reforms. Further the commitment to education was combined with the idea of equality of results. From this viewpoint providing the same opportunity is not enough.

1.3. Some of the missing links in educational discussions should be mentioned here, because of their importance to our approach

At this point it seems appropriate to emphasize some actual conditions.

1.3.1. External conditions

1. educational inflation (Bourdieu & Passeron 1970; Hansen 2003; Beck 1992; Livingstone 1998, 2009) – a trend towards underemployment, over-qualification, and over-education as an outcome of the strengthening of human capital. Meaning that youngsters with lesser formal education are forced out of jobs they can manage, while over-qualified youngsters are taking over.
2. financial crisis – still a wide public and political interest in education: more formal education as the answer number one. But is more education in fact useable in jobs that don't demand such higher skills and knowledge. A trend appears to be that we educate far beyond what the labour market can consume. A principle discussion on the aims of education (Bildung) – concerning family, leisure time, political activity/democracy.
3. smaller cohorts – opening new options, but also much more demanding than before (the most recent changes in the act on active policy on labour market came into force August 1st this year. Unskilled young persons – who are loosing their jobs – are now given instructtion to start an education. Young people under the age of 25 and without being the breadwinner of a family are after 13 weeks of unemployment ordered to education. Municipalities, companies and vocational schools are ordered to cooperate in order to offer qualifying education combined with practical trainee jobs.

1.3.2. Internal conditions

1. resources – do the schools and institutions have the resources to meet young people with special needs?
2. motivation (educational thinking, formal/informal, evaluation of competences) – how do we motivate young people for 'interesting' education aimed at 'boring' jobs?
3. alternate ways of doing things – first enfolding a broad concept of education, formation and Bildung; second creating learning environments which are 'fit for fight', meaning that such environments are aiming at developing an overall orientation (not just one aim, but

more aims; not just one way of learning, but a broad variety; not just for the future job, but also for future family, personal development, and societal responsibility as a citizen, etc.).

1.4. An inherent contradiction

The reflections above have tried to show a red thread – that of empowering youngsters to contribute actively in order to open as many options themselves as possible by means of education for all.

Referring back to Bourdieu's analysis such educational interventions may still provide young persons with cultural capital. In a broader context, however, this is in no way innocent. A plausible explanation is (partly based on Desjardins & Rubinson 2009: 26-27): Towards the end of the 1990s policy-makers had somehow unwilling come to the insight that while the 'new economy' promises an increased productivity and an improved standard of living, it also introduces a new set of transitions and adjustment challenges for society, industry and individuals. If not met properly, these challenges could augment and even strengthen the permanent exclusion or marginalisation of segments of the population and exacerbate social and economic divisions. These concerns have partly shifted the policy agenda in the direction of "inclusive liberalism" (see e.g. Craig & Porter 2005; Mahon & McBride 2008). Mahon & McBride argue that while "inclusive liberalism" shares certain features with neo-liberalism, it differs in other important aspects. The differences can be found in "inclusive liberalism's" emphasis on the idea of investing in people who demonstrate they are willing to take responsibility for their own development and providing more incentives and 'carrots rather than sticks' within a supply-side approach. It is, of course, presently difficult to judge whether or not what we see are minor adjustments to neo-liberalism or if something more fundamental has occurred.

Recognising market failures, and growing concerns about large groups not participating fully in social and economic life, the 'softer' version of the economic paradigm can be read as a shift in balance between the three classic institutional arrangements. The market still has a central role, but the responsibilities of the individual and the state are visible and apparently increasing, too. The newer rhetoric is one of shared responsibilities. A closer reading of the text might lead one to be more sceptical, since what stands out in recent policy documents is the stress on the responsibility of the individuals for their own learning. This narrowness in approaching the state's responsibility may be understood as "inclusive liberalism" in the sense that it does invoke a form of inclusiveness – although it also has strong neo-liberal features. It does not seem that there has been a shift back to Keynesianism.

1.5. Responsibility – individual or societal?

This section of the article aims at understanding societal responsibility.

A sort of new spirit has developed over the past decades – a fundamental change of societal responsibility. Zygmunt Bauman has framed that development as a shift from a society of producers to a society of consumers in his interesting analysis (1998), including new forms of marginalization and social exclusion. This means that the overall, hegemonic slogan is: work or perish! And he continues by explaining that the new poor are seen as abnormal, and that an old trend is to some extent in a revival, namely that that the best way out is to get rid of them. In brief we are facing severe challenges, if Bauman's analysis is to be taken seriously. Translated into education the making of a consumer is more important than producing producers.

Further Bauman states "in the industrial phase of modernity one fact was beyond all questioning: that everyone must be a producer first, before anything else. In 'modernity mark two', the consumers' modernity, the brute unquestionable fact is that one needs to be consumer first, before one can think of becoming anything in particular" (ibid.: 26). The consequences may be rather overwhelming: a steady working career is no longer a widely available option. Permanent, well guarded and assured jobs are now a rarity. New vacancies tend to be fixed term, until further notice and part-time. The catchword is flexibility, and this stands for a game of 'hire and fire' with very few rules attached. In his conclusion he underlines that the prospect of constructing a lifelong identity on the foundation of work is dead and buried (ibid.: 27).

A change from 'work ethic' to 'work aesthetic' – the latter is depending on choice of style, etc. – will cause immense challenges to our capability approach. The work ethic conveyed a message of equality (ibid.: 33), while the work aesthetic emphasizes distinction and elevates some professions on the cost of other types of work which are regarded as so uniformly abject and worthless that they can not become objects of willing, unforced choice. Jobs in the first category are 'interesting; jobs in the second are 'boring'. The young generation prefers interesting and not boring jobs – although young people might not have the competencies to get into an interesting job. The result is that unequal conditions and chances are not interpreted as inequality, but rather as an anomic state of the individual.

The society of producers had a vision of full employment; the society of consumers does not care about full employment. The norm once was that you should get a job and those not able of getting one was seen as abnormal. Originally the persistent presence of the poor tended to be explained by the shortage of work or the shortage of will to work. But the labour market has undergone changes as well. Robert Castel points at a development splitting up the labour market in different sectors: that of full integration, that of partly integration and that of decoupling. It should not be necessary to continue this argumentation at this spot. The outcome of this development is new forms of poverty, meaning that you are excluded form whatever passes for a 'normal life' or cut off from the chances of whatever passes in a given society for a 'happy life', and resulting in falling self-esteem, feelings of shame or guilt.

In brief we are in fact facing a complicated situation. I will now mention some trends of the nexus welfare state and lifelong education.

The above presented further implies a break with the traditional welfare state policy by demanding a direct responsibility of individuals to better their situation. Or perhaps the policy only breaks with a certain interpretation of the welfare state apparatus – that of the provider, offering opportunities and not claiming that people should do something and not just let the professionals take care. Where the former welfare state promoted a vague idea of a humanistic inspired paradigm of education, today's national policy debates are almost exclusively driven by an economic paradigm of lifelong learning. One might conclude – comparing with e.g. the shift of paradigm from lifelong education to lifelong learning – that welfare and social assistance get linked to willingness to take any work, and readiness to undertake some form of labour market training program to enhance employability prospects (Crouch, Finegold & Sako 1999: 5). The emphasis on learning rather than education as promoted in the conceptualisation of lifelong learning seems to be well suited for a neo-liberal agenda. This increased attention on the individual's responsibility for his and her own learning is closely embedded in a changing understanding and articulation of the very concept of lifelong learning and signals a move away from a preoccupation with education to a focus on learning (Griffin 1999; Rubenson 1999). As observed by Tujnman & Broström (2002: 103) "the emphasis on "learning" rather than "education" is highly significant because it reduces the traditional preoccupation with structures and institutions and instead focuses on the individual. ….the realisation of lifelong learning depends to a large degree on the capacity and motivation of individuals to take care of their own learning".

The responsibility of persons to make adequate provisions for the creation and preservation of their own human capital seems to become a common characteristic in Europe. The value system of individualisation is embedded in a new ethics which is based on the principle of duty to oneself (Beck & Beck-Gernsheim 2002: 38). Failure in the labour market or as a parent is increasingly seen to be an outcome of an individual's decision with regard to education and training (Holzer 1996). Thus, under neo-liberal globalization acquisition of skills and competencies has become the social rationalization for accepting unequal opportunities, poverty and inequalities (Bourdieu 1998).

To conclude on part 1 a national cause has to be reinvented. When educational progress is linked to popular movements and gets broad national support, it seems to become lasting progress. However, we cannot reinvent a national cause in the old sense of the concept. Nowadays it has to be combined with an international aspect, with collective rights, achieving equality and strengthening democracy.

2. Our research on CA

2.1. The local interpretation

In the optic of the capabilities approach the Danish case story of our ongoing analysis shows following: the importance of educational resources does not exclusively lie in increasing professional skills and economic productivity of a person. The major part lies in reducing inequalities and empowering people in order to have an integrated and active life in the community at large, and to face the requirements of a knowledge-based economy. And we are not alone, since the Ministry of Education has supported a very likely idea. With this approach, the further focus has been dwelling on: 1) how the different programmes/agencies, we are studying, are situated in the nexus «education-employment-community/social integration»; 2) which factors favour (or prevent) the conversion of educational resources into capabilities "to chose and to act" people's own life/job; 3) how and when capability for learning is enhanced, and it transforms into capability for work.

We understand capability for learning as a key concept also in assessing the long term effects of the programmes of education and training, because it manages to consider the whole personal career and a perspective of lifelong learning consistent with the dynamics of the technological change, knowledge based societies and the expectations of school and the education system as a whole.

2.2. Higher standards of education for all

The Danish government has decided to meet the global challenge by lifting the level of public education as well as demanding lifelong education of each and every one. 85% of the young generation should accomplish 12 years of schooling 2010 – and 95% in 2015. The state is offering opportunities – meaning that young people have a right to spend 12 years in school + 1 year of kindergarten class (13 years). Then young people are expected to use their right – since it is not only a right, but also a duty. Those not capable of using that right have been looked upon as 'vasted lives' or 'deviants'. Since 2007 the right has been extended to include even youngsters with special needs. They are offered via a rather flexible arrangement.

The new Act on Education has been a success. For the moment being about 1400 young people are participating in a wide number of schools, residential homes, production schools, high schools, etc.

Usually they are not valued to be members of the smart set. As so called "target group" one may believe they are homogeneous. In fact they differ very much – some have had problems with schooling, others have a diagnosis (ADHD, Asperger's Syndrom, Autism, etc.); but one trend is similar: they have been very lonely, sometimes isolated, excluded from the good company of peers.

The diversity of the providing organizations matches somehow the diversity of their "costumers". This trait characterizes a strong tradition of Danish pedagogy and educational supply – the tendency of state supported free schools which are taking differences of young persons seriously in account and offer them overall solutions: school, workshops, digs, food, etc. under one and same roof.

2.3. *The projects – education*

We are following two large projects – including a broad variety of institutions, a large number of teachers, pedagogues, etc. as well as a large number of young people with special needs. An important artefact is the individual plan of education which every person uses as her or his way through the educational programme. Some old problems have been turned upside down. The intention is that the staff members are responsible for creating the necessary scaffolding and contacts between the different organizations. Former the young person should make arrangements with schools, employers, administration, etc. on his own. But facing that many members of the "target group" are not capable of doing such due to lack of experiences, the organizations have taken over that responsibility. The staff coordinates activities between school, employer, recreation centres or clubs and the community meaning that the young person is not stopped by obstacles due to non-existing experience of how to contact who, when, where and often for how long. The outcome seems optimistic. When young people are supported by a team of professionals, a major obstacle has been pushed away. They are no longer up against the Great Wall of China, since the professionals have the contacts and networks in companies, municipalities, different organizations etc.

The individual plan of each young male or female by and large runs around the clock and in all settings. This might reintroduce Goffman's nightmare of an asylum, but it does not seem so. As we are still in medias res, we can only present some reflections and first outcomes.

Concerning conversion of factors enhancing or the opposite – we have by now gained some insight. The learning platform for the group of young people mentioned seems to be a practical one. They are getting into "communities of practice" following the 'master' during the day, learning his skills by observing and trial and error. Practical tasks are not only a way to motivate students, but a way to learn more about how things run in a company, among workers in everyday situations and settings. The craftsman is so to say the role model of the young people. This implies that staff members are organising the daily routines – one meets at 7 in the morning, is welcomed by the peers and the master, sits around the table with a cup of coffee, exchanging the latest daily news or small talking, waiting and prepared to listen to the activities of the day, is then beginning the duties of the day, having lunch together and finishing the day by resuming what did or did not function. One might call that setting a cognitive apprenticeship. The outcome is astonishing: students labelled as young people with learning disabilities are equipped with videos, PDA, and instructions and are becoming rather fast learners. Some young people remarked that they could not read and write. Nevertheless, they have learned to read and write simple information about their craft, about how to fill out applications for jobs, about how to use a bank account and other everyday necessities. This is not a miracle, but rather an outcome of the learning environment. They understand that it is necessary to read and understand instructions when acting like a carpenter or service worker in elderly care. At some institutions 'stronger' and 'weaker' students are making teams – for example one is driver, while the other is navigating (for an earlier research see e.g. Gudmundsson & Rosendal Jensen 2005).

2.4. The projects – workplace

To bridge the gap between schooling and working place counsellors have a special task to fulfil. They contact firms, introduce the young person and follow her or him through the first difficult months of getting acquainted with the rituals, habits, and expectations of the work place. The main obstacle here is that each context has its own logic of meaning. In order to act in a competent way the young person has to learn to fit into a different logic of meaning than he is used to. By getting knowledge about mobility and relations young people are experiencing how to handle such transitions. You have to show up every morning at 7 o'clock in the firm. This means that you cannot drink too many beers or smoke marihuana the evening before. If you haven't arrived, the counsellor contacts the firm and personally fetches the young person and brings him to the job. Experiences show that one day off soon grows to a week off, and then the young person is too ashamed to show up ever again. Therefore, the counsellor has to be ready and take immediate action. This is somehow a new trend – former young people would fight for their collective rights (Rosendal Jensen 2007).

Seen through a personal dimension many young people underline the close relationship with their teachers as well as their peer group. The expect respect, acknowledgement, and trust.

From side of the institutional dimension it is obvious that the institutions try to adjust their structure, learning arrangements, etc. to the level of the young persons. Of course this openness does not involve a total change of every routine or the daily structure. But the institutions are open in order to meet the needs of their "costumers" and continue the necessary support plus the control demanded from municipalities. They have to act costumer-friendly.

In a societal dimension young persons with special needs are on their way to become citizens. The intention is that they continue education – e.g. get into further education after completing their basis education of 3 years – or at least have become active citizens. Quite a challenge one might argue.

We have identified some barriers which may be interesting for an international audience. First – dispositional barriers, the participants' experience or understanding of his own capacities or capabilities. Second – situational barriers, embedded in the participants' actual situation, e.g. lack of resources and difficulties getting into a community either at institutions or workplaces. Third – institutional barriers, usually as an outcome of practices where the participant is lacking social, vocational or personal competencies or the institution does not care enough about integrating newcomers.

In general ambitions are high and promising, but practices still have to be developed.

References

Bauman, Z. (1998): Work, consumerism and the new poor. Buckingham/Philadelphia.

Beck, U. (1992): Risk Society: Towards a New Modernity. London.

Beck, U. & Beck-Gernsheim, E. (2002): Individualization. London.

Bourdieu, P. (1998): Acts of Resistance: Against the Tyranny of the Market. New York.

Bourdieu, P. & Passeron, J-C. (1970): La Reproduction: Elements pour une théorie du système d'enseignement. Paris.

Craig, D. & Porter, D. (2005): The third way and the third world: poverty reduction and social inclusion strategies in the rise of 'inclusive' liberalism. Review of International Political Economy 12, 2.

European Commission (2000): A Memorandum on Lifelong Learning. Luxembourg: Office for Official Publications of the European Commission.

Griffin, C. (1999): Lifelong learning and social democracy. International Journal of Lifelong Education, 18, 4, 329-342.

Gudmundsson, G. & Rosendal Jensen, N. (2005): Pædagogik for unge med særlige behov: en forskningsbaseret udredning om, 'hvad der virker'. København.

Hansen, E.J. (2003): Uddannelsessystemerne i sociologisk perspektiv. København.

Hernes, G. (1973): Om ulikhetens reproduksjon. København.

Holzer, H. (1996): What Employers Want. New York.

Livingstone, D.W. (1998): The Education-Jobs-Gap: Underemployment or Economic Democracy. Boulder, Colo.

Livingstone, D.W. (Ed.) (2009): Education & Jobs: Exploring the Gaps. Toronto.

Mahon, R. & McBride, S. (Eds.) (2008): The OECD and Transnational Governance. Vancouver.

Rosendal Jensen, N. (2007): Den nye faglige ungdom. In: Jensen, K. & Rosendal Jensen, N. (Eds.): Staten og den institutionelle pædagogik. Pædagogisk sociologi bind 1. København, 107-126.

Rubenson, K. (1999): Adult education and training: The poor cousin: An analysis of OECD reviews of national policies for education. Scottish Journal of Adult Education, 5, 2, 5-32.

Sen, A. (1979): Equality of What? The Tanner Lecture on Human Values. Delivered at Stanford University May 22.

Stehr, N. (1994): Arbeit, Eigentum und Wissen: Zur Theorie von Wissensgesellschaften. Frankfurt am Main.

Stehr, N. (1999): Paper presented at the conference "Globalitás – tudástársadalom – lokalitás" of the Third Millenium Foundation, Fot, Hungary, December 28.

Gunter Graf, Oscar Germes-Castro & Bernhard Babic

Approaching Capabilities with Children in Care – An international Project to Identify Values of Children and Young People in Care

Introduction

SOS Children's Villages is a non-governmental and non-denominational child-focused organisation that provides direct services in the areas of care, education and health for children at risk of losing, or who have already lost, parental care. The organisation also builds the capacity of the children's caregivers, their families and communities to provide adequate care. Finally, SOS Children's Villages also advocates for the rights of children without parental care. Globally speaking, the organisation currently offers 74.700 children a home in a family-based setting and supports another 171.600 in their families of origin. Through its programmes and services the organisation strives to enable these children and young people to live a life according to their own culture and religion and to be active members of their community.

From this point of view the links between the organisation's efforts and the central ideas of the capability approach (CA) are obvious. However, the approach has not yet been applied systematically on the situation of and the work with children and youth in care. Therefore SOS Children's Villages and the International Research Center Salzburg (IFZ) started a research project to clarify to which extent the CA can serve as a framework to analyse youth and family related services in different cultural contexts. We want to find out which capabilities[1] are valuable for the respondents (children, youths, caregivers, parents and others) from two different countries (Nicaragua and Namibia) and to investigate how well the support they receive from SOS Children's Villages and others meets their needs. This knowledge shall enable the organisation to create processes and tools to enhance and optimise its quality and programme development. In this paper we introduce the project and explain its participative design.[2]

---

1 The word "capability" can be used in many different meanings (see Crocker 2008: 168ff. and Robeyns 2005: 100). In this article we use it primarily in the sense of "the capability set of a person" and "the functionings or combination of functionings feasible for a person" (the elements of a capability set).

2 The project was also presented and discussed at the International Conference of the Human Development and Capability Association, September 2009 in Lima, Peru. For more details

The Project "Approaching Capabilities with Children in Care"

Using the terminology of the CA, one could say that the efforts of SOS Children's Villages aim at enabling children and young people to live a flourishing life they have reason to choose and value. Of course, this shall not conceal the fact that SOS Children's Villages has not yet applied the CA systematically to its work. In fact, for the organisation it is an open question whether the CA is really suitable for deciding upon processes for the support of children and youths in care and to rate them in a second step, although there are many promising references that indicate that the CA could serve as an adequate framework for these purposes. However, a more detailed examination of this topic inevitably leads to additional questions. Because of the cultural differences between the countries and territories in which SOS Children's Villages operates, it is e.g. necessary to take a very close look at what a flourishing life in the sense of the CA means in a particular cultural context. This includes the necessity to know which capabilities are valued by the children, youths and families SOS Children's Villages supports, especially if one agrees that the assessment of policies, programmes and services should not only take place "on the basis of their impact on incomes, but whether or not they expand the real freedoms that people value", as suggested by UNESCO (2002: 33). At the same time, it has to be taken into account that the question of how to select relevant capabilities is not clearly answered yet (Schokkaert 2008: 16ff.). Furthermore the statements of other authors concerning the CA in relation to children have to be considered.

Challenges of the Capability Approach concerning Children

In the last decades the capability approach has undoubtedly emerged as the leading alternative to standard economic frameworks for thinking about many important social issues. Many scientists consider it as the appropriate theoretical basis for addressing questions of poverty, inequality and development and it is a well-known fact that some of the approach's central ideas have even influenced the Human Development Index.

Many theoretical aspects of the capability approach have been discussed extensively by scholars from different fields of expertise, but something that has to be explored further is the relationship between the capability approach and children. The leading capability scholars, Amartya Sen and Martha Nuss-

---

see Babic, Germes-Castro and Graf 2009.

baum, have not addressed the issue in detail and many questions still have to be answered. When dealing with children, both Sen and Nussbaum seem to have a strong tendency to see them primarily as the agents they will become one day (Nussbaum 2000, 89ff.; Sen 2006: part VI; Saito 2003: 25ff.). Their future capabilities are considered as the point of reference in the capability framework, and decisions by caregivers and social institutions should be made essentially by referring to the freedom that children will enjoy later on. For children, the reasoning continues, certain functionings have to be guaranteed. This will help them to enjoy valuable capabilities when they are adults, but their agency in the present state of being a child is widely neglected in the works of Sen and Nussbaum. Sen for example clearly expresses this point of view when he answers the question how he thinks the capability approach is applicable to children, since children are not mature enough to make decisions by themselves. According to Saito (2003: 25) his response is the following one: "If the child does not want to be inoculated, and you nevertheless think it is a good idea for him/her to be inoculated, then the argument may be connected with the freedom that this person will have in the future by having the measles shot now. The child when it grows up must have more freedom. So when you are considering a child, you have to consider not only the child's freedom now, but also the child's freedom in the future." Now, one could argue that the CA is only applicable to children if you consider the person's capabilities in terms of his/her life span (Saito 2003: 25; see also Sen 2006: 10). According to this point of view it is the freedom they will enjoy in the future that counts and influences decisively what we owe to children.

One problem with this conception widely present in the capability approach literature is the undifferentiated use of the term "child". Sen for example doesn't make clear how he understands it, seeming to presuppose that children normally are incapable of making their own decisions (Sen 2006: 9). He seems to equate children with very young human beings and mainly addresses questions of justice arising in this context, stressing the importance of the structural conditions a good society has to provide for people who are so young that they are not able to decide for themselves (Sen 2006: 10). However, in many important contexts the word "child" is used differently: The article 1 of the United Nations Convention on the Rights of the Child (UNCRC) for example defines a child as any "human being below the age of eighteen years unless under the law applicable to the child, majority is attained earlier" (UN 1990). Now obviously this category of human beings is highly heterogeneous, ranging from infants not being able to survive on their own to young persons capable of earning their own money, driving a car and even having children on their own. And while it is clear that it is not reasonable to attribute to a 5-month-old the capability to make important decisions for her/himself we consider many youths as responsible persons being able to choose the kind of life they have reason to value. When understanding childhood in such a broad way, it is clear that it involves many different levels and stages. Different children possess diverse levels of agency and hence the question if and to what extend children are the subjects of capabilities has to be discussed more carefully. Maturity and the ability to live an independent life is not something that is simply given or not. It has to be seen as a process, as something that develops and grows over time. But here another problem arises. As Leßmann (2009) points out, Sen's formal description of capability sets is best seen as a comparative static model, capturing primarily which functionings are feasible (to a specific person) at a specific point in time.[3] He does not consider explicitly how capability sets change over time and how they are linked temporally. Especially when dealing with the complexities of human development and the question how the process of learning can be conceptualised in the CA framework, one sees that this theoretical shortcoming restricts the applicability of the CA in its current form: It is not clear how to deal with the well-known facts (i) that a person needs time to develop functionings and to expand her/his capability set (e.g. through learning) and (ii) that a person's capability set is constantly changing over time. Therefore Leßmann's demand that the CA needs to be complemented with a model of temporal interaction that allows to link capability sets temporally seems to be crucial (see Leßmann 2009: 11).

If we adopt the definition of the word "child" as used in the UNCRC (and thus going beyond Sen's understanding of the term), there are good reasons to conclude that it is wrong to deprive children, as a group, of capabilities. It is also clear that this issue has to be treated in a sophisticated way, paying sufficient attention to the different levels of agency existing in this target group. But if children are agents it is important to involve them in the process of selecting and evaluating their capabilities. In this context one can also point to some research projects explicitly conducted in the framework of the capability approach. The studies conducted by Biggeri, Libanora, Mariani & Menchini (2005), Biggeri & Anich (2009) and Young (2006) clearly indicate that participative approaches open up important possibilities for the selection of children's capabilities. If children are given suitable and age-appropriate opportunities they are able to form and express their views on a variety of matters, helping us to understand concepts like "children's well being" and "children's capabilities" in an adequate and comprehensive manner.

3 It is interesting to observe that he does not even include a time point explicitly in his definition of the capability set of a person (for example Sen 1992: 39ff.). Nevertheless it is obvious, that it only makes sense to refer to such a set at a specific moment in time.

Child participation as a necessary completion

Child participation, it can be argued, is therefore a necessary completion of the CA if it should be applied to children. And although the idea of involving children in the conceptualisation and evaluation of their capabilities is fairly new in the theoretical framework of the CA, it can be stated that in other contexts during the last decades, child participation has been a common topic for different stakeholders at different levels, such as policy makers, organisations working for and with children and also for the scientific community. One major reason for this phenomenon is the adaptation and ratification of the mentioned UNCRC twenty years ago, which shows that the above outlined view that many children can be seen as agents and participants in actions affecting them, is nowadays a widely accepted one. The most quoted UNCRC article in regard to participation is article 12:

1. States Parties shall assure to the child who is capable of forming his or her own views the right to express those views freely in all matters affecting the child, the views of the child being given due weight in accordance with the age and maturity of the child.
2. For this purpose, the child shall in particular be provided the opportunity to be heard in any judicial and administrative proceedings affecting the child, either directly, or through a representative or an appropriate body, in a manner consistent with the procedural rules of national law. (UN 1990)

Although this UN article might not give a precise definition of children's participation, it definitely introduces new attitudes towards children: They are no longer seen as recipients of services or passive beneficiaries of adults care or care provided by the State, but as the subjects of rights and participants in actions affecting them (see also Lansdown 2003: 1).

In our project we acknowledge this shift in thinking about childhood: We consider it important to involve children in the selection and evaluation of their capabilities and claim that this is one of the most significant ways to understand the type of life they value.

Lansdown and Hart, both child participation experts with consultancy experience for organisation such as UNICEF, have shown empirical evidence that children (even small children aged 8 and below) are capable of explaining their ideas, points of views and experiences to adults and other stakeholders. Lansdown states in her book "*Can you hear me?*" that "Young children have insights, perspectives, ideas and experiences that are unique to them. Indeed, they have a great deal to teach adults about their lives" (Lansdown 2005: 10). Lansdown bases this statement on the results of participation studies conducted by her, and on other examples such as the ones provided by

Hart in the UNICEF document "Children's participation: The theory and practice of involving young citizens in community development and environmental care" (Hart 1997). This document describes how child participation and child initiatives have managed to develop into regular governmental programmes in several countries.

Furthermore, participation of children in alternative care in research projects is not a new topic for SOS Children's Villages. The involvement of children and youths has helped the organisation to better understand their views and concerns in order to improve services which aim at supporting children to live "the life they have a reason to choose and value". The organisation relies on child participation when developing measures or conducting new projects. The Quality4Children project, which was conducted in cooperation with the Fédération Internationale des Communautés Educatives (FICE) and the International Foster Care Organisation (IFCO), can serve as a good example in this context. Within the framework of this initiative, over 150 children and youths from 26 European countries were asked about their best experiences in alternative child care; out of their narrations (among others) quality standards for out-of-home child care were elaborated. In the meantime these standards have been recognised by entities such as the European Commission and the Council of Europe (Quality4Children 2007).

Based on our own experiences and the findings of other empirical studies that confirm that children and youths are able to express their views and knowledge on subjects concerning their life, we plan to involve children and youths in the framework of "Approaching Capabilities with Children in Care". Children aged between 8 and 13 years and youths between the age of 14 and 18 will compose half of the research sample; they will be asked what the "flourishing life" they would like to live looks like.

The following part describes the methods which will be applied to ensure child involvement in an adequate form.

Methodological considerations

Although it is difficult and complex to state in detail what the CA is (see for example Sen 1999), there seems to be a wide consensus among scholars from different disciplines that it can be seen as a broad normative framework for different evaluative exercises (Robeyns 2005: 94). It is deeply connected with value judgements and the notion of freedom: people – maybe the phrase used most in the CA literature – should have the freedom to lead the kind of life they have reason to choose and to value, and social institutions have the task to provide the structural conditions to make this possible; any research based on the CA has to take this into account. Therefore it is crucial to find out what people – in a specific social, cultural and economic context – value (for a helpful discussion of this topic see Robeyns 2006). Having concluded that children and youths can indeed be considered as agents, it is a priority for us to involve them in the process of conceptualising their capabilities and in the generation of value judgements regarding their own lives. Consequently, we will ask young people living inside and outside programmes run by SOS Children's Villages about their values, the life they would like to lead later on, how they assess their chances to realise their plans, what kind of support they already receive and what kind of (additional) support they need to achieve their goals. Furthermore, their families of origin, co-workers of SOS Children's Villages and partner organisations as well as other relevant persons shall also be involved, in order to realise a multi-perspective approach on the question what the life of the young people should look like later on, what they should be able to be, and what they should be able to do as adults. That is among others to avoid distortions such as adaptive preferences by the young people, which could emerge if their perspective would be the only one to be taken into account (see Biggeri 2007: 6).

Due to the explorative character of the study and the necessity to get an in-depth understanding of the respondents' views and values, mainly qualitative investigations will be carried out. Thereby the adequate involvement of children and youths is given a high weight. This means that they should have sufficient opportunities to contribute in a way that is appropriate to their communicational abilities and needs. As was pointed out above these can vary widely within our primary target group (children/youths who lost parental care or are at risk of loosing it) and we want to offer them different alternatives to choose from concerning the method of data collection. Younger children might have problems to express themselves verbally and would rather prefer to draw a picture concerning their life in the future, as suggested in particular projective approaches (see Soley & Smith 2008). Youths, in contrast, might prefer to tell us about their plans and conceptions in a narrative interview (Schütze 1977). For others it could be more attractive to talk about these topics with a peer in the manner of 'storytelling' (Rafetseder 2004; Reinmann-Rothmeier et al. 2000). No matter how the vision of a child or youth of his/her future was created, after he/she finished telling it, he/she will be asked to explain it in more detail in a semi-structured qualitative interview (Lamnek 2005: 329ff.), which will be focused on this vision. For adults, conducting focus group discussions (Lamnek 2005: 408) combined with a semi-structured qualitative interview will be an effective way to get relevant information concerning the research topic.

We expect that out of the triangulation of the different data it will be possible to extract a culturally and regionally adequate notion of a flourishing life the young people who have been interviewed have reason to choose and value. On the one hand, this notion could provide us with reliable criteria to assess and optimise the work of SOS Children's Villages. On the other hand, we hope that the gathered information can also support the development of new programmes and services.

If we achieve these results, the next step would be to develop tools and/or guidelines on the basis of the experiences we gather by conducting the field studies, which would enable us to also apply them as a formally standardised process in other countries (Babic, Germes-Castro & Graf 2009).

Timeline and project structure

As was indicated before, the research project "Approaching Capabilities with children in care" is not exclusively conducted by SOS Children's Villages. Since March 2009, when the project started, the organisation has been co-operating with the International Research Center Salzburg (IFZ), an Institute of Advanced Studies in Social Ethics dedicated to scholarship and research in the area of social challenges. The Center is linked to the University of Salzburg – mainly to the Center for Ethics and Poverty Research – as well as with King's College London. The interdisciplinary and cutting edge research at the Center is focused on resilience and capabilities, on poverty alleviation and solidarity, on decent work and questions of work ethos.

On the side of SOS Children's Villages, its umbrella organisation SOS-Kinderdorf International with headquarters in Innsbruck, Austria, and the German association of SOS Children's Villages are involved. The first one is responsible for the project management and is conducting the study together with the IFZ. The latter mainly provides financial support. Representatives of these three bodies constitute the steering group of the project, which meets at regular intervals.

Field studies are taking place in Nicaragua and in Namibia, between October 2009 and March 2010. Therefore the project management, located at SOS-Kinderdorf International, is supported by local coordination teams that consist of a representative of the involved national association of SOS Children's Villages and a member of the project research team. The local representatives in both countries chair the local advisory boards while the member of the project research team leads the local research.

Government and community officials as well as experts form relevant academic fields are part of the advisory boards. Additionally, representatives of the participating programmes and facilities run by SOS Children's Villages or its partner organisations and youth representatives have a seat there, too.

The local research team consists mainly of people with experience in qualitative research, interns, trainees from universities in the case of Namibia, and a social researcher in Nicaragua. Young people from SOS programmes, who are not participating in the investigations as respondents, are also members of the local research teams.

In the course of 2010, preliminary presentations to show the first findings of the studies will take place in Namibia and Nicaragua. The international project "Approaching Capabilities with Children in Care" is planned to be finalised by February 2011 with a presentation of the final results.

References

Babic, B., Germes-Castro, O. & Graf, G. (2009): Approaching Capabilities with Children in Care. Paper presented at the International Conference of the Human Development and Capability Association, September 2009; Lima, Peru.

Biggeri, M. (2007): Choosing dimensions in the case of children's wellbeing. In: Maitreyee, No. 7, February 2007, 4-7.

Biggeri, M., Libanora, R. Mariani, S. & Menchini, L. (2005): Children Conceptualizing their Capabilities: Results of a Survey Conducted during the First Children's World Congress on Child Labour. In: Journal of Human Development, 7, 1, 59-83.

Biggeri, M. & Anich, R. (2009): The Deprivation of Street Children in Kampala: Can the Capability Approach and Participatory Methods Unlock a New Perspective in Research and Decision Making? In: Mondes en Dévéloppement, 37, 2, 146, 73-93.

Crocker, D. (2008): Ethics of Global Development. Agency, Capability, and Deliberative Democracy. Cambridge.

Hart, R.A. (1997): Children's participation: The theory and practice of involving young citizens in community development and environmental care. UNICEF, New York.

Lamnek, S. (2005): Qualitative Sozialforschung. Lehrbuch, Weinheim.

Lansdown, G. (2005): Can you hear me? – The right of young children to participate in decisions affecting them. Working papers in Early Childhood Development 36, 15-16.

Leßmann, O. (2009): Capability and Learning to Choose. In: Studies in Philosophy and Education. DOI 10.1007/s11217-009-9123-9.

Nussbaum, M. (2000): Women and human development: the capabilities approach. Cambridge.

Quality4Children (2007): Quality4Children Standards for Out-of-Home Child Care in Europe. As downloaded from http://www.quality4children.info/navigation/cms,id,31,nodeid,31,_country,at,_language,en.html in November 2009.

Rafetseder, G. (2004): Storytelling. A Handbook for Organisational Storytelling. Innsbruck.

Reinmann-Rothmeier, G., Erlach, C. & Neubauer, A.(2000): Erfahrungsgeschichten durch Story-Telling – eine multifunktionale Wissensmanagement-Methode. München.

Robeyns, I. (2005): The Capability Approach – a theoretical survey. In: Journal of Human Development, 6, 1, 93-114.

Robeyns, I. (2006): The Capability Approach in Practice. In: The Journal of Political Philosophy, 14, 3, 351-376.

Saito, M. (2003): Amartya Sen's Capability Approach to Education: A Critical Exploration. In: Journal of Philosophy of education, 37, 1, 17-33.

Schokkaert, E. (2008): The capabilities approach. As downloaded from http://ssrn.com/abstract=1084821 in November 2009.

Schütze, F. (1977): Die Technik des narrativen Interviews in Interaktionsfeldstudien dargestellt an einem Projekt zur Erforschung von kommunalen Machtstrukturen. Bielefeld.

Sen, A. (1992): Inequality Reexamined. Cambridge MA.

Sen, A. (1999): Commodities and Capabilities. Oxford & New York.

Sen, A. (2006): Children and Human Rights. Institute for Human Development Foundation Day Lecture delivered on December 19, 2006, New Delhi.

Soley, L. & Smith, A.L. (2008): Projective Techniques for Social Science and Business Research. Milwaukee.

UN (1990): Convention on the Rights of the Child. As downloaded from http://www2.ohchr.org/english/law/pdf/crc.pdf in November 2009.

UNESCO (2002): Education for All: Is the world on track? EFA Global Monitoring Report 2002. Paris: UNESCO .

Young, Marion (2006): Defining valued learning and capability. As downloaded from http://www.capabilityapproach.com/pubs/5_3_Young.pdf in November 2009.

Zoe Clark & Franziska Eisenhuth

Beyond Futurority – A Capabilities Perspective on Childhood and Youth

Beyond a functionings approach for children

Until now there is only a minor debate about a capabilities perspective on childhood and youth or in other words about the development of capabilities and the process of becoming capable agent during these life stages. It seems to be commonsense that during childhood and youth primarily the development of functionings has to be taken into account in respect to developing future capabilities, due to the fact the CA, as all liberal theories of justice, implies the individuals' capacity for autonomy, a feature which most liberal theories do not attribute to children (Ballet 2007).

Amartya Sen primarily puts emphasis on children's future capabilities. Even if he concedes, that also children should have certain latitude of choice, he insists that this freedom is affected with regard to their future: "It is the freedom they will have in the future rather than the present that should be considered" (Saito 2003).

Also Martha Nussbaum (2006b) points out, that within a capabilities perspective obligatory school attendance during childhood can be legitimized in order to produce mature adult capabilities.

Beyond these functionings approaches to the wellbeing of children there are some authors who recently started to develop a capability perspective on childhood.

For example both Mario Biggeri and Maria Laura Di Tommaso adapt Martha Nussbaum's list of basic human capabilities. Biggeri (Biggeri et. al. 2006) uses it to explore relevant capabilities for all children, Di Tommaso (2007) formulates a special list of capabilities for children in developing countries. So Biggeri as well as Di Tommaso are defining age specific capabilities, which they consider to be relevant during childhood and youth.

Jérôme Ballet and Hilde Bojer are going one step back behind this attempt and tackle the theoretical question in how far the capabilities approach (CA) can actually be applied to children. Ballet (2007) advocates a "weak self-determination principle" for children meaning that children should be in a position to make choices, but within a framework which prevents harmful choices.

Bojer (2004) combines the idea of capabilities with Rawls' theory of justice to conceptualize "the good of children". Contrarily to Rawls, who explicitly excludes children from the social contract he proposes, Bojer argues for distribution over the life-cycle, using Rawls' thought experiment of the original position as argument: As all parties in the original situation know that they will start their life as helpless infants they would secure favourable conditions during childhood.

In our contribution we would like to make another attempt to frame justice for young people from a capabilities perspective, in deepening the argument why young people should not only become functioning, but also be deemed as capable agents.

Justice for young people

Nancy Fraser (2008) offers a fruitful systematization for a meta-reflection on concepts of justice. She draws a distinction between the "who of justice", the "what of justice" and the "how of justice":

Working on these three questions we will frame the following questions:

- *Who* can be regarded as a participant in social justice? Here we will bring the argument forward that also children and adolescents should be addressees of social justice.
- *What* could be the objects of distribution for young people? Here we are arguing that it can be also capabilities and not only functionings.
- *How* can young people be taken into account as capable agents, even though they are dependent on care?

As mentioned above, one dominant perception stresses the importance of childhood and youth as a source for capable adulthood. Within this argumentation the early stages of life are not considered as intrinsically valuable, but tend to get reduced to instruments for later adulthood. Such an exclusively instrumental way of addressing childhood and youth seems to be contradictory to fundamental theoretical assumptions of justice within the CA.

Located in the tradition of political liberal theory the CA employs an ethical individualism, which considers the individual subject as the unit of moral concern. Accordingly, Nussbaum (2006b) emphasizes the importance to treat every person as his or her own end, rather than an instrument (e.g. for the community or the economy). This basic assumption makes it quite implausible to immolate early life stages to later adult ones, as children and young people are not taken into account as current but as future addressees of social justice.

There is only little doubt about causal correlations between early periods of life and the further development of individuals. However we will reason within the following sections why young people should be included within overall yardsticks of equal justice from a capabilities perspective.

Equality for whom?

The proponents of the CA insist on treating each individual as its own end and as the unit of moral concern. Within this section we would like to question how this is synergizing with the model of citizenship suggested by Nussbaum and which other possibilities are there in order to identify the "who of justice".

Following Nussbaum (2006b), the state is the institution which is in charge for distributing capabilities. The group of people who are entitled to express claims with respect to social justice to the state are "citizens". Thereby, Nussbaum's conceptualization of citizens contains more than a formal status of full members of a nation state, but describes an ideal of well-educated subjects who are reflective, who can reason logically and who can thereby participate in forming and perpetuating democracy.

As a consequence of this model, Nussbaum addresses the importance of education for the cultivation of citizenship (e.g. Nussbaum 2002; 2006a). In some texts she thereby focuses on the role of higher education to prepare undergraduates for citizenship and to shape them for democracy. So by implication undergraduates may not be conceived as full citizens because they still have to be prepared and to be shaped. Yet they are not fully excluded from the status of citizenship either: Nussbaum points to their right to vote and their ongoing participation in political life (Boman et al. 2002). Hence developing and exercising citizenship appear as simultaneous and overlapping processes in the case of undergraduates.

Nevertheless, this paradigm all the more excludes young people under 18 years from the status of citizenship. Even though it seems reasonable for each individual in a democracy to develop functionings for decision making and deliberation during childhood and youth, it is still problematic to postpone children's and young people's capability to participate in forming justice to their future adulthood.

We are therefore challenging this concept of citizenship as a condition for being a recipient of justice in terms of the CA. This model largely ignores children's and young people's current well-being.

One alternative approach of deliberative participation is developed by Jean-Michel Bonvin (2009), with his concept of capability for voice. He states that one should have the opportunity to participate in every public decision and action by which one is "concerned".

Nancy Fraser (2008) suggests an analogical frame of parity of participation. She advocates that everybody who is subjected by a given governance structure which govern their interaction, should have the opportunity to participate in negotiations concerning these structures. With this "all-subjected" approach of participation she develops a frame, which is able to identify the institutional levels of governance within globalized times. These may be local and national but also transnational.

James Bohman (1996) elaborates how "deliberative democracy" can be realized to guarantee equal participation among persons. He as well as Bonvin and Fraser claims inclusion of everyone who is "affected" by a decision.

Clearly, young people are concerned or affected by certain public decisions in the sense of Bonvin or Bohman, and they are subjected by several institutions in the sense of Fraser. Taking these authors serious, this would be a matter of fact which should allow them to participate, even though they are no full citizens in respect to Nussbaum yet.

Hence young people have to be entitled to participate in decision making processes in their families, schools and recreational facilities, but also in public action which affect their everyday lives. It is crucial to define how this participation can be conceptualized as the dilemma remains: Participating in democratic contests over justice requires functionings, like bringing arguments forward and comprehending the points of the other involved persons. These functionings have cognitive preconditions and they have to be practiced. Young people may not yet have full capacities in both aspects; the younger they are, the less probable it is that they have these capacities.

Summarizing the "equality for whom" question, we state that participation of children and young people has to be claimed in order to include them in struggles about justice. In the following sections, we will make some suggestions concerning the realization of this participation.

Equality of what?

In order to discuss the "equality of what" in respect to young people we will now consider the instrumental as well as the intrinsic value of childhood and youth.

As the foregoing argumentation indicated, there is still an instrumental role of childhood and youth that has to be taken into account, even if young people are recognized as an end in themselves instead as means for e.g. human capital. The achievement of functionings in order to act as capable adult in the future plays an important role during this stage of life. Hence a functioning approach towards young people can be legitimized regarding to their future freedoms. But focussing on the development of young people's functionings does not imply anything about the provision and distribution of functionings.

In order to ensure the development of functionings, the family is often consulted as 'natural unit' (Nussbaum 2006b: 250) of provision and concern. Thus the responsibility for children's needs is often reduced to a family issue. But even if the family can provide basic capabilities, like love and care, and functionings, like different forms of interaction, it also has to be recognized as an institution which is constitutively pervaded by power structures.

On the one hand, in particular parents have the possibility to take various decisions which essentially affect their children's living conditions, for example in terms of their education, nutrition, leisure. This power is largely unquestioned, perpetuated by traditions and institutionalized by laws. So the distribution of goods and subsequently also of capabilities between children and their parents or legal guardians has to be taken into account. As Nussbaum puts it (but in view of women): "seeing other family members as recipients of the largesse of a beneficent altruist is not the same thing as seeing them as agents, each with a life to live, deserving of both respect and resources" (2006b: 65).

On the other hand, parents are themselves equipped with unequal sets of capabilities and functionings. Accordingly the dependency of children on their family comes along with unequal starts to life and is consequently reproducing social inequality. Thus also the distribution of functionings and capabilities among children has to be recognized.

On the basis of this assumption we advocate to localize the responsibility for young people's set of functionings outside the private sphere, but conceptualize it as a part of public policy. We thus consider functionings as a social good which is an issue of equal distribution. As mentioned the family may be one provider for the needs of their children, but the interpersonal dependency of young people within their families should not exclude them from social justice in terms of a publically provided distribution of functionings.

Beyond this functioning approach we suggest assuming childhood and youth as a capability in itself as these are important periods of life, where parts of "Bildung"[1] in the sense of human development and cultural self formation takes place.

The opportunity to spend childhood and youth in terms of a moratorium is distributed quite unequally within national and global contexts. A moratorium is defined as the liberty of an enforcement of wage labour and provision for oneself and others, while having the right of being cared for. Whether

1 "Bildung" is a German term which cannot be translated to English one to one. One aspect of this term is education but beyond it can be understood as cultural self-formation.

somebody is able to choose this moratorium depends highly on class, gender and origin. While some people are forced to early economic independence from their parents or adapt their preference to early labour market participation, others have the possibility to delay different kinds of work and instead of that participate in formal, non-formal and informal kinds of "Bildung".

This kind of moratorium offers several ways of opportunities for developing functionings. Thus we suggest considering youth and childhood in terms of moratoriums as valuable social goods, which offer latitudes for human development. According to these assumptions we propose to conceptualize the possibility of choosing and defining a good childhood and youth as a capability in itself. While young people might not be able to make a decision about a good life as a whole, they are able to have reasonable desires in respect to a good childhood and youth.

In order to make this freedom of choice available, age specific capabilities are needed as preconditions for these decisions. In order to devise such age specific capabilities it seems to be necessary to differentiate between particular age groups. Babies and very small children are very limited in their ability to make decisions concerning the conversion of capabilities into functionings. (But still there are spaces for decisions, for example the time for and amount of food, the beginning of speaking, using the toilette and so on.) In particular the relevance of specific capabilities for childhood and youth has to be differentiated in order to grasp a yardstick of capabilities that is as broad and adequate as possible.

Summarizing the "equality of what" question, we would like to advocate for an equal distribution of functionings in respect to future capabilities. But beyond this functionings approach for young people we suggest to ensure capabilities as freedom of choice in order to enable young people to make decisions about a good childhood and youth. Defining a moratorium during childhood and youth as a capability means not to immolate these life stages to later adulthood, but treat it as an own valuable end and as part of human development.

Equality how?

In order to make some tentative suggestions for the "how of justice" we go back to the dilemma how to take young people into account as addressees for justice, even though they are dependent on advocacy and care.

According to Bonvin (2009), everybody should have the possibility to make reasonable choices about their personal conversion of capabilities into functionings. Beyond this, as mentioned before, every person who is concerned by a public decision should be allowed to participate within the process of decision-making in terms of deliberation. But the distinction of self-determined adults versus dependent and non-autonomous young people excludes the latter from these two kinds of freedoms. So we have to clarify how the status of self-determination as a major precondition for the availability of opportunity freedom and processual freedom is defined and might be redefined. For this purpose we can use two important criteria of self-determination which Micha Brumlik (2004) suggests:

1. Persons need to be able to have a coherent habit of language.
2. Persons need to have an adequate basis of information, in order to be able to phrase a plausible argument.

There has to be a debate about the measurement of plausibility and hierarchical assessment of different basis of information, but we will leave this debate out now.

However it can be reasoned out of the second aspect, that self-determination and autonomy might not be attributes of a person *per se*. Instead of categorizing young people as autonomous or not, the question if they are able to have a capability for voice has to be related to different situations and processes of decision making. As comprehensive self-determination is always an ideal, the assumption that young people are comprehensively lacking self-determination might be counterfactual in respect to various concerns.

So even if young people have not reached the status of full autonomy and self-determination, which is an ideal typical yardstick anyway, their autonomy and self-determination might be recognized punctually. This punctuality can be related to a capability for voice, in order to include young people within claims for social justice. Consequently children should not only be seen as passive recipients of schooling, welfare, social services, but should be allowed to realize a capability for voice, in order to recognize them as current subjects of moral concern, instead of future citizens.

For reflection on the performance level of participation, James Bohman (1996) delivers fruitful thoughts. As he points out it is crucial for successful deliberation that participants have the ability to convince the other persons involved. Different types of "deliberative inequalities" hinder this task and should be considered in the case of young people: Power asymmetries affect the potential participants' access to the public sphere which is the place of deliberative debates. Furthermore, communicative inequalities affect the ability to initiate deliberation about the potential participants' concerns, to participate verbally in deliberation processes and to influence their outcome.

Young people (as other individuals, depending on the context) are only marginally represented in the public sphere and tend to lack a sufficient vocabulary in which to express their needs and perspectives publicly. To overcome the exclusion that goes along with these aspects, Bohman suggests relying on groups as "corrective capacity" (: 132): If young people form a group, they both pool their power and their communicative abilities and thus they are more likely to gain a capability for voice and succeed to act strategically as a collective actor in the public sphere. For this purpose, Bohman proposes to mobilize already existing informal networks and to search for the support of law and political power.

But this is not to be understood as a perfectionist yardstick in order to force young people into deliberation. Referring to Bonvin's notion of passive empowerment, it has to be possible that individuals choose not to attend public actions of deliberation without this decision resulting in new disadvantages for them. This would be the case if individual children could rely on stakeholders who acted on their behalf.

We would like to conclude that even if paternalistic treatments of young people might be reasonable and necessary in certain cases, they still have to be legitimized. Following our suggestion of punctual self-determination, it has to be legitimized if paternalistic and advocatory decision making is necessary or if young persons are able to argue for themselves.

Furthermore the exclusion of young people out of public decisions concerning them has to be legitimized. For example the organization of schools might be object of deliberative processes, where it seems to be an obligation to state reasons if young people are excluded.

Beyond, the question still remains how to develop autonomy and self-determination during childhood and youth in respect to future adulthood. Therefore the aims of education or "Bildung" have to be discussed.

Summarizing the "how of justice" question, not only realized functionings and skill capabilities have to be taken into account in order to include young people as current addressees of social justice, but also opportunity capabilities that allow access to participation and self-determination.

Conclusion

To sum up, we are arguing that in a capabilities perspective, children and young people have to be included as agents into conceptions of justice in order to reduce intergenerational inequality. This inclusion is complicated by the fact that young people's abilities punctually differ from the ideal of autonomous adults, which underlies the conception of justice the CA proposes. While this dilemma cannot be resolved *per se*, several conceptual considerations allow considering children and young people as entitled addressees of social justice.

Summarizing the above, we argue that children and young people should be conceptualized as addressees of justice because their subjection to governance structures entitles them to influence these structures. Contents of the justice for young people should be both current capabilities which are enabling them to live a valuable youth, and functionings with a view to future capabilities. Even though we cannot expect reasonable and far-ranging decisions from young people in every single situation, their participation in deliberation processes still can be conceptualized.

References

Ballet, J. (2007): Children's Autonomy, Education and Capabilities. University of Versailles Saint-Quentin-en-Yvelines. First Draft, September 2007.

Biggeri, M., Libanora, R., Mariani, S. & Menchini, L. (2006): Children Conceptualizing their Capabilities: Results of a Survey Conducted during the First Children's World Congress on Child Labour. In: Journal of Human Development, 7, 1, 59-83.

Bohman, J. (1996): Public Deliberation. Pluralism, Complexity, and Democracy. Cambridge.

Bojer, H. (2004): Social justice and the rights of children. University of Oslo, June 28, 2004. [online: http://mora.rente.nhh.no/projects/EqualityExchange/Portals/0/articles/bojer4.pdf]

Boman, Y., Gustavsson, B. & Nussbaum, M. (2002): A discussion with Martha Nussbaum on "Education for Citizenship in an Era of Global Connection". In: Studies in Philosophy and Education, 21, 305-311.

Bonvin, J.-M. (2009): Der Capability Ansatz und sein Beitrag für die Analyse gegenwärtiger Sozialpolitik. In: Soziale Passagen, 1, 8-22.

Brumlik, M. (2004): Advokatorische Ethik – zur Legitimation pädagogischer Eingriffe. Berlin/Wien.

Di Tommaso, M.L. (2007): Children capabilities: A structural equation model for India. In: The Journal of Socio-Economics 36, 436-450.

Fraser, N. (2008): Scales of Justice. Reimagining Political Space in a Globalizing World. Cambridge.

Nussbaum, M. (2002): Education for Citizenship in an Era of Global Connection. In: Studies in Philosophy and Education, 21, 289-303.

Nussbaum, M. (2006a): Education and Democratic Citizenship: Capabilities and Quality Education. In: Journal of Human Development, 7, 3, 385-395.

Nussbaum, M. (2006b): Women and human development. Cambridge.

Saito, M. (2003): Amartya Sen's Capability Approach to Education: A critical Exploration. In: Journal of Philosophy of Education, 37, 1.

Contributors

Babic, Bernhard, SOS-Kinderdorf International, Programme Development, Innsbruck, Austria, mail: bernhard.babic@sos-kd.org

Ballet, Jérôme, University of Versailles Saint-Quentin-en-Yvelines (UVSQ), Center of Ethics and Economics for Environment and Development (C3ED), France, mail: jballetfr@yahoo.fr

Bartelheimer, Peter, Georg-August-Universität Göttingen, Soziologisches Forschungsinstitut (SOFI), Germany, mail: peter.bartelheimer@sofi.uni-goettingen.de

Biggeri, Mario, Dept. of Economics, University of Florence, Italy, mail: Mario.biggeri@unifi.it

Büttner, R., Georg-August-Universität Göttingen, Soziologisches Forschungsinstitut (SOFI), Germany, mail: rene.buettner@sofi.uni-goettingen.de

Cameron, John, Erasmus University Rotterdam, International Institute of Social Studies (ISS), The Netherlands, mail: Cameron@iss.nl

Clark, Zoe, Universität Bielefeld, Research School "Education and Capabilities", Germany, mail: zoe.clark@uni-bielefeld.de

Comim, Flavio, University of Cambridge, St. Edmund's College, Capability and Sustainability Centre, UK, mail: fvc1001@cam.ac.uk

Dean, Hartley, London School of Economics, Department of Social Policy, UK, mail: h.dean@lse.ac.uk

Edelstein, Wolfgang, Director emeritus, Max-Planck-Institut für Bildungsforschung, Forschungsbereich Entwicklung und Sozialisation, Berlin, Germany, mail: Edelstein@mpib-berlin.mpg.de

Eisenhuth, Franziska, Universität Bielefeld, Research School "Education and Capabilities", Germany, mail: feisenhuth@uni-bielefeld.de

Gaertner, Wulf, Universität Osnabrück, FB Wirtschaftswissenschaften/-VWL/Theoretische Volkswirtschaftslehre, Germany, mail: wulf.gaertner@-uni-osnabrueck.de

Germes-Castro, Oscar, SOS-Kinderdorf International, Programme Development, Innsbruck, Austria, mail: Oscar.GermesCastro@sos-kd.org

Graf, Gunter, Internationales Forschungszentrum Salzburg, Austria, mail: ggraf@ifs-salzburg.at

Grundmann, Matthias, Westfälische Wilhelms-Universität Münster, Institut für Soziologie, Germany, mail: Matthias.Grundmann@uni-muenster.de

Leßmann, Ortrud, Helmut-Schmidt-Universität Hamburg, Projekt GeNECA (Gerechte Nachhaltige Entwicklung auf der Grundlage des Capability Ansatzes), Germany, mail: o.lessmann@web.de

Muñiz Castillo, Mirtha R., Maastricht University, Maastricht Graduate School of Governance, The Netherlands, mail: mirtha.munizcastillo@maastrichtuniversity.nl

Otto, Hans-Uwe, Universität Bielefeld, Bielefeld Center for Edcuation and Capability Research, Germany, mail: hansuwe.otto@uni-bielefeld.de

Rosendal Jensen, Niels, Aarhus University, Danish School of Education, Department of Education, DK, mail: nrj@dpu.dk

Sadlowski, Iris, Eberhard-Karls-Universität Tübingen, Wirtschafts- und Sozialwissenschaftliche Fakultät, Institut für Politikwissenschaft, Germany, mail: iris.sadlowski@t-online.de

Salais, Robert, Humboldt-Universität zu Berlin, Centre Marc Bloch (CMB), Germany, mail: robert.salais@cmb.hu-berlin.de

Schäfer, Heinrich W., Universität Bielefeld, Fakultät für Geschichtswissenschaft, Philosophie und Theologie, Fakultät für Soziologie, Germany, mail: heinrich.schaefer@uni-bielefeld.de

Schmidt, Tanja, Georg-August-Universität Göttingen, Soziologisches Forschungsinstitut (SOFI), Germany, mail: tanja.schmidt@sofi.uni-goettingen.de

Steinhoff, Annekatrin, Westfälische Wilhelms-Universität Münster, Institut für Soziologie, Germany, mail: annekatrin.steinhoff@uni-muenster.de

Volkert, Jürgen, Hochschule Pforzheim, Fakultät für Wirtschaft und Recht, mail: juergen.volkert@hs-pforzheim.de

Watts, Michael, Cambridge Admissions Office, Widening Participation Initiatives Officer, UK, mail: mw362@cam.ca.uk

Wüst, Kirsten, Hochschule Pforzheim, Fakultät für Wirtschaft und Recht, mail: kirsten.wuest@hs-pforzheim.de

Ziegler, Holger, Universität Bielefeld, Fakultät für Erziehungswissenschaft, AG 8 Soziale Arbeit, Germany, mail: holger.ziegler@uni-bielefeld.de

Index